SINGLE LEVEL
HOME PLANS

ALL NEW 7TH EDITION

GARLINGHOUSE

Library of Congress No.: 98-75665
ISBN: 0-938708-86-4
Covers & Interior Layouts by Debra Novitch

TABLE OF CONTENTS

Publisher
JAMES D. MCNAIR III

Editorial Staff
DEBRA COCHRAN, SUE BARILE

Submit all Canadian plan orders to:
The Garlinghouse Company
60 Baffin Place, Unit #5
Waterloo, Ontario N2V 1Z7

Canadians Order only: 1-800-561-4169
Fax#: 1-800-719-3291
Customer Service#: 1-519-746-4169

PLAN: 20100

Photography by John Ehrenclou

WIDE-OPEN AND CONVENIENT

TOTAL LIVING AREA	1,737 SQ. FT
MAIN AREA	1,737 SQ. FT.
BASEMENT	1,727 SQ. FT.
GARAGE	484 SQ. FT.
BEDROOMS	THREE
BATHROOMS	2 FULL
FOUNDATION	BASEMENT, SLAB OR CRAWL SPACE

DESIGN BY THE GARLINGHOUSE COMPANY

Stacked windows fill the wall in the front bedroom of this one-level home, creating an attractive facade. Around the corner, two more bedrooms and two full baths complete the bedroom wing, set apart for bedtime quiet. Notice the elegant vaulted-ceiling in the master bedroom, the master tub and shower illuminated by a skylight, and a dual vanity in both baths. Active areas enjoy a spacious feeling. Look at the high, sloping ceilings in the fire-placed living room, the sliders that unite the breakfast room and kitchen with an adjoining deck, and the vaulted ceilings in the formal dining room off the foyer. The photographed home may have been modified to suit individual tastes.

MAIN AREA

1

PRICE CODE B

STATELY HOME

With a traditional, elegant exterior and lively interior spaces, this three bedroom executive home makes both everyday life and entertaining a breeze. A palladian window floods the foyer with light for a dramatic entrance alluding to a surprising, open floor plan. Whip up a gourmet meal in the well-planned kitchen while chatting with family and friends in the large Great room with cathedral ceiling, fireplace, and built-in cabinets. The screened porch, breakfast area, and master suite access the deck with optional spa. The large master suite, located in the rear for privacy, features a luxurious skylit bath with separate shower, corner whirlpool tub, and separate vanities. A skylit bonus room above the garage adds space when needed. This plan is available with a crawl space or a basement foundation. Please specify when ordering. The photographed home may have been modified to suit individual tastes.

attic access

down

skylights

BONUS RM.
21-9 x 16-7

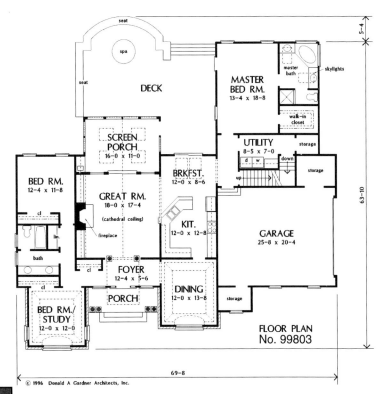

seat

spa

DECK

seat

SCREEN PORCH
16-0 x 11-0

BED RM.
12-4 x 11-8

cl

bath

lin.

cl

GREAT RM.
18-0 x 17-4

(cathedral ceiling)

fireplace

cl

FOYER
12-4 x 5-6

PORCH

BED RM./ STUDY
12-0 x 12-0

BRKFST.
12-0 x 8-6

KIT.
12-0 x 12-8

DINING
12-0 x 13-8

MASTER BED RM.
13-4 x 18-8

master bath

skylights

walk-in closet

UTILITY
8-5 x 7-0

storage

d w

down

storage

up

GARAGE
25-8 x 20-4

storage

5-4

63-10

69-8

FLOOR PLAN
No. 99803

Photography by Jon Riley of Riley & Riley Photography

TOTAL LIVING AREA	1,977 SQ. FT
MAIN FLOOR	1,977 SQ. FT.
BONUS AREA	430 SQ. FT.
GARAGE	610 SQ. FT.
BEDROOMS	3
BATHROOMS	2 FULL
FOUNDATION	BASEMENT OR CRAWL SPACE

DESIGN BY DONALD A. GARDNER
ARCHITECTS, INC.

PLAN: 99803

PERFECT COMPACT RANCH

This Ranch home features a large sunken Great room, centralized with a cozy fireplace. The master bedroom has an unforgettable bathroom with a super skylight. The huge three-car plus garage can include a work area for the family carpenter. In the center of this home, a kitchen includes an eating nook for family gatherings. The porch at the rear of the house has easy access from the dining room. One other bedroom and a den, which can easily be converted to a bedroom, are on the opposite side of the house from the master bedroom. The photographed home may have been modified to suit individual tastes.

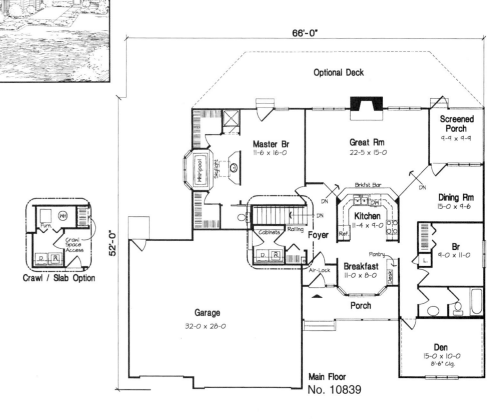

Crawl / Slab Option

66'-0"

Optional Deck

Master Br
11-6 x 16-0

Great Rm
22-5 x 15-0

Screened Porch
9-9 x 9-9

Whirlpool

Skylight

Brkfst Bar

DN

DN

Dining Rm
15-0 x 9-6

Kitchen
11-4 x 9-0

DW

Cabinets

Railing

Foyer

Ref.

Pantry

Br
9-0 x 11-0

Air-Lock

Breakfast
11-0 x 8-0

Desk

Porch

Garage
32-0 x 28-0

Den
15-0 x 10-0
8'-6" Clg.

Main Floor
No. 10839

52'-0"

Crawl Space Access

Furn.

Photography by John Ehrenclou

TOTAL LIVING AREA	1,738 SQ. FT
MAIN FLOOR	1,738 SQ. FT.
BEDROOMS	TWO
BATHROOMS	2 FULL
BASEMENT	1,083 SQ. FT.
GARAGE	796 SQ. FT.
FOUNDATION	BASEMENT, SLAB OR CRAWL SPACE

DESIGN BY THE GARLINGHOUSE COMPANY

PLAN: 10839

VICTORIAN CHARM

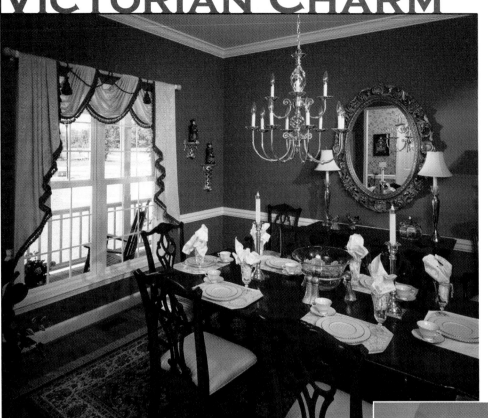

This home combines the Victorian charm of yesteryear with a plan designed for today's families. Accented by columns, the Great room with fireplace is vaulted, while the foyer, dining room, kitchen, breakfast bay, and bedroom/study boast impressive ten foot ceilings. With double door entry, the secluded master suite features a tray ceiling, walk-in closet, and private, skylit bath. Two additional bedrooms are located on the opposite side of the house and share a full bath with linen closet. Front and back porches extend the living space to the outdoors, and the two-car garage offers storage space. The photographed home may have been modified to suit individual tastes.

Photography by Jon Riley of Riley & Riley Photography

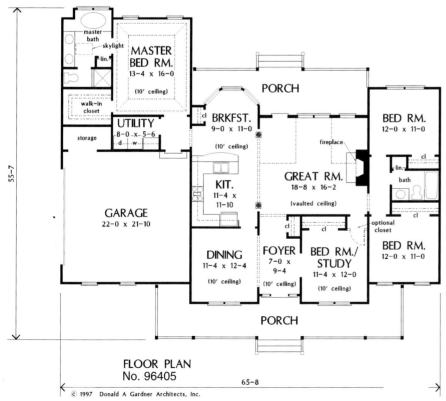

FLOOR PLAN
No. 96405

65-8

© 1997   Donald A Gardner Architects, Inc.

TOTAL LIVING AREA	1,903 SQ. FT.
MAIN FLOOR	1,903 SQ. FT.
GARAGE & STORAGE	531 SQ. FT.
BEDROOMS	FOUR
BATHROOMS	2 FULL
FOUNDATION	CRAWL SPACE

DESIGN BY DONALD A. GARDNER
ARCHITECTS, INC.

PLAN: 96405

GROWING FAMILIES

Great privacy as well as an open great room for gathering make this exciting three bedroom country home perfect for the active young family. The Great room features a fireplace, cathedral ceiling, and built-in bookshelves. The kitchen is designed for efficient use with its food preparation island and pantry. The master suite with cathedral ceiling, walk-in closet, and a luxurious bath provides a welcome retreat. A second floor bonus room makes a perfect study or play area. This plan is available with a basement or crawl space foundation. Please specify when ordering. The photographed home may have been modified to suit individual tastes.

Photography by Jon Riley of Riley & Riley Photography

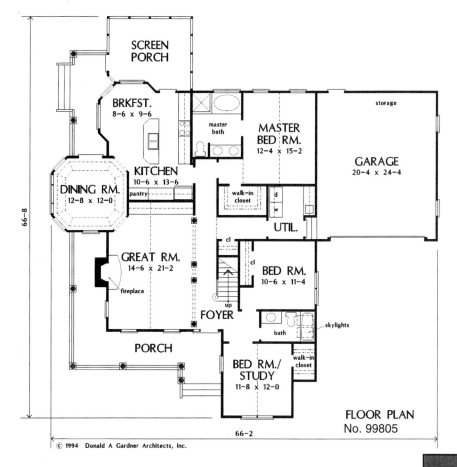

SCREEN PORCH

BRKFST.
8-6 x 9-6

master bath

MASTER BED RM.
12-4 x 15-2

storage

GARAGE
20-4 x 24-4

KITCHEN
10-6 x 13-6

pantry

DINING RM.
12-8 x 12-0

walk-in closet

d
w

UTIL.

cl

GREAT RM.
14-6 x 21-2

fireplace

cl

BED RM.
10-6 x 11-4

up

FOYER

PORCH

bath

skylights

walk-in closet

BED RM./ STUDY
11-8 x 12-0

66-8

66-2

FLOOR PLAN
No. 99805

© 1994   Donald A Gardner Architects, Inc.

TOTAL LIVING AREA	1,787 SQ. FT
MAIN FLOOR	1,787 SQ. FT.
BONUS ROOM	326 SQ. FT.
BEDROOMS	THREE
BATHROOMS	2 FULL
GARAGE	521 SQ. FT.
FOUNDATION	BASEMENT OR CRAWL SPACE

DESIGN BY DONALD A. GARDNER
ARCHITECTS, INC.

PLAN: 99805

CATHEDRAL CEILING

The clever use of interior space plus cathedral and tray ceilings give this graceful home a feeling much larger than its 1,737 square feet. A cathedral ceiling and columns provide tremendous impact in the Great room, while the octagonal shape of the dining room provides plenty of windows for ample light. This shape is repeated in the open breakfast bay. The kitchen features a center island and a pantry. The master bedroom, with tray ceiling, is privately situated with a luxurious bath. The front bedroom with its cathedral ceiling and large circle-top window doubles as a study. Wrapping porches at front and rear of the home invite quiet relaxation. The photographed home may have been modified to suit individual tastes.

Photography by Jon Riley of Riley & Riley Photography

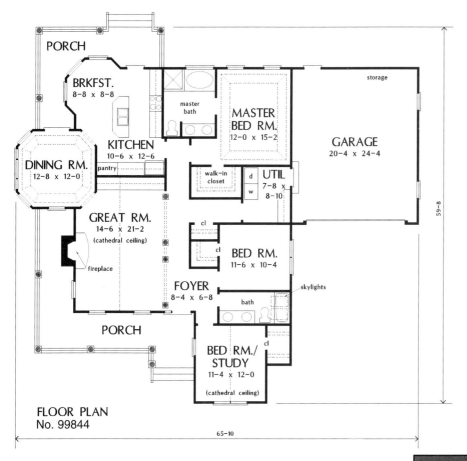

PORCH

BRKFST.
8-8 x 8-8

master bath

MASTER BED RM.
12-0 x 15-2

storage

KITCHEN
10-6 x 12-6

GARAGE
20-4 x 24-4

DINING RM.
12-8 x 12-0

pantry

walk-in closet

d w

UTIL
7-8 x 8-10

59-8

GREAT RM.
14-6 x 21-2
(cathedral ceiling)

fireplace

cl

cl

BED RM.
11-6 x 10-4

FOYER
8-4 x 6-8

skylights

bath

PORCH

cl

BED RM./
STUDY
11-4 x 12-0

(cathedral ceiling)

FLOOR PLAN
No. 99844

65-10

TOTAL LIVING AREA	1,737 SQ. FT.
MAIN FLOOR	1,737 SQ. FT.
GARAGE & STORAGE	517 SQ. FT.
BEDROOMS	THREE
BATHROOMS	2 FULL
FOUNDATION	CRAWL SPACE

DESIGN BY DONALD A. GARDNER
ARCHITECTS, INC.

PLAN: 99844

Perfect for a beachfront lot, this elevated plan sits one level off the ground. This is high enough to slip two cars and a boat underneath. Round top windows and brick facing behind the porch give this getaway the polish of a year round home. The house gains a sense of volume from a wide-open plan, a vaulted ceiling and lots of breeze catching windows. The efficient L-shape kitchen has an easy flow into the bedroom/living area. The screen porch is perfect to take in an ocean view. No materials list is available for this plan. The photographed home may have been modified to suit individual tastes.

Photography Supplied by The Meredith Corporation

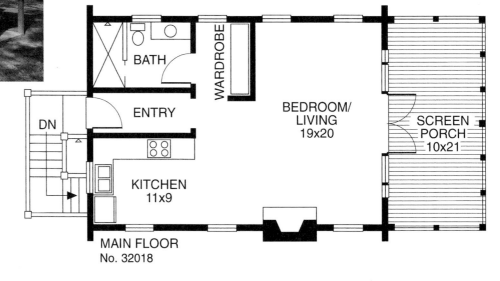

TOTAL LIVING AREA	663 SQ. FT.
MAIN FLOOR	663 SQ. FT.
BEDROOMS	1
BATHROOMS	1 FULL
FOUNDATION	POST

DESIGN BY THE MEREDITH CORPORATION

WIDTH 23'-6"
DEPTH 41'-2"

BATH

WARDROBE

ENTRY

DN

BEDROOM/
LIVING
19x20

SCREEN
PORCH
10x21

KITCHEN
11x9

MAIN FLOOR
No. 32018

PLAN: 32018

Photography by Jon Riley of Riley & Riley Photography

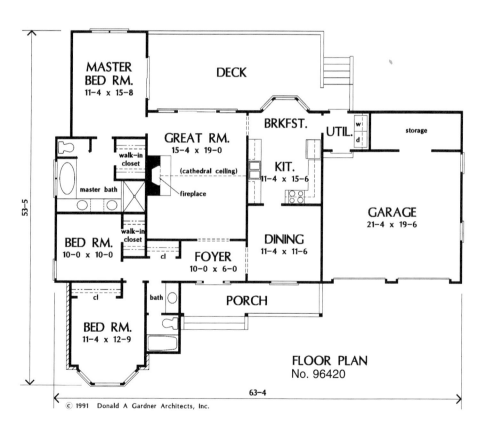

MASTER BED RM.
11-4 x 15-8

DECK

GREAT RM.
15-4 x 19-0

walk-in closet

(cathedral ceiling)

master bath

fireplace

BRKFST.

UTIL.

w/d

storage

KIT.
11-4 x 15-6

walk-in closet

BED RM.
10-0 x 10-0

cl

FOYER
10-0 x 6-0

DINING
11-4 x 11-6

GARAGE
21-4 x 19-6

53-5

cl

bath

PORCH

BED RM.
11-4 x 12-9

FLOOR PLAN
No. 96420

63-4

© 1991 Donald A Gardner Architects, Inc.

Multi-paned bay window, dormers, cupola, covered porch, and a variety of building materials add romance to this efficient Country cottage. The foyer opens to a formal dining room and a large Great room with fireplace and cathedral ceiling. Step onto the expansive deck from the Great room or from the private master suite. Relax in the luxurious master bath with garden tub, separate shower, dual sink vanity, and walk-in closet. Two family bedrooms up front share another full bath, while a utility/mudroom is conveniently located off the kitchen and rear doors.
The photographed home may have been modified to suit individual tastes.

TOTAL LIVING AREA	1,512 SQ. FT.
MAIN FLOOR	1,512 SQ. FT.
BEDROOMS	THREE
BATHROOMS	2 FULL
GARAGE & STORAGE	516 SQ. FT.
FOUNDATION	CRAWL SPACE

DESIGN BY DONALD A. GARDNER ARCHITECTS, INC.

PLAN: 96420

Photography Supplied by Design Basics, Inc.

Columns and arched transoms are focal points of this ranch home elevation. The ten-foot entry has formal views of the dining room and the Great room which features a brick fireplace . The large island kitchen offers an angled range and a pantry. The sunny breakfast room has an atrium door to the back yard. The separate bedroom wing provides optimum privacy. The master suite includes a whirlpool bath with a sloped ceiling, a double vanity and a walk-in closet. This plan is available with a basement or slab foundation. Please specify when ordering. The photographed home may have been modified to suit individual tastes.

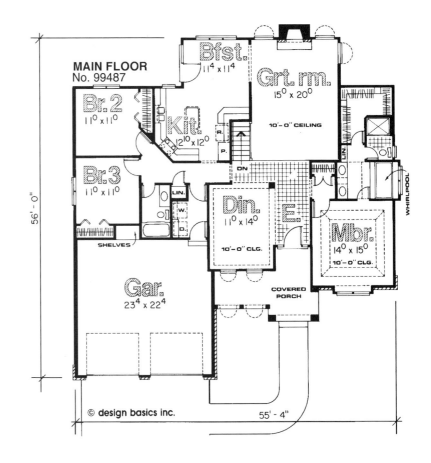

TOTAL LIVING AREA	1,806 SQ. FT
MAIN FLOOR	1,806 SQ. FT.
BEDROOMS	THREE
BATHROOMS	2 FULL
GARAGE	548 SQ. FT.
FOUNDATION	BASEMENT OR SLAB

DESIGN BY DESIGN BASICS, INC.

PLAN: 99487

CLASSIC DESIGN

Photography by John Ehrenclou

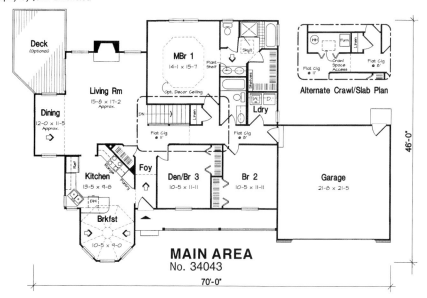

Deck (Optional)

Living Rm
15-8 x 17-2
Approx.

Dining
12-0 x 11-5
Approx.

MBr 1
14-1 x 15-7

Plant Shelf

Skylt

Opt. Decor Ceiling

Flat Clg • 11'

Ldry

Flat Clg • 8'

Alternate Crawl/Slab Plan

Crawl Space Access

Flat Clg • 11'

Flat Clg • 8'

Kitchen
13-5 x 9-8

Foy

Den/Br 3
10-5 x 11-11

Br 2
10-5 x 11-11

Garage
21-8 x 21-5

Brkfst
10-5 x 9-0

MAIN AREA
No. 34043

70'-0"

46'-0"

This convenient, one-level plan is perfect for the modern family with a taste for classic design. Traditional Victorian touches in this three-bedroom beauty include a romantic, railed porch and an intriguing breakfast tower just off the kitchen. You will love the step-saving arrangement of the kitchen between the breakfast and formal dining rooms. Enjoy the wide-open living room with sliders out to a rear deck, and the handsome master suite with its skylit, compartmentalized bath. Notice the convenient laundry location on the bedroom hall. The photographed home may have been modified to suit individual tastes.

TOTAL LIVING AREA	1,583 SQ. FT
MAIN AREA	1,583 SQ. FT.
BEDROOMS	THREE
BATHROOMS	2 FULL
BASEMENT	1,573 SQ. FT.
GARAGE	484 SQ. FT.
FOUNDATION	BASEMENT, SLAB OR CRAWL SPACE

DESIGN BY THE GARLINGHOUSE COMPANY

PLAN: 34043

SIMPLY CHARMING

Photography Supplied by The Meredith Corporation

A simple covered entry mimics the gables on the two halves of the home. Two bedrooms and bath occupy one side of this home while a hall passes the courtyard deck and leads to the dramatic living room and kitchen on the opposite side. The courtyard deck and a screen porch expand living spaces out doors. High ceilings and gable windows keep the interior light and airy. The photographed home may have been modified to suit individual tastes.

MAIN FLOOR
No. 32122

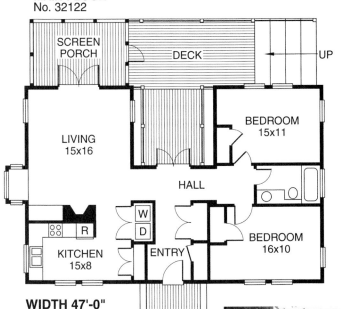

WIDTH 47'-0"
DEPTH 45'-6"

TOTAL LIVING AREA	1,112 SQ. FT.
MAIN FLOOR	1,112 SQ. FT.
BEDROOMS	TWO
BATHROOMS	1 FULL
BASEMENT	484 SQ. FT.
FOUNDATION	BASEMENT OR CRAWL SPACE

DESIGN BY THE MEREDITH CORPORATION

PLAN: 32122

MULTIPLE GABLES

Photography Supplied by Studer Residential Design

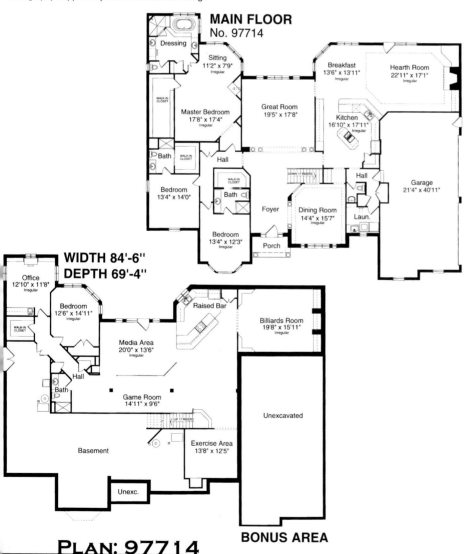

MAIN FLOOR
No. 97714

Dressing

Sitting
11'2" x 7'9"
Irregular

Breakfast
13'6" x 13'11"
Irregular

Hearth Room
22'11" x 17'1"
Irregular

WALK-IN CLOSET

Master Bedroom
17'8" x 17'4"
Irregular

Great Room
19'5" x 17'8"

Kitchen
16'10" x 17'11"
Irregular

Bath

WALK-IN CLOSET

Hall

Hall

Garage
21'4" x 40'11"

Bedroom
13'4" x 14'0"

WALK-IN CLOSET

Bath

Foyer

DOWN 17 RISERS

Dining Room
14'4" x 15'7"
Irregular

Laun.

Bedroom
13'4" x 12'3"
Irregular

Porch

WIDTH 84'-6"
DEPTH 69'-4"

Office
12'10" x 11'8"
Irregular

Bedroom
12'6" x 14'11"
Irregular

Raised Bar

WALK-IN CLOSET

Media Area
20'0" x 13'6"
Irregular

Billiards Room
19'8" x 15'11"
Irregular

Hall

Bath

Game Room
14'11" x 9'6"

Unexcavated

Basement

UP 17 RISERS

Exercise Area
13'8" x 12'5"

Unexc.

BONUS AREA

PLAN: 97714

Exquisite columns, 13 ft. ceiling heights and detailed ceiling treatments decorate the dining room and Great room. The gourmet kitchen with island and snack bar combine with the spacious breakfast room hearth room. The luxurious master bedroom suite with sitting area and fireplace is complemented by a deluxe dressing room with whirlpool tub, shower and dual vanities. Blueprints come with a design for a billiard room, secondary kitchen, media area, exercise area, full bath and additional bedrooms for the bonus area. No materials list is available for this plan. The photographed home may have been modified to suit individual tastes.

TOTAL LIVING AREA	3,570 SQ. FT
MAIN FLOOR	3,570 SQ. FT.
BONUS AREA	2,367 SQ. FT.
BASEMENT	1,203 SQ. FT.
BEDROOMS	THREE
BATHROOMS	3 FULL, 1 HALF
FOUNDATION	BASEMENT

DESIGN BY STUDER RESIDENTIAL DESIGN

Photography by Jon Riley of Riley & Riley Photography

Dual porches, gables, and circle-top windows give this home its special country charm. The foyer, expanded by a vaulted ceiling, introduces a formal colonnaded dining room. The kitchen features columns and an island for easy entertaining. The vaulted Great room is always bright with light from the circle-top clerestory. Extra room for growth is waiting in the skylit bonus room. The front bedroom doubles as a study for versatility. A tray ceiling adds volume to the private master suite that has a bath with sky-light, garden tub, dual vanity, and both linen and walk-in closets. The photographed home may have been modified to suit individual tastes.

TOTAL LIVING AREA	1,832 SQ. FT
MAIN FLOOR	1,832 SQ. FT.
BONUS AREA	425 SQ. FT.
BEDROOMS	THREE
BATHROOMS	2 FULL
GARAGE	562 SQ. FT.
FOUNDATION	CRAWL SPACE

DESIGN BY DONALD A. GARDNER ARCHITECTS, INC.

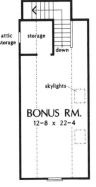

BONUS RM.
12-8 x 22-4

attic storage

storage

down

skylights

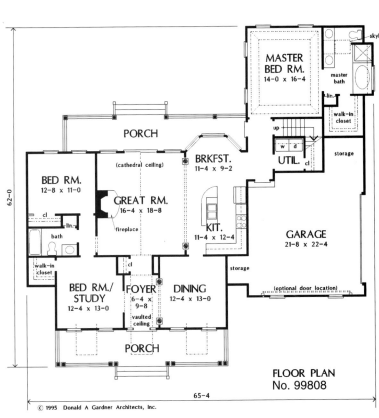

PORCH

BED RM.
12-8 x 11-0

GREAT RM.
16-4 x 18-8
(cathedral ceiling)
fireplace

BRKFST.
11-4 x 9-2

KIT.
11-4 x 12-4

MASTER BED RM.
14-0 x 16-4

master bath

walk-in closet

UTIL.

storage

GARAGE
21-8 x 22-4

walk-in closet

bath

BED RM./ STUDY
12-4 x 13-0

FOYER
6-4 x 9-8
vaulted ceiling

DINING
12-4 x 13-0

storage

(optional door location)

PORCH

62-0

65-4

FLOOR PLAN
No. 99808

© 1995 Donald A Gardner Architects, Inc.

PLAN: 99808

DRAMATIC RANCH

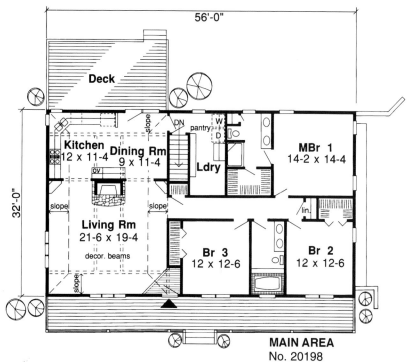

56'-0"

Deck

Kitchen
12 x 11-4

Dining Rm
9 x 11-4

pantry

DN

W
D

Ldry

MBr 1
14-2 x 14-4

slope

slope

Living Rm
21-6 x 19-4

decor. beams

slope

32'-0"

slope

lin.

Br 3
12 x 12-6

Br 2
12 x 12-6

MAIN AREA
No. 20198

The exterior of this ranch home is all wood with interesting lines. More than an ordinary ranch home, it has an expansive feeling to drive up to. The large living area has a stone fireplace and decorative beams. The kitchen and dining room lead to an outside deck. The laundry room has a large pantry, and is off the eating area. The master bedroom has a wonderful bathroom with a huge walk-in closet. In the front of the house, there are two additional bedrooms with a bathroom. This house offers one floor living and has nice big rooms.

TOTAL LIVING AREA	1,792 SQ. FT.
MAIN AREA	1,792 SQ. FT.
BEDROOMS	THREE
BATHROOMS	2 FULL
BASEMENT	818 SQ. FT.
GARAGE	857 SQ. FT.
FOUNDATION	BASEMENT

DESIGN BY THE GARLINGHOUSE COMPANY

PLAN: 20198

This Traditional design is accented by the use of gable roofs and the blend of stucco and brick to form a truly spectacular exterior. This home has the look and feel of a much larger home. Entering the den, we find a high vaulted ceiling with built-in cabinets and a fireplace. The dining room is open to the den creating the Great room feel for this area. The U-shaped kitchen features built-in appliances. The bedrooms are designed in a split fashion. The master bedroom is located to rear of the plan and features a private bath. This plan is available with a crawl space or slab foundation. Please specify when ordering.

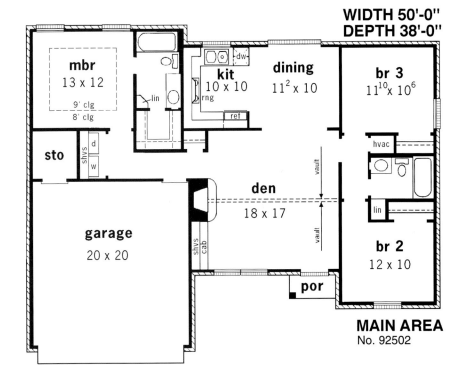

WIDTH 50'-0"
DEPTH 38'-0"

mbr
13 x 12
9' clg
8' clg

sto

kit
10 x 10
rng
ref
dw

dining
11^2 x 10

br 3
11^{10}x 10^6

hvac

den
18 x 17
vault
vault

garage
20 x 20

br 2
12 x 10

por

MAIN AREA
No. 92502

TOTAL LIVING AREA	1,237 SQ. FT.
MAIN AREA	1,237 SQ. FT.
BEDROOMS	THREE
BATHROOMS	2 FULL
GARAGE	436 SQ. FT.
FOUNDATION	SLAB OR CRAWL SPACE

DESIGN BY RICK GARNER

PLAN: 92502

BUDGET BEAUTY

B. NATHAN

© Donald A. Gardner Architects, Inc.

Not only have the rear and sides of this home been squared off for easy, economical building, but other architectural elements also add a rare smoothness. Square columns with chamfered corners adorn the front porch. A partially open kitchen easily serves the generous breakfast area. The dining room, front bedroom, and master suite feature tray ceilings. The master bath includes separate shower and garden tub, skylight, dual vanities, and enclosed toilet. This plan is available with a basement or crawl space foundation. Please specify when ordering.

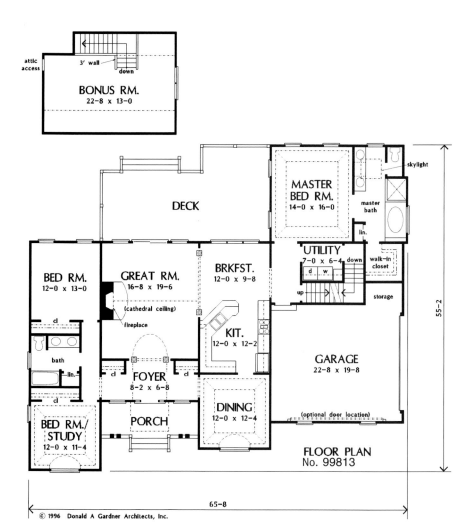

TOTAL LIVING AREA	1,959 SQ. FT
MAIN FLOOR	1,959 SQ. FT.
BONUS AREA	385 SQ. FT.
BEDROOMS	THREE
BATHROOMS	2 FULL
GARAGE	484 SQ. FT.
FOUNDATION	BASEMENT OR CRAWL SPACE

DESIGN BY DONALD A. GARDNER ARCHITECTS, INC.

© 1996 Donald A Gardner Architects, Inc.

PLAN: 99813

This home features a well designed floor plan, offering convenience and style. The living room includes a two-sided fireplace shared with the dining room. An U-shaped kitchen is equipped with a peninsula counter/breakfast bar. The private master suite includes a whirlpool tub, a double vanity and a step-in shower. A large walk-in closet adds ample storage space to the suite. The secondary bedroom and the den/guest room share use of the full hall bath.

TOTAL LIVING AREA	1,625 SQ. FT.
MAIN AREA	1,625 SQ. FT.
BEDROOMS	THREE
BATHROOMS	2 FULL
BASEMENT	1,625 SQ. FT.
GARAGE	455 SQ. FT.
FOUNDATION	BASEMENT, SLAB OR CRAWL SPACE

DESIGN BY THE GARLINGHOUSE COMPANY

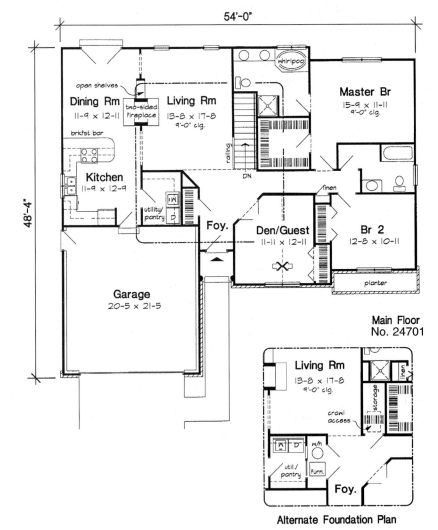

Main Floor
No. 24701

Alternate Foundation Plan

PLAN: 24701

© Donald A. Gardner Architects, Inc.

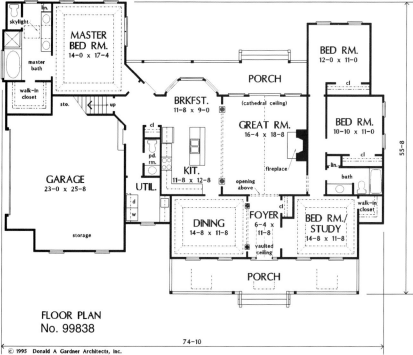

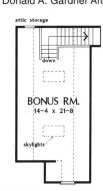

attic storage

down

BONUS RM.
14-4 x 21-8

skylights

Exciting volumes and nine-foot ceilings add elegance to this open plan. Sunlight fills the foyer from a vaulted dormer and streams through an opening into the Great room's cathedral ceiling. The dining room, delineated from the foyer by columns, features a tray ceiling. Children's bedrooms share a full bath. The front bedroom doubles as a study and is accented by a tray ceiling. The master suite is highlighted by a tray ceiling and includes a skylit bath with garden tub, private toilet, double vanity, and spacious walk-in closet. A skylit bonus room provides opportunity for expansion.

TOTAL LIVING AREA	2,192 SQ. FT
MAIN FLOOR	2,192 SQ. FT.
BONUS ROOM	390 SQ. FT.
BEDROOMS	FOUR
BATHROOMS	2 FULL, 1 HALF
GARAGE	582 SQ. FT.
FOUNDATION	CRAWL SPACE

DESIGN BY DONALD A. GARDNER ARCHITECTS, INC.

FLOOR PLAN
No. 99838

74-10

PLAN: 99838

EXTRA TOUCHES

You don't have to sacrifice style when buying a smaller home. Notice the palladian window with a fan light above at the front of the home. The entrance porch includes a turned post entry. Once inside, the living room is topped by an impressive vaulted ceiling. A fireplace accents the room. A decorative ceiling enhances both the master bedroom and the dining room. The kitchen includes a peninsula counter. A private bath and double closet highlight the master suite.

TOTAL LIVING AREA	1,312 SQ. FT.
MAIN AREA	1,312 SQ. FT.
BEDROOMS	THREE
BATHROOMS	2 FULL
BASEMENT	1,293 SQ. FT.
GARAGE	459 SQ. FT.
FOUNDATION	BASEMENT, SLAB, OR CRAWL SPACE

DESIGN BY THE GARLINGHOUSE COMPANY

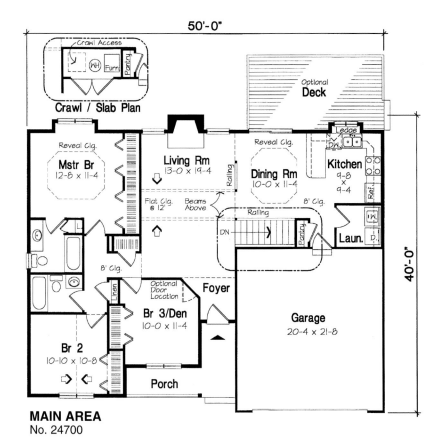

MAIN AREA
No. 24700

PLAN: 24700

If you are looking for traditional country styling, this is the home for you. The dining room is to the right of the foyer and includes direct access to the kitchen and built-in cabinets. The kitchen is made more efficient by the peninsula counter/eating bar extending counter space and provides a perfect place for meals on the go. The den is enhanced by a vaulted ceiling and a lovely fireplace. The master suite is tucked into a private corner and pampered by a five piece master bath. The two additional bedrooms are on the opposite side of the home and share the full bath located in the hall. This plan is available with a crawl space or slab foundation. Please specify when ordering.

WIDTH 66'-10"
DEPTH 46'-10"

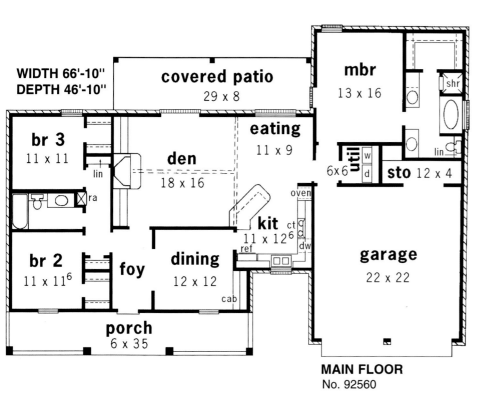

MAIN FLOOR
No. 92560

TOTAL LIVING AREA	1,660 SQ. FT
MAIN FLOOR	1,660 SQ. FT.
BEDROOMS	THREE
BATHROOMS	2 FULL
GARAGE	544 SQ. FT.
FOUNDATION	CRAWL SPACE OR SLAB

DESIGN BY RICK GARNER

PLAN: 92560

"WELCOME HOME"

© Donald A. Gardner Architects, Inc.

This plan's wide front porch and its comfortable design encourages relaxation. A center dormer lights the foyer, as columns punctuate the entry to the dining room and Great room. The spacious kitchen has an angled countertop and is open to the breakfast bay. Tray ceilings add elegance to the dining room and the master bedroom. A second master suite is located on the opposite end of the home and features an optional arrangement for the physically challenged. A skylit bonus room is located over the garage and provides room for growth.

TOTAL LIVING AREA	2,349 SQ. FT
MAIN AREA	2,349 SQ. FT.
BONUS ROOM	435 SQ. FT.
BEDROOMS	FOUR
BATHROOMS	3 FULL
GARAGE	615 SQ. FT.
FOUNDATION	CRAWL SPACE

DESIGN BY DONALD A. GARDNER ARCHITECTS, INC.

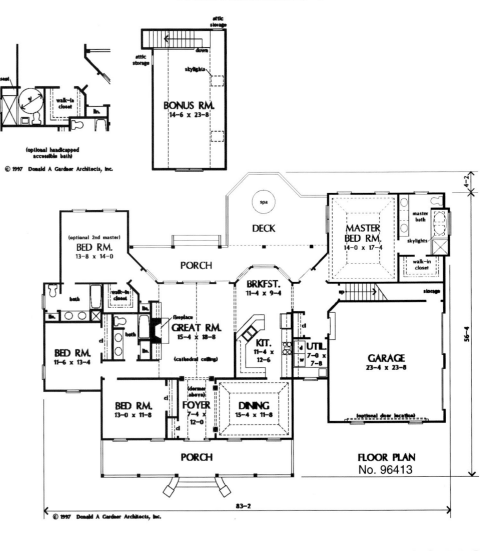

(optional handicapped accessible bath)

© 1997 Donald A Gardner Architects, Inc.

BONUS RM.
14-6 x 23-8

FLOOR PLAN
No. 96413

© 1997 Donald A Gardner Architects, Inc.

PLAN: 96413

© Donald A. Gardner Architects, Inc.

B. NATHAN

Dormers cast light and interest into the foyer for a grand first impression that sets the tone in a home full of today's amenities. The Great room, articulated by columns, features a cathedral ceiling and is conveniently located adjacent to the breakfast room and kitchen. Tray ceilings and picture windows with circle tops accent the front bedroom and dining room. A secluded master suite includes a bath with skylight, garden tub, separate shower, dual vanity and spacious walk-in closet. This plan is available with a crawl space or a basement foundation. Please specify when ordering.

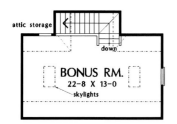

attic storage
down
BONUS RM.
22-8 X 13-0
skylights

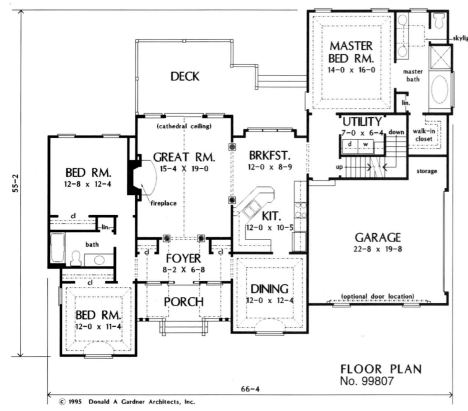

DECK

(cathedral ceiling)

MASTER BED RM.
14-0 x 16-0

master bath

skylight

lin.

UTILITY
7-0 x 6-4   down   lin.

walk-in closet

GREAT RM.
15-4 x 19-0

BRKFST.
12-0 x 8-9

d   w

up

storage

BED RM.
12-8 x 12-4

fireplace

cl   lin.

bath

KIT.
12-0 x 10-5

GARAGE
22-8 x 19-8

cl

FOYER
8-2 X 6-8

cl

cl

DINING
12-0 x 12-4

(optional door location)

BED RM.
12-0 x 11-4

PORCH

55-2

66-4

© 1995 Donald A Gardner Architects, Inc.

FLOOR PLAN
No. 99807

TOTAL LIVING AREA	1,879 SQ. FT.
MAIN FLOOR	1,879 SQ. FT.
BONUS AREA	360 SQ. FT.
BEDROOMS	THREE
BATHROOMS	2 FULL
GARAGE	485 SQ. FT.
FOUNDATION	BASEMENT OR CRAWL SPACE

DESIGN BY DONALD A. GARDNER ARCHITECTS, INC.

PLAN: 99807

© 1993 Donald A. Gardner Architects, Inc.

QUAINT AND COZY COTTAGE

TOTAL LIVING AREA	1,864 SQ. FT
MAIN FLOOR	1,864 SQ. FT.
BONUS AREA	420 SQ. FT.
GARAGE & STORAGE	614 SQ. FT.
BEDROOMS	THREE
BATHROOMS	2 FULL, 1 HALF
FOUNDATION	BASEMENT OR CRAWL SPACE

DESIGN BY DONALD A. GARDNER ARCHITECTS, INC.

With porches front and back, this country home surprises with an open floor plan featuring a large Great room with cathedral ceiling. Nine-foot ceilings add volume throughout the home. A central kitchen opens to the breakfast area and Great room for easy entertaining. A bonus room over the garage makes expanding easy. This plan is available with a basement or crawl space foundation. Please specify when ordering.

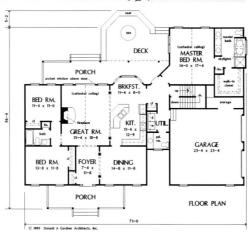
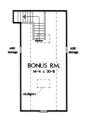

FLOOR PLAN

© 1993 Donald A Gardner Architects, Inc.

PRICE CODE D

DETAILED CHARMER

TOTAL LIVING AREA	1,307 SQ. FT
MAIN AREA	1,307 SQ. FT.
BASEMENT	1,298 SQ. FT.
GARAGE	462 SQ. FT.
BEDROOMS	THREE
BATHROOMS	2 FULL
FOUNDATION	BASEMENT, SLAB OR CRAWL SPACE

DESIGN BY THE GARLINGHOUSE COMPANY

Walk past the charming front porch, in through the foyer and you'll be struck by the exciting, spacious living room. Complete with high sloping ceilings and a beautiful fireplace. The large master bedroom has its own private bath, and a decorative ceiling. The dining room provides decorative ceiling details, and a full slider out to the deck. The kitchen includes a double sink and an attractive bump-out window.

MAIN AREA

Slab/Crawl Space Option

28

PRICE CODE A

GREAT STARTER HOME

TOTAL LIVING AREA	1,576 SQ. FT
MAIN FLOOR	1,576 SQ. FT.
BASEMENT	1,454 SQ. FT.
GARAGE	576 SQ. FT.
BEDROOMS	THREE
BATHROOMS	2 FULL
FOUNDATION OR CRAWL SPACE	BASEMENT, SLAB

DESIGN BY THE GARLINGHOUSE COMPANY

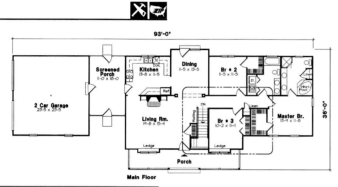

Main Floor

93'-0"

36'-0"

2 Car Garage 23-5 x 23-5

Screened Porch 11-0 x 18-0

Kitchen 13-8 x 11-5

Dining 11-5 x 13-5

Br # 2 11-5 x 11-5

Living Rm. 14-8 x 15-4

Br # 3 10-2 x 11-11

Master Br. 13-4 x 11-8

Porch

Alternate Crawl/Slab Plan

Br # 2 10-2 x 11-11

Furn.

Crawl Access

Ledge

This functional, all on one level, home plan features a lovely country porch entry into a spacious living room that is accented by a fireplace. The efficient U-shaped kitchen has direct access to both the dining and the living room. A screened porch is accessed directly from the kitchen. The master bedroom includes a private double vanity bath with a whirlpool tub and separate shower. The two additional bedrooms share a full double vanity bath which has the added convenience of a laundry center.

PRICE CODE B

ATTENTION GETTING DETAIL

TOTAL LIVING AREA	2,735 SQ. FT
MAIN FLOOR	2,735 SQ. FT.
GARAGE	561 SQ. FT.
BEDROOMS	FOUR
BATHROOMS	3 FULL
FOUNDATION	CRAWL SPACE OR SLAB

DESIGN BY RICK GARNER

WIDTH 68'-10"
DEPTH 67'-4"

mbr 15 x 21⁴ raised clg

sto 8⁶ x 8

util 8⁶ x 9

garage 21 x 22

porch 8 x 30⁸

eating 13 x 11

kit 13 x 13

den 18 x 24 raised clg

dining 14 x 12

foy

porch

br 4 14 x 12

br 3 14 x 12

br 2 14 x 12

MAIN FLOOR

This spacious four bedroom home features a formal foyer leading directly into the den. The den is expansive, topped by a raised ceiling, and focuses on a cozy fireplace. The kitchen uses an angled extended counter, and flows into the den and eating area. The dining area includes an a boxed bay window. The split bedroom plan insures privacy for the master bedroom. Crowned in a raised ceiling and pampered by a plush, whirlpool bath, the master suite is sure to please. This plan is available with a crawl space or slab foundation, Please specify when ordering.

PRICE CODE F

PLAN: 96468

© Donald A. Gardner Architects, Inc.

BONUS ROOM EXPANDS FAMILY SPACE

TOTAL LIVING AREA	1,864 SQ. FT
MAIN FLOOR	1,864 SQ. FT.
BONUS ROOM	319 SQ. FT.
GARAGE & STORAGE	503 SQ. FT.
BEDROOMS	THREE
BATHROOMS	2 FULL
FOUNDATION	CRAWL SPACE

DESIGN BY DONALD A. GARDNER ARCHITECTS, INC.

The space flows easily from the sunlit foyer into a generous Great room with cathedral ceiling, while interior accent columns define the open kitchen and breakfast bay. The master bedroom, located off the Great room, features a tray ceiling and back porch access, and the well-appointed master bath is separated from the bedroom by closets. A new design twist puts two more bedrooms just steps away from the bonus room.

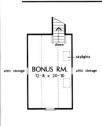

FLOOR PLAN

© 1996 Donald A Gardner Architects, Inc.

PRICE CODE D

PLAN: 99840

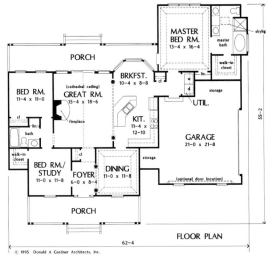

© Donald A. Gardner Architects, Inc.

PORCHES GALORE

TOTAL LIVING AREA	1,632 SQ. FT
MAIN FLOOR	1,632 SQ. FT.
GARAGE & STORAGE	561 SQ. FT.
BEDROOMS	THREE
BATHROOMS	2 FULL
FOUNDATION	CRAWL SPACE

DESIGN BY DONALD A. GARDNER ARCHITECTS, INC.

Porches front and back, gables, and dormers provide special charm to this Country home. The Great room has a cathedral ceiling, fireplace, and a clerestory window. Columns divide the open Great room from the kitchen and breakfast bay. A tray ceiling and columns dress up the formal dining room. The master suite with tray ceiling and back porch access is privately-located in the rear. The skylit master bath features whirlpool tub, shower, dual vanity, and spacious walk-in closet.

FLOOR PLAN

© 1995 Donald A Gardner Architects, Inc.

PRICE CODE D

BEST OF BOTH WORLDS

TOTAL LIVING AREA	1,954 SQ. FT
MAIN FLOOR	1,954 SQ. FT.
BONUS ROOM	436 SQ. FT.
GARAGE & STORAGE	649 SQ. FT.
BEDROOMS	THREE
BATHROOMS	2 FULL, 1 HALF
FOUNDATION	CRAWL SPACE

DESIGN BY DONALD A. GARDNER
ARCHITECTS, INC.

PRICE CODE D

© Donald A. Gardner Architects, Inc.

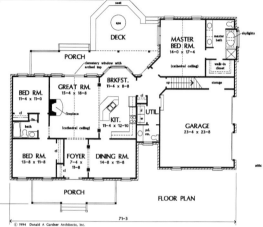

FLOOR PLAN

This plan offers the best of both worlds for those torn between traditional and country style. You get all the room you need in just 1,954 square feet thanks to an open floor plan and covered porches in this three bedroom country home. Cathedral ceilings add volume to the master suite which is located in the rear for privacy. Its well-appointed skylit bath features a whirlpool tub, separate shower, and a dual vanity.

VERSITILE DESIGN

TOTAL LIVING AREA	1,590 SQ. FT
MAIN FLOOR	1,590 SQ. FT.
GARAGE & STORAGE	506 SQ. FT.
BEDROOMS	3
BATHROOMS	2 FULL
FOUNDATION	CRAWL SPACE

DESIGN BY DONALD A. GARDNER
ARCHITECTS, INC.

© Donald A. Gardner Architects, Inc.

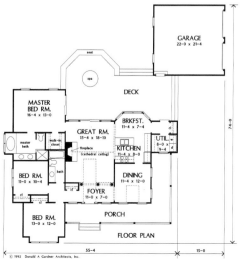

FLOOR PLAN

Country on the outside and contemporary on the inside, this three-bedroom charmer celebrates country life with a wrap-around porch and a large rear deck. Columns dramatically open the foyer to a generous Great room which in turn opens to the kitchen/breakfast area for a feeling of spaciousness. Natural light penetrates from dormer windows into the foyer and dining room. The master suite is privately located at the rear, while two front bedrooms share a second full bath.

PRICE CODE D

© Donald A. Gardner Architects, Inc.

COMPACT COUNTRY COTTAGE

TOTAL LIVING AREA	1,310 SQ. FT
MAIN FLOOR	1,310 SQ. FT.
GARAGE & STORAGE	455 SQ. FT.
BEDROOMS	THREE
BATHROOMS	2 FULL
FOUNDATION	CRAWL SPACE

DESIGN BY DONALD A. GARDNER ARCHITECTS, INC.

Multi-paned bay window, dormers, cupola and a covered porch give this compact country cottage visual impact. The foyer opens to a large Great room, with fireplace and cathedral ceiling. Two front bedrooms, one with bay window, the other with walk-in closet, share an ample bath. The master suite is privately located at the rear with walk-in closet and private bath with double vanity.

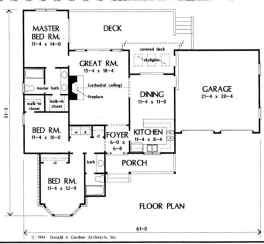

PRICE CODE C

© 1993 Donald A. Gardner Architects, Inc.

HOME BUILDERS ON A BUDGET

TOTAL LIVING AREA	1,498 SQ. FT
MAIN FLOOR	1,498 SQ. FT.
GARAGE & STORAGE	427 SQ. FT.
BEDROOMS	THREE
BATHROOMS	2 FULL
FOUNDATION	CRAWL SPACE

DESIGN BY DONALD A. GARDNER ARCHITECTS, INC.

We kept all the Country charm when we down-sized one of our most popular plans for home builders on a budget. Columns punctuate the open, one-level floor plan and connect the foyer and kitchen/breakfast room to the large Great room with cathedral ceiling and fireplace. Tray ceilings lift the master bedroom, dining room, and bedroom/study out of the ordinary. The private master suite features a garden tub, double vanity, walk-in closet, separate shower, and operable skylights.

PRICE CODE C

Design by
Vaughn A. Lauban Designs

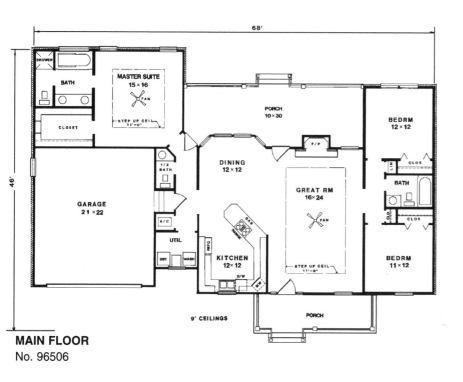

MAIN FLOOR
No. 96506

Attractive Ceiling Treatments and Open Layout

- This plan features:
  — Three bedrooms
  — Two full and one half baths
- Great Room and Master Suite with step-up ceiling treatments
- A cozy fireplace providing warm focal point in the Great Room
- Open layout between Kitchen, Dining and Great Room lending a more spacious feeling
- Five-piece, private Bath and walk-in closet in the pampering Master Suite
- Two additional Bedrooms located at opposite end of home

MAIN FLOOR — 1,654 SQ. FT.
GARAGE — 480 SQ. FT.

TOTAL LIVING AREA:
1,654 SQ. FT.

Design by
The Garlinghouse Company

Refer to **Pricing Schedule A** on the order form for pricing information

Large Living in a Small Space

■ This plan features:

— Three bedrooms

— Two full baths

■ A sheltered entrance leads into an open Living Room with a corner fireplace and a wall of windows

■ A well-equipped Kitchen features a peninsula counter with a Nook, a Laundry and clothes closet, and a built-in Pantry

■ A Master Bedroom with a private Bath

■ Two additional Bedrooms that share full hall Bath

MAIN FLOOR — 993 SQ. FT.
GARAGE — 390 SQ. FT.
BASEMENT — 987 SQ. FT.

TOTAL LIVING AREA:
993 SQ. FT.

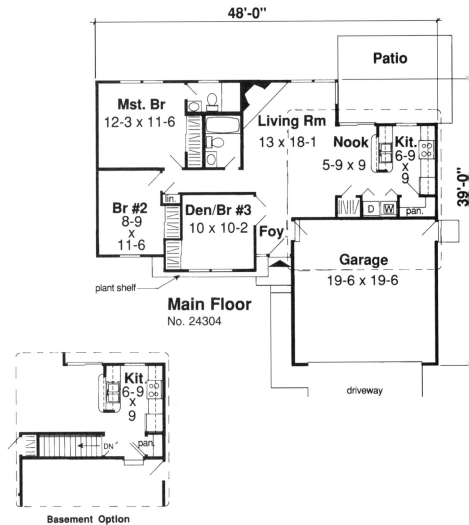

48'-0"

Patio

Mst. Br
12-3 x 11-6

Living Rm
13 x 18-1

Nook
5-9 x 9

Kit.
6-9 x 9

Br #2
8-9 x 11-6

Den/Br #3
10 x 10-2

Foy

lin.

39'-0"

D   W   pan.

plant shelf

Garage
19-6 x 19-6

Main Floor
No. 24304

driveway

Kit
6-9 x 9

DN   pan.

Basement Option

To order your Blueprints, call 1-800-235-5700

Design by
Frank Betz Associates, Inc.

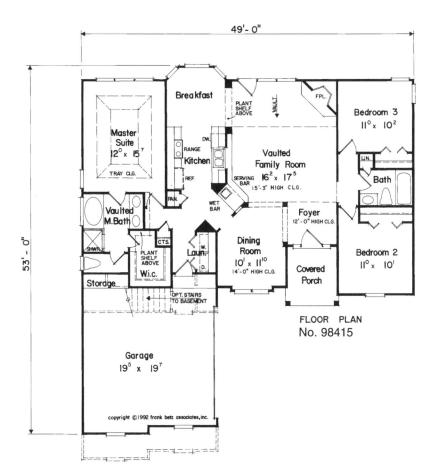

49'- 0"

53' - 0"

Breakfast

PLANT SHELF ABOVE

VAULT

FPL

Master Suite
12⁰ x 15⁷
TRAY CLG.

RANGE

DW.

Kitchen

REF.

PAN.

Bedroom 3
11⁰ x 10²

Vaulted Family Room
16² x 17⁵
15'-3" HIGH CLG.

SERVING BAR

LIN.

Bath

Vaulted M.Bath

WET BAR

Foyer
12'- 0" HIGH CLG.

SHWR.

PLANT SHELF ABOVE

CTS.

Laun.

W.

D.

Dining Room
10¹ x 11¹⁰
14'-0" HIGH CLG.

Bedroom 2
11⁰ x 10¹

Wi.c.

Storage

OPT. STAIRS TO BASEMENT

Covered Porch

FLOOR PLAN
No. 98415

Garage
19⁵ x 19⁷

copyright ©1992 frank betz associates, inc.

Split Bedroom Plan

◾ This plan features:

— Three bedrooms

— Two full baths

◾ A tray ceiling gives a decorative touch to the Master Bedroom

◾ A full Bath located between the secondary Bedrooms

◾ A corner fireplace and a vaulted ceiling highlight the Family Room

◾ A wetbar/serving bar and a built-in Pantry add to the convenience of the Kitchen

◾ The formal Dining Room is crowned in an elegant high ceiling

◾ An optional basement, crawl space or slab foundation — please specify when ordering

MAIN FLOOR — 1,429 SQ. FT.
BASEMENT — 1,472 SQ. FT.
GARAGE — 438 SQ. FT.

TOTAL LIVING AREA:
1,429 SQ. FT.

Design by
The Garlinghouse Company

Refer to **Pricing Schedule A** on the order form for pricing information

Family Favorite

■ This plan features:

— Three bedrooms

— Two full baths

■ An open arrangement with the Dining Room that combines with ten foot ceilings to make the Living Room seem more spacious

■ Glass on three sides of the Dining Room which overlooks the Deck

■ An efficient, compact Kitchen with a built-in Pantry and peninsula counter

■ A Master Suite with a window seat, a compartmentalized private Bath and a walk-in closet

■ Two additional Bedrooms that share a full hall closet

MAIN AREA — 1,359 SQ. FT.
BASEMENT — 1,359 SQ. FT.
GARAGE — 501 SQ. FT.

TOTAL LIVING AREA:
1,359 SQ. FT.

MAIN AREA
No. 20156

Refer to **Pricing Schedule A** on the order form for pricing information

Design by
Jannis Vann & Associates, Inc.

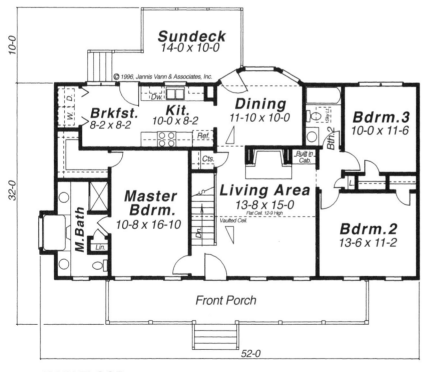

© 1996, Jannis Vann & Associates, Inc.

Sundeck
14-0 x 10-0

Brkfst.
8-2 x 8-2

W.D.

Dw.

Kit.
10-0 x 8-2

Ref.

Cts.

Dining
11-10 x 10-0

Bth.2

Skylt.

Bdrm.3
10-0 x 11-6

Built-in Cab.

Master Bdrm.
10-8 x 16-10

M. Bath

Lin.

Living Area
13-8 x 15-0
Flat Ceil. 12-9 High
Vaulted Ceil.

Bdrm.2
13-6 x 11-2

L.

Front Porch

10-0

32-0

52-0

MAIN FLOOR
No. 98912

Simply Cozy

◼ This plan features:
— Three bedrooms
— Two full baths

◼ Quaint front porch shelters Entry into the Living Area which is showcased by a massive fireplace and built-ins

◼ Formal Dining Room with Sun Deck access accented by a bay of glass

◼ Efficient, galley Kitchen with Breakfast Area, laundry facilities and outdoor access

◼ Secluded Master Bedroom offers a roomy walk-in closet and plush Bath with dual vanity and a garden window tub

◼ Two additional Bedrooms with ample closets share a full Bath with a skylight

MAIN FLOOR — 1,325 SQ. FT.
BASEMENT — 556 SQ. FT.
GARAGE — 724 SQ. FT.

TOTAL LIVING AREA:
1,325 SQ. FT.

Design by
The Garlinghouse Company

Refer to **Pricing Schedule C** on the order form for pricing information

Central Living Room

■ This plan features:

— Four bedrooms

— Two full baths

■ Sheltered entrance leads into fieldstone Foyer and spacious Living Room with a Terrace beyond

■ Formal Dining Room opens to Living Room and Kitchen for easy entertaining

■ An efficent Kitchen offers Laundry facilities and loads of counter and storage space

■ Comfortable Family Room convenient to Garage and outdoors

■ Quite corner Master Bedroom enjoys a walk-in closet and private Bath

MAIN AREA — 2,022 SQ. FT.
BASEMENT — 2,022 SQ. FT.
GARAGE — 576 SQ. FT.

TOTAL LIVING AREA:
2,022 SQ. FT.

MAIN FLOOR
No. 9846

To order your Blueprints, call 1-800-235-5700

Design by
Studer Residential Design, Inc.

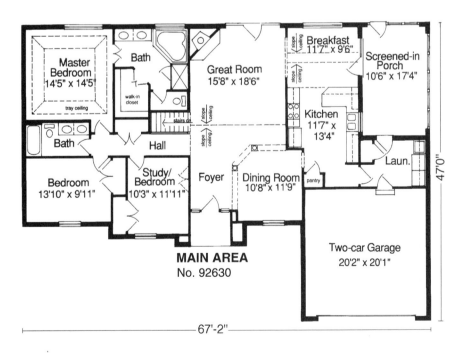

MAIN AREA
No. 92630

Master Bedroom 14'5" x 14'5"
tray ceiling

Bath

walk-in closet

Great Room 15'8" x 18'6"

Breakfast 11'7" x 9'6"

Screened-in Porch 10'6" x 17'4"

Kitchen 11'7" x 13'4"

Bath

Hall

stairs dn

Laun.

Bedroom 13'10" x 9'11"

Study/ Bedroom 10'3" x 11'11"

Foyer

Dining Room 10'8" x 11'9"

pantry

Two-car Garage 20'2" x 20'1"

47'0"

67'-2"

Charming Brick Ranch

▪ This plan features:

— Three bedrooms

— Two full baths

▪ Sheltered entrance leads into open Foyer and Dining Room defined by columns

▪ Vaulted ceiling spans Foyer, Dining Room, and Great Room with corner fireplace and atrium door to rear yard

▪ Central Kitchen with separate Laundry and Pantry easily serves Dining Room, Breakfast Area and Screened Porch

▪ Luxurious Master Bedroom offers tray ceiling and French doors to Bath

▪ No materials list is available for this plan

MAIN AREA —1,782 SQ. FT.
GARAGE — 407 SQ. FT.
BASEMENT — 1,735 SQ. FT.

TOTAL LIVING AREA:
1,782 SQ. FT.

Design by
Living Designs

Refer to **Pricing Schedule A** on
the order form for pricing information

Inviting Porch Has Dual Function

■ This plan features:

— Three bedrooms

— One full and one three-quarter baths

■ An inviting, wrap-around Porch Entry with sliding glass doors leading right into a bayed Dining Room

■ A Living Room with a cozy feeling, enhanced by the fireplace

■ An efficient Kitchen opening to both Dining and Living Rooms

■ A Master Suite with a walk-in closet and private Master Bath

■ An optional basement, slab or crawl space foundation — please specify when ordering

MAIN FLOOR — 1,295 SQ. FT.
GARAGE — 400 SQ. FT.

TOTAL LIVING AREA:
1,295 SQ. FT.

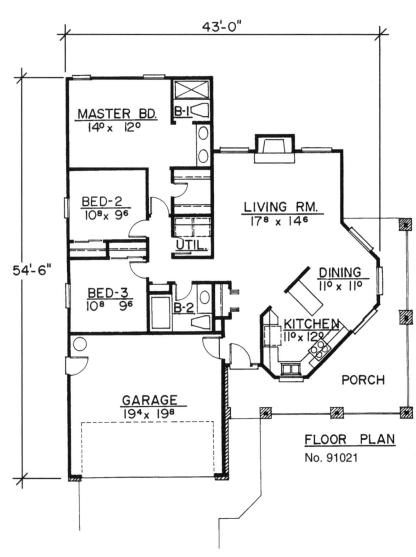

43'-0"

54'-6"

MASTER BD.
14⁰ x 12⁰

B-1

BED-2
10⁸ x 9⁶

UTIL.

LIVING RM.
17⁸ x 14⁶

BED-3
10⁸ 9⁶

B-2

DINING
11⁰ x 11⁰

KITCHEN
11⁰ x 12⁸

PORCH

GARAGE
19⁴ x 19⁸

FLOOR PLAN
No. 91021

To order your Blueprints, call 1-800-235-5700

Design by
Urban Design Group

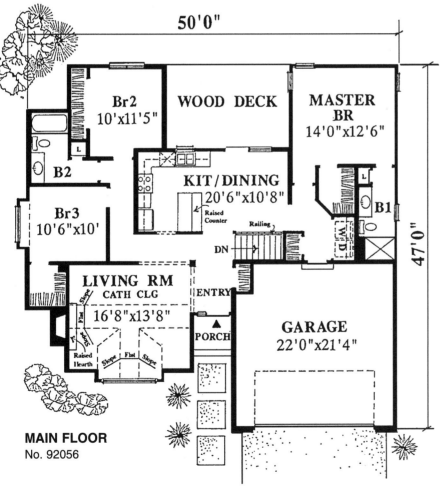

MAIN FLOOR
No. 92056

Split-Bedroom Floor Plan

■ This plan features:
— Three bedrooms
— One full and one three-quarter bath
■ Outstanding Living Room with a cathedral ceiling and boxed bay window
■ Combination Kitchen and Dining Room with a raised peninsula counter/snack bar
■ Wood rear deck expanding living space to the outdoors
■ Secluded Master Bedroom Suite with private three-quarter bath
■ Two additional bedrooms with ample closet space

MAIN FLOOR — 1,425 SQ. FT.
BASEMENT — 1,425 SQ. FT.

TOTAL LIVING AREA:
1,425 SQ. FT.

PLAN NO. 94640

Design by
Chatham Home Planning, Inc.

Refer to **Pricing Schedule D** on the order form for pricing information

Family Room at Heart of the Home

■ This plan features:

— Four bedrooms

— Three full baths

■ The Living Room and Dining Room are to the right and left of the Foyer

■ The Dining Room with French doors opens to the Kitchen

■ An extended counter maximizes the work space in the Kitchen

■ The Master Bedroom is equipped with a double vanity Bath, two walk-in closets and a linear closet

■ A cozy fireplace and a decorative ceiling highlight the Family Room

■ No materials list is available for this plan

MAIN FLOOR — 2,558 SQ. FT.
GARAGE — 549 SQ. FT.

TOTAL LIVING AREA:
2,558 SQ. FT.

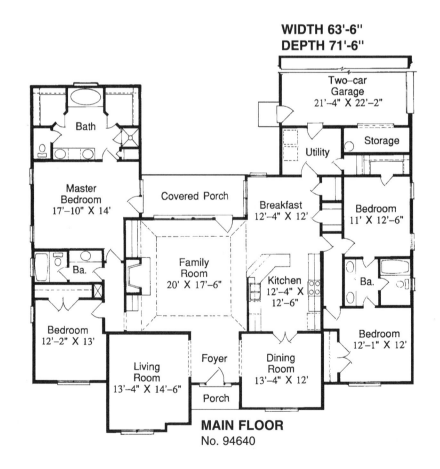

WIDTH 63'-6"
DEPTH 71'-6"

MAIN FLOOR
No. 94640

To order your Blueprints, call 1-800-235-5700

Design by
Wickes Lumber Company

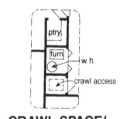

CRAWL SPACE/ SLAB OPTION

ptry.
furn
w. h.
crawl access

Bow Window Adds to Curb Appeal

■ This plan features:

— Three bedrooms

— Two full baths

■ Curb appeal is enhanced by a beautiful bow window in the Living Room, and by the front Porch

■ A Dining Room that is separated from the Kitchen by only a peninsula counter/eating bar

■ More than ample counter space, a double sink and a Laundry Center in the Kitchen

■ A Master Bedroom with a private full Bath and his-n-her closets

■ Two additional bedrooms that share a full hall bath

MAIN AREA — 1,373 SQ. FT.
GARAGE — 400 SQ. FT.

TOTAL LIVING AREA:
1,373 SQ. FT.

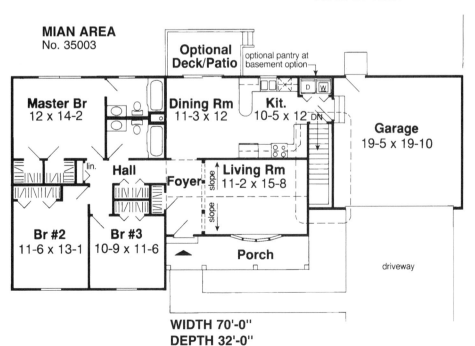

MIAN AREA
No. 35003

Optional Deck/Patio

optional pantry at basement option

Master Br 12 x 14-2

Dining Rm 11-3 x 12

Kit. 10-5 x 12   DN

D W

Garage 19-5 x 19-10

lin.

Hall

Foyer **Living Rm** 11-2 x 15-8

slope

Br #2 11-6 x 13-1

Br #3 10-9 x 11-6

Porch

driveway

WIDTH 70'-0"
DEPTH 32'-0"

Design by
Fillmore Design Group

Refer to **Pricing Schedule E** on
the order form for pricing information

Brick Magnificence

■ This plan features:

— Four bedrooms

— Three full baths

■ Large windows and attractive
brick detailing using segmented
arches give fantastic curb appeal

■ Convenient Ranch layout allows
for step-saving one floor ease

■ A fireplace in the Living Room
adds a warm ambience

■ The Family Room sports a
second fireplace and built-in
shelving

■ Two additional Bedrooms include
private access to a full double
vanity Bath

■ No materials list is available for
this plan

MAIN FLOOR — 2,858 SQ. FT.
GARAGE — 768 SQ. FT.

TOTAL LIVING AREA:
2,858 SQ. FT.

89' - 7"

68' - 4"

3-Car-Gar
24x32

Patio Area

BrkfstRm
13x10
10'Clg.

Patio Area

MstrBed
17x14

LivRm
17x15
10'Clg.

Kit
13x14
10'Clg.

FamilyRm
16x17
10'Clg.

Util
8'Clg.

Study
11x11

Ent/Gallery
11'Clg.

Bed#4
12x12
8'Clg.

FmlDin
12x13
11'Clg.

Bed#3
12x12
10'Clg.

Bed#2
14x11

Main Floor
No. 92243

To order your Blueprints, call 1-800-235-5700

Refer to **Pricing Schedule C** on the order form for pricing information

Design by
Homeplanners

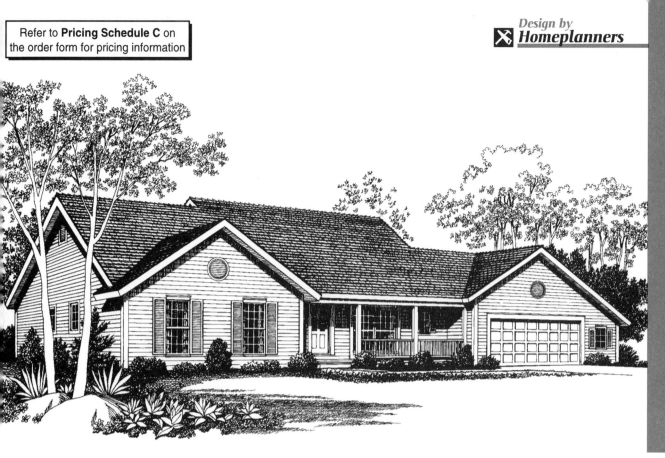

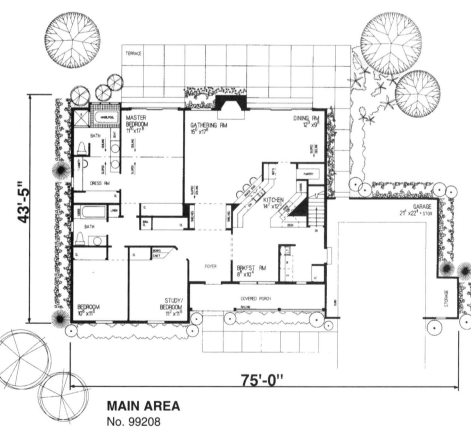

MAIN AREA
No. 99208

43'-5"

75'-0"

Cozy Traditional with Style

■ This plan features:

— Three bedrooms

— Two full baths

■ A convenient one-level design

■ A galley-style Kitchen that shares a snack bar with the spacious Gathering Room

■ A focal point fireplace making the Gathering Room warm and inviting

■ An ample Master Suite with a luxury Bath which contains a whirlpool tub and separate Dressing Room

■ Two additional Bedrooms, one that could double as a Study, located at the front of the house

MAIN AREA — 1,830 SQ. FT.
BASEMENT — 1,830 SQ. FT.

TOTAL LIVING AREA:
1,830 SQ. FT.

Design by
Donald A. Gardner Architects, Inc.

Refer to **Pricing Schedule C** on the order form for pricing information

© 1993 Donald A. Gardner Architects, Inc.

Economical Three Bedroom

■ This plan features:
— Three bedrooms
— Two full baths

■ Dormers above the covered Porch casts light into the Foyer

■ Columns punctuate the entrance to the Great Room/ Dining Room Area with a shared cathedral ceiling and a bank of operable skylights

■ Kitchen with a Breakfast Counter, open to the Dining Area

■ Private Master Bedroom with a tray ceiling and luxurious Bath featuring a double vanity, separate shower, and skylights over the whirlpool tub

MAIN FLOOR — 1,322 SQ. FT.
GARAGE & STORAGE — 413 SQ. FT.

TOTAL LIVING AREA:
1,322 SQ. FT.

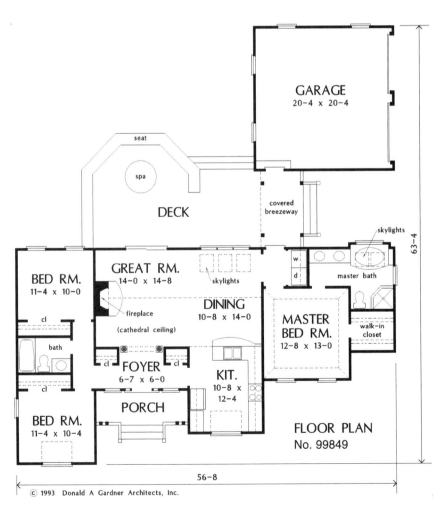

© 1993 Donald A Gardner Architects, Inc.

To order your Blueprints, call 1-800-235-5700

Design by
Rick Garner

Classically Appointed

■ This plan features:

— Three bedrooms

— Two full baths

■ The recessed front Entry leads into a formal foyer

■ The Kitchen is U-shaped and features a wall oven

■ There is an eating bay that over-looks the back Porch and is open to the Kitchen

■ The Master Suite has a full Bath, and a walk-in closet

■ Two large secondary Bedrooms share a Bath in the hall

■ An optional slab or crawl space foundation — please specify when ordering

MAIN FLOOR — 1,856 SQ. FT.
GARAGE — 521 SQ. FT.

TOTAL LIVING AREA:
1,856 SQ. FT.

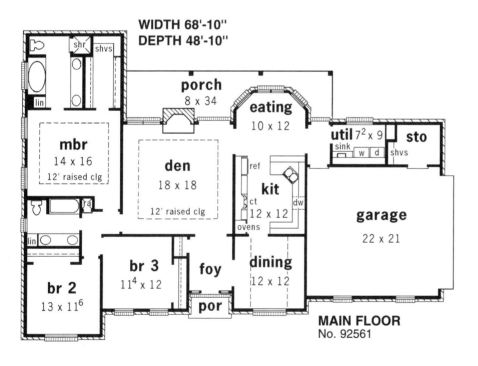

WIDTH 68'-10"
DEPTH 48'-10"

porch
8 x 34

eating
10 x 12

util 7² x 9
sink

sto
shvs

mbr
14 x 16
12' raised clg

den
18 x 18
12' raised clg

ref

kit
ct
12 x 12
ovens
dw

garage
22 x 21

br 3
11⁴ x 12

foy

dining
12 x 12

br 2
13 x 11⁶

por

MAIN FLOOR
No. 92561

Design by
Design Basics, Inc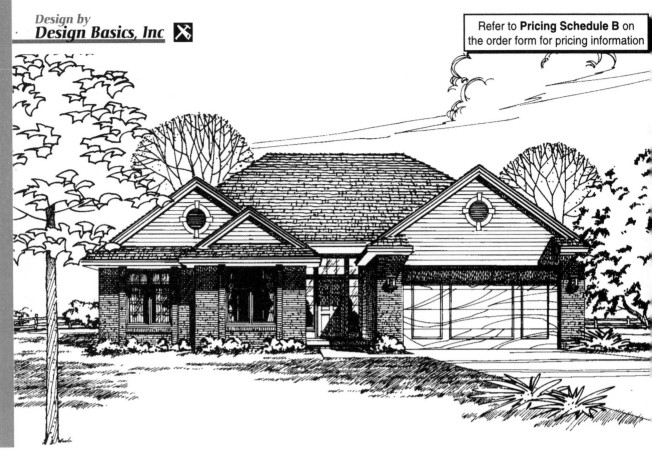

Refer to **Pricing Schedule B** on the order form for pricing information

Ten Foot Entry

■ This plan features:

—Three bedrooms

—Two full baths

■ Large volume Great Room highlighted by a fireplace flanked by windows

■ See-through wetbar enhancing the Breakfast Area and the Dining Room

■ Decorative ceiling treatment giving elegance to the Dining Room

■ Fully equipped Kitchen with a planning desk and a Pantry

■ Roomy Master Bedroom suite has a volume ceiling and special amenities; a skylighted dressing bath area, plant shelf, a large walk-in closet, a double vanity and a whirlpool tub

MAIN FLOOR — 1,604 SQ. FT.
GARAGE — 466 SQ. FT.

TOTAL LIVING AREA:
1,604 SQ. FT.

MAIN FLOOR
No. 94986

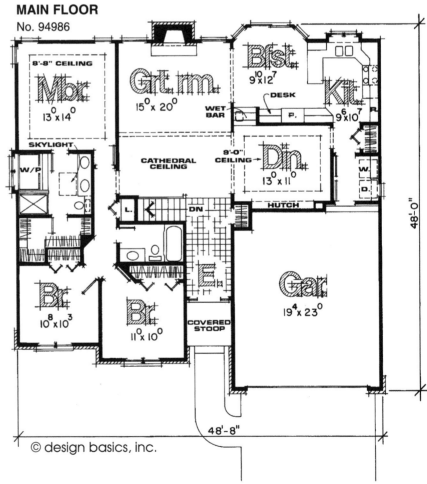

© design basics, inc.

Design by
National Home Planning Services

Truly Western Approach to the Ranch House

■ This plan features:

— Four bedrooms

— Three full baths

■ Authentic ranch styling with long loggia, posts and braces, hand-split shake roof and cross-buck doors

■ A Texas-sized hexagonal, sunken Living Room with two solid walls, one with a fireplace.

■ A porch surrounding the Living Room on three sides

■ A Master Suite with a private Master Bath

■ An efficient well-equipped Kitchen flowing into the Family Room

MAIN FLOOR — 1,830 SQ. FT.
BASEMENT — 1,830 SQ. FT.
GARAGE — 540 SQ. FT.

TOTAL LIVING AREA:
1,830 SQ. FT.

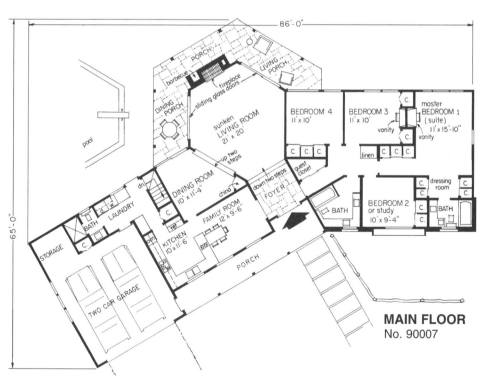

MAIN FLOOR
No. 90007

Design by
The Garlinghouse Company

Refer to **Pricing Schedule A** on the order form for pricing information

Simple Lines Enhanced by Elegant Window Treatment

■ This plan features:

— Two bedrooms (optional third)

— Two full baths

■ A huge, arched window that floods the front room with natural light

■ A homey, well-lit Office or Den

■ Compact, efficient use of space

■ An efficient Kitchen with easy access to the Dining Room

■ A fireplaced Living Room with a sloping ceiling and a window wall

■ A Master Bedroom sporting a private Master Bath with a roomy walk-in closet

MAIN AREA — 1,492 SQ. FT.
BASEMENT — 1,486 SQ. FT.
GARAGE — 462 SQ. FT.

TOTAL LIVING AREA:
1,492 SQ. FT.

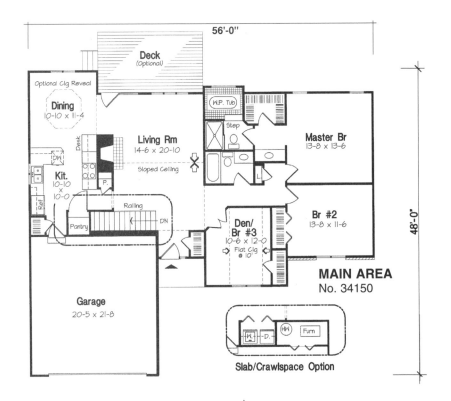

56'-0"

Deck (Optional)

Optional Clg Reveal

Dining
10-10 x 11-4

W.P. Tub

Step

Master Br
13-8 x 13-6

Desk

Living Rm
14-6 x 20-10

Sloped Ceiling

Kit.
10-10 x 10-0

P.

Railing

Br #2
13-8 x 11-6

Pantry

DN

Den/
Br #3
10-6 x 12-0
Flat Clg @ 10'

48'-0"

Garage
20-5 x 21-8

MAIN AREA
No. 34150

Slab/Crawlspace Option

W. D. HW Furn

To order your Blueprints, call 1-800-235-5700

Design by
Perfect Plan

One Story Country Home

▧ This plan features:

— Three bedrooms

— Two full baths

▧ A Living Room with a high ceiling that slopes and a heat-circulating fireplace at the rear wall

▧ An efficient Kitchen that adjoins the Dining Room that views the front Porch

▧ A Dinette Area for informal eating in the Kitchen that can comfortably seat six people

▧ A Master Suite arranged with a large dressing area

MAIN AREA — 1,367 SQ. FT.
BASEMENT — 1,267 SQ. FT.
GARAGE — 431 SQ. FT.

TOTAL LIVING AREA:
1,367 SQ. FT.

FLOOR PLAN No. 99639

50'-0"
21'-4"
33'-10"

TERR.

whirlpool tub 5'-6"
shr.
M.B.R.
heat-circul. f.p.
L.R.
dw
al. gl. dr.
DINETTE
KIT. 14'-8" x 12'-4"
TWO CAR GAR. 21'-0" x 19'-6"

glass blocks
t.v.
skylight above
ref.
16'-6 x 15'-2 AVE.
13'-0 x 20'-6 high ceiling
w. d.
dn.

DRESSING
c.
W.I.C.
L.
D.R. 11'-4" x 10'-0"
STOR.

c.
c.
B.R. 11'-0 x 12'-0 high ceiling
B.R. 10'-6 x 10'-0
P.
columns
railing

Design by
The Garlinghouse Company

Refer to **Pricing Schedule C** on the order form for pricing information

Central Courtyard Features Pool

■ This plan features:

— Three bedrooms

— Two full baths

■ A central Courtyard complete with a Pool

■ A secluded Master Bedroom accented by a skylight, a spacious walk-in closet, and a private Bath

■ A convenient Kitchen easily serving the Patio for comfortable outdoor entertaining

■ A detached two-car Garage

MAIN AREA — 2,194 SQ. FT.
GARAGE — 576 SQ. FT.

TOTAL LIVING AREA:
2,194 SQ. FT.

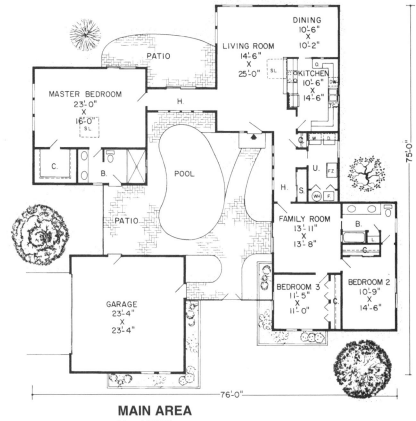

MAIN AREA
No. 10507

To order your Blueprints, call 1-800-235-5700

Refer to **Pricing Schedule A** on the order form for pricing information

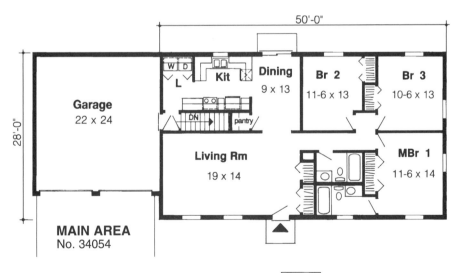

Ranch Provides Great Kitchen Area

■ This plan features:

— Three bedrooms

— Two full baths

■ A Dining Room with sliding glass doors to the backyard

■ Access to the Garage through the Laundry Room

■ A Master Bedroom with a private full Bath

■ A two-car Garage

MAIN AREA — 1,400 SQ. FT.
BASEMENT — 1,400 SQ. FT.
GARAGE — 528 SQ. FT.

TOTAL LIVING AREA:
1,400 SQ. FT.

Floor plan — MAIN AREA, No. 34054

50'-0"

28'-0"

Garage 22 x 24

W D / L / Kit

Dining 9 x 13

Br 2 11-6 x 13

Br 3 10-6 x 13

DN / pantry

Living Rm 19 x 14

MBr 1 11-6 x 14

MAIN AREA No. 34054

Alternate Plan w/ Crawlspace

W D / L / Kit 10 x 13

Dining 9 x 13

F

Design by
Frank Betz Associates, Inc.

Refer to **Pricing Schedule B** on
the order form for pricing information

Easy One Floor Living

■ This plan features:

—Three bedrooms

—Two full baths

■ A spacious Family Room topped
by a vaulted ceiling and highlighted by a large fireplace and a
French door to the rear yard

■ A pantry and a peninsula counter
adding more efficiency to the
Kitchen

■ A crowning tray ceiling over the
Master Bedroom and a vaulted
ceiling over the Master Bath

■ A vaulted ceiling over the cozy
Sitting Room in the Master Suite

■ An optional basement, crawl
space or slab foundaiton —
please specify when ordering

MAIN FLOOR — 1,671 SQ. FT.
BASEMENT — 1,685 SQ. FT.
GARAGE — 400 SQ. FT.

TOTAL LIVING AREA:
1,671 SQ. FT.

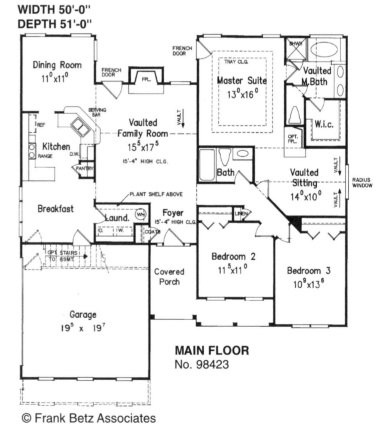

WIDTH 50'-0"
DEPTH 51'-0"

MAIN FLOOR
No. 98423

© Frank Betz Associates

To order your Blueprints, call 1-800-235-5700

Design by
Ahmann Design, Inc.

MAIN FLOOR PLAN
No. 93190

SCREEN PORCH
31'8" X 9'8"

NK.
10'0" X 18'0"

KIT.
10'4" X 15'0"

PAN.

GRT. RM.
VAULTED CEILING
17'8" X 22'0"

MBR.
14'8" X 15'4"

DIN
10'-1 1/8" CEILING
12'0" X 11'6"

BOFFIT

BOFFIT
VAULTED CEILING

LINEN
DOWN

LIN
LIN

BR. #3
11'8" X 13'0"

BR. #2
10'-1 1/8" CEILING
13'0" X 13'4"

3 CAR GAR.
26'0" X 48'0"

73'-0"

58'-8"

Luxury on One Level

■ This plan features:

— Three bedrooms

— Two full and one half baths

■ Covered front Porch leads into entry and Great Room with vaulted ceiling

■ Huge Great Room perfect for entertaining or family gatherings with a cozy fireplace

■ Arched soffits and columns impact the formal Dining Room

■ Country-size Kitchen with a Pantry, work island, eating Nook with Screen Porch beyond, and nearby Laundry/Garage entry

■ Master Bedroom offers a walk-in closet and a luxurious Bath

■ No materials list is available for this plan

MAIN FLOOR — 2,196 SQ. FT.
BASEMENT — 2,196 SQ. FT.

TOTAL LIVING AREA:
2,196 SQ. FT.

Design by
Vaughn A. Lauban Designs ✖

Refer to **Pricing Schedule A** on
the order form for pricing information

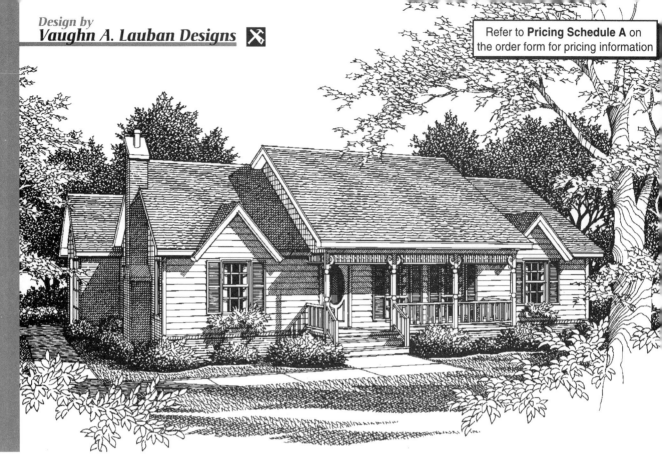

Country Charmer

- This plan features:
  —Three bedrooms
  —Two full baths
- Quaint front Porch is perfect for sitting and relaxing
- Great Room opening into Dining Area and Kitchen
- Corner deck in rear of home accessed from Kitchen and Master Suite
- Master Suite with a private Bath, walk-in closet and built-in shelves
- Two large secondary bedrooms in the front of the home share a hall Bath
- Two-car Garage located in the rear of the home

MAIN FLOOR — 1,438 SQ. FT.
GARAGE — 486 SQ. FT.

TOTAL LIVING AREA:
1,438 SQ. FT.

MAIN FLOOR
No. 96509

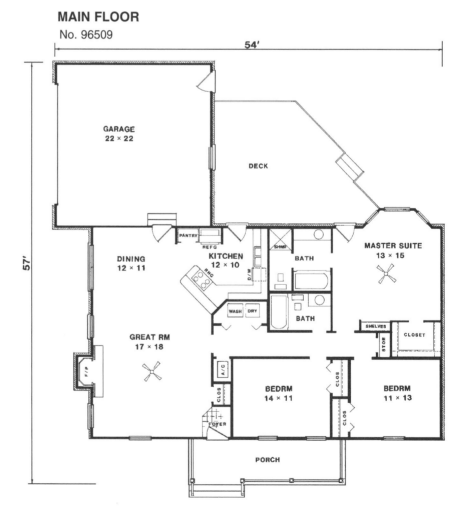

To order your Blueprints, call 1-800-235-5700

Design by
Rick Garner

European Style

■ This plan features:

— Four bedrooms

— Three full and one half baths

■ Central Foyer between spacious Living and Dining rooms

■ Hub Kitchen with extended counter and nearby Utility/ Garage entry

■ Spacious Den with a hearth fireplace between built-ins

■ Master Bedroom wing with decorative ceiling, plush Bath with two walk-in closets

■ Three additional Bedrooms with ample closets and full Baths

■ Choice of basement or crawl space foundation — please specify when ordering

MAIN FLOOR — 2,727 SQ. FT.
GARAGE — 569 SQ. FT.

TOTAL LIVING AREA:
2,727 SQ. FT.

WIDTH 70'-10"
DEPTH 64'-5"

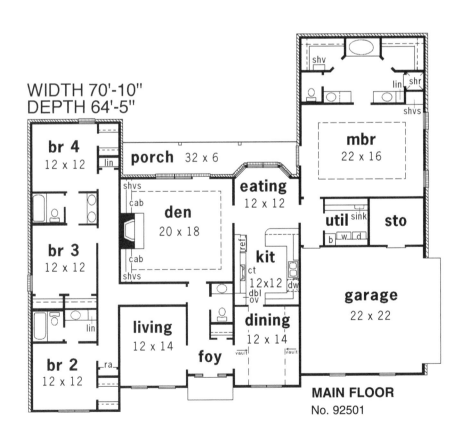

MAIN FLOOR
No. 92501

Design by
The Garlinghouse Company

Brick Home with Four Bedrooms

- This plan features:
— Four bedrooms
— Two and one half baths

- Four roomy bedrooms, including the Master Bedroom

- A centrally located Family Room including a fireplace, wetbar, and access to the Patio

- A large Dining Room at the front of the home for entertaining

- An interesting Kitchen and Nook with an adjoining Utility Room

MAIN FLOOR — 2,070 SQ. FT.
GARAGE — 474 SQ. FT.

TOTAL LIVING AREA:
2,070 SQ. FT.

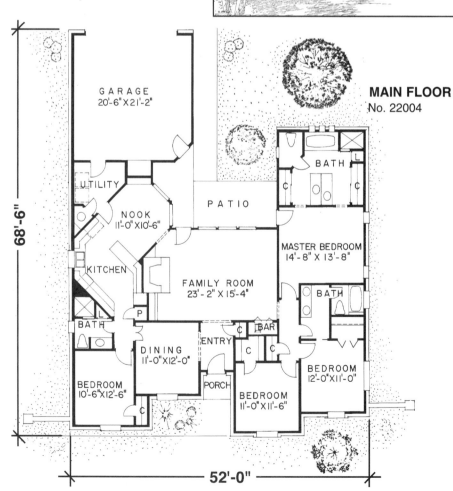

MAIN FLOOR No. 22004

To order your Blueprints, call 1-800-235-5700

Design by
The Garlinghouse Company

Carefree Convenience

■ This plan features:

— Three bedrooms

— Two full baths

■ A galley Kitchen, centrally located between the Dining, Breakfast and Living Room areas

■ A huge Family Room which exits onto the Patio

■ A Master Suite with double closets and vanity

MAIN AREA — 1,600 SQ. FT.
GARAGE — 465 SQ. FT.

TOTAL LIVING AREA:
1,600 SQ. FT.

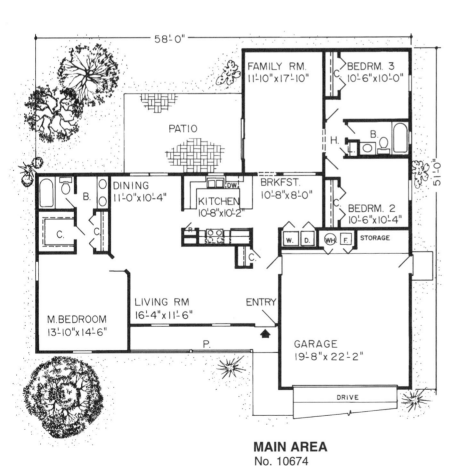

MAIN AREA
No. 10674

Design by
The Garlinghouse Company

Refer to **Pricing Schedule D** on the order form for pricing information

Home Recalls the South

■ This plan features:

— Three bedrooms

— Two full and one half baths

■ A Master Bedroom Suite with a private Study

■ Fireplaces enhancing the formal Living Room and spacious Family Room

■ A lovely, screened porch/patio skirting the Family Room and the Kitchen

■ A Utility Room with access into the Storage and Garage areas

MAIN AREA — 2,466 SQ. FT.
BASEMENT — 1,447 SQ. FT.
GARAGE — 664 SQ. FT.

TOTAL LIVING AREA:
2,466 SQ. FT.

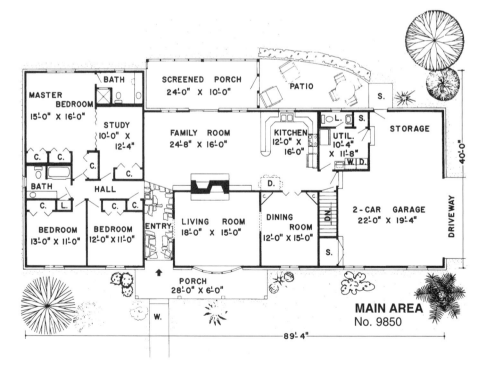

MASTER BEDROOM 15'-0" X 16'-0"
BATH
STUDY 10'-0" X 12'-4"
BATH
BEDROOM 13'-0" X 11'-0"
BEDROOM 12'-0" X 11'-0"
HALL
ENTRY
SCREENED PORCH 24'-0" X 10'-0"
PATIO
FAMILY ROOM 24'-8" X 16'-0"
KITCHEN 12'-0" X 16'-0"
UTIL. 10'-4" X 11'-8"
W.D.
STORAGE
S.
LIVING ROOM 18'-0" X 15'-0"
DINING ROOM 12'-0" X 15'-0"
2-CAR GARAGE 22'-0" X 19'-4"
DRIVEWAY
40'-0"
PORCH 28'-0" X 6'-0"
W.
89'-4"
MAIN AREA No. 9850

To order your Blueprints, call 1-800-235-5700

Design by
Perfect Plan

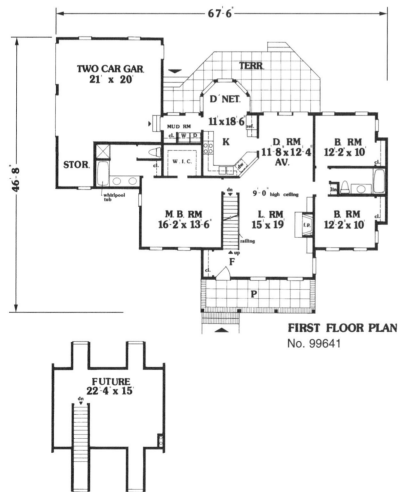

67'-6"

TWO CAR GAR.
21' x 20'

TERR.

D´NET.
11' x 18'-6"

46'-8"

STOR.

MUD RM
cl. W D

K

W. I. C.

whirlpool tub

D. RM.
11'-8" x 12'-4"
AV.

B. RM.
12'-2" x 10'

M. B. RM
16'-2" x 13'-6"

9'-0" high ceiling

L. RM
15 x 19

f.p.

B. RM.
12'-2" x 10'

dn
up
railing

F

cl.

P

FIRST FLOOR PLAN
No. 99641

FUTURE
22'-4" x 15'

dn

SECOND FLOOR PLAN

Southern Traditional Flavor

■ This plan features:

— Three bedrooms

— Two full baths

■ A varied roof line with dormers and a charming colonnaded front porch sheltering the entrance

■ Living Room enhanced by nine-foot ceilings and a bookcase flanked fireplace

■ Two mullioned French doors leading from the Dining Room to the rear terrace

■ Master Suite with walk-in closet and a compartmented Bath with a separate stall shower, whirlpool tub and double vanity

FIRST FLOOR — 1,567 SQ. FT.
SECOND FLOOR(BONUS) — 462 SQ. FT.
BASEMENT — 1,567 SQ. FT.
GARAGE — 504 SQ. FT.

TOTAL LIVING AREA:
1,567 SQ. FT.

Design by
Donald A. Gardner Architects, Inc.

Refer to **Pricing Schedule C** on
the order form for pricing information

© 1995 Donald A Gardner Architects, Inc.

Amenities of a Larger Home

■ This plan features:
— Three bedrooms
— Two full baths

■ A continuous cathedral ceiling in the Great Room, Kitchen, and Dining Room giving a spacious feel to this efficient plan

■ Skylighted Kitchen with a seven foot high wall

■ Master Bedroom opens up with a cathedral ceiling and contains a walk-in closet and dual vanity

■ Cathedral ceiling as the crowing touch to the front Bedrooms/ Study

MAIN FLOOR — 1,253 SQ. FT.
GARAGE & STORAGE — 420 SQ. FT.

TOTAL LIVING AREA:
1,253 SQ. FT.

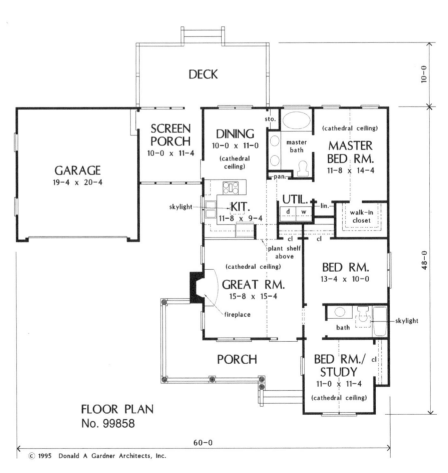

FLOOR PLAN
No. 99858

© 1995   Donald A Gardner Architects, Inc.

To order your Blueprints, call 1-800-235-5700

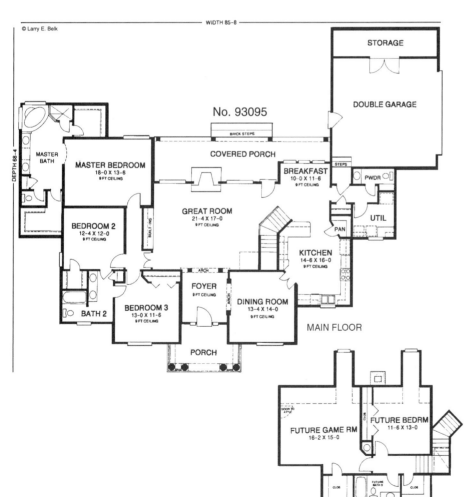

WIDTH 85-8

© Larry E. Belk

DEPTH 68-4

STORAGE

DOUBLE GARAGE

MASTER BATH

No. 93095

BRICK STEPS

COVERED PORCH

MASTER BEDROOM
18-0 X 13-6
9 FT CEILING

BREAKFAST
10-0 X 11-6
9 FT CEILING

PWDR

GREAT ROOM
21-4 X 17-0
9 FT CEILING

BEDROOM 2
12-4 X 12-0
9 FT CEILING

BUILT-INS

STEPS

UTIL

PAN

KITCHEN
14-6 X 16-0
9 FT CEILING

ARCH

FOYER
9 FT CEILING

BEDROOM 3
13-0 X 11-6
9 FT CEILING

DINING ROOM
13-4 X 14-0
9 FT CEILING

BATH 2

MAIN FLOOR

PORCH

DOOR TO ATTIC

FUTURE GAME RM
16-2 X 15-0

FUTURE BEDRM
11-6 X 13-0

CLO.

FUTURE BATH 3

CLO.

BONUS AREA

Stately Elegance

▪ This plan features:

— Three bedrooms

— Two full and one half baths

▪ Elegant columns frame Entry into Foyer and expansive Great Room beyond

▪ Efficient Kitchen ideal for busy cook with walk-in Pantry, Breakfast Area and access to formal Dining Room, Laundry and Garage

▪ A private Master Bedroom suite boasts a plush Bath with two huge, walk-in closets, a double vanity, and whirlpool tub

▪ Staircase in Kitchen Area leads to expandable second floor

▪ An optional slab or crawl space foundation — please specify when ordering

MAIN FLOOR — 2,409 SQ. FT.
GARAGE — 644 SQ. FT.

TOTAL LIVING AREA:
2,409 SQ. FT.

Design by
Ahmann Designs, Inc.

Refer to **Pricing Schedule C** on
the order form for pricing information

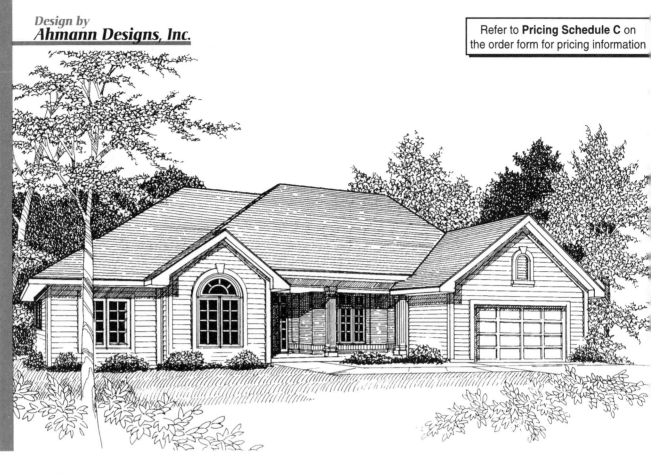

Distinctive Ranch

■ This plan features:

— Three bedrooms

— Two full baths

■ This hipped roofed Ranch has an exterior that mixes brick and siding

■ The Great room has a cathedral ceiling, and a rear wall fireplace

■ The Kitchen has a center island and opens into the Nook

■ The Dining Room features a high ceiling and a bright front window

■ The two-car Garage could easily be expanded to three with a door placed in the rear Storage Area

■ No materials list is available for this plan

MAIN FLOOR — 1,802 SQ. FT.
BASEMENT — 1,802 SQ. FT.

TOTAL LIVING AREA:
1,802 SQ. FT.

MAIN FLOOR PLAN
No. 93143

To order your Blueprints, call 1-800-235-5700

Design by
The Garlinghouse Company

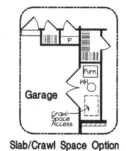

Garage

Crawl Space Access

Slab/Crawl Space Option

Easy Living

■ This plan features:

— Three bedrooms

— Two full baths

■ A dramatic sloped ceiling and a massive fireplace in the Living Room

■ A Dining Room crowned by a sloping ceiling and a plant shelf also having sliding doors to the Deck

■ A U-shaped Kitchen with abundant cabinets, a window over the sink and a walk-in Pantry

■ A Master Suite with a private full Bath, decorative ceiling and walk-in closet

■ Two additional Bedrooms that share a full Bath

MAIN FLOOR — 1,456 SQ. FT.
BASEMENT — 1,448 SQ. FT.
GARAGE — 452 SQ. FT.

TOTAL LIVING AREA:
1,456 SQ. FT.

50'- 0"

45' - 4"

(Optional) Deck

Dining
12-0 x 9-9

Plant Shelf Above

Sink

Kitchen
9-4 x 13-4

Range

Ref

Desk

Decor. Clg. (Optional)

MBR #1
11-8 x 14-0

Living Rm
12-2 x 19-4

Foyer

DN

Railing

Garage
19-4 x 23-6

Den/BR #3
10-5 x 11-6

BR #2
10-5 x 10-5

MAIN FLOOR
No. 20164

Design by
Perfect Plan ⚒

Refer to **Pricing Schedule A** on
the order form for pricing information

Formal Balance

■ This plan features:

— Three bedrooms

— Two full baths

■ A cathedral ceiling in the Living
Room with a heat-circulating
fireplace as the focal point

■ A bow window in the Dining
Room that adds elegance as well
as natural light

■ A well-equipped Kitchen that
serves both the Dinette and the
formal Dining Room efficiently

■ A Master Bedroom with three
closets and a private Master Bath
with sliding glass doors to the
Master Deck with a hot tub

MAIN FLOOR — 1,476 SQ. FT.
BASEMENT — 1,361 SQ. FT.
GARAGE — 548 SQ. FT.

TOTAL LIVING AREA:
1,476 SQ. FT.

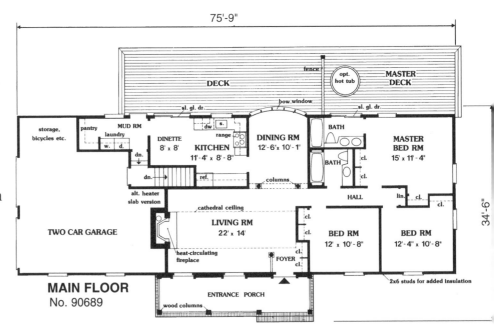

MAIN FLOOR
No. 90689

To order your Blueprints, call 1-800-235-5700

Design by
L.M. Brunier & Associates, Inc.

Four-Bedroom Charmer

▪ This plan features:

— Four bedrooms

— Two full baths

▪ A vaulted ceiling in the naturally lighted entry

▪ A Living Room with a masonry fireplace, large windowed bay and vaulted ceiling

▪ A coffered ceiling and built-in china cabinet in the Dining Room

▪ A large Family Room with a wood stove alcove

▪ An island cooktop, built-in Pantry and a telephone desk in the efficient Kitchen

▪ A luxurious Master Bedroom with whirlpool garden tub, walk-in closet and double sink vanity

▪ A Study with a window seat and built-in bookshelves

MAIN AREA— 2,185 SQ. FT.

TOTAL LIVING AREA:
2,185 SQ. FT.

MAIN AREA
No. 91346

WIDTH — 58'-0"
DEPTH — 60'-0"

PLAN NO. 92546

Design by
Rick Garner

Refer to **Pricing Schedule E** on
the order form for pricing information

Symmetrical and Stately

■ This plan features:

— Four bedrooms

— Two full and one half baths

■ Double columned Porch leads into the open Foyer, the Dining Room accented by an arched window and pillars, and a spacious Den

■ Decorative ceiling crowns the Den with a hearth fireplace and built-in shelves

■ Large, efficient Kitchen with a peninsula serving counter, a Breakfast area, adjoining the Utility and the Garage

■ Master Bedroom suite has a decorative ceiling and dual vanity

■ An optional crawl space or slab foundation — please specify when ordering

MAIN FLOOR — 2,387 SQ. FT.
GARAGE — 505 SQ. FT.

TOTAL LIVING AREA:
2,387 SQ. FT.

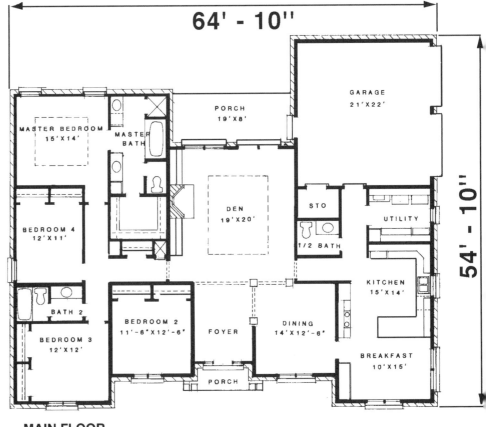

MAIN FLOOR
No. 92546

68   To order your Blueprints, call 1-800-235-5700

Design by
Donald A. Gardner Architects, Inc.

© 1993 Donald A Gardner Architects, Inc.

Traditional Beauty

■ This plan features:

— Three bedrooms

— Two full baths

■ Traditional beauty with large arched windows, round columns, covered porch, brick veneer and an open floor plan

■ Clerestory dormers above covered Porch

■ Cathedral ceiling and fireplace enhancing the Great Room

■ Island Kitchen with Breakfast area accessing the large Deck with an optional spa

■ Tray ceiling over the Master Bedroom, Dining Room and Bedroom/Study

■ Dual vanity, separate shower, and whirlpool tub in the Master Bath

MAIN FLOOR — 1,576 SQ. FT.
GARAGE — 465 SQ. FT.

TOTAL LIVING AREA:
1,576 SQ. FT.

FLOOR PLAN

No. 99802

© 1993 Donald A Gardner Architects, Inc.

DECK

spa

MASTER BED RM.
13-4 x 13-8

master bath

skylights

walk-in closet

storage

w d

BRKFST.
11-4 x 7-8

fireplace

BED RM.
11-4 x 11-0

GREAT RM.
15-4 x 16-10
(cathedral ceiling)

KITCHEN
11-4 x 10-0

GARAGE
20-0 x 19-8

cl

bath

cl

FOYER
8-2 x 5-10

cl

cl

DINING RM.
11-4 x 11-4

BED RM./ STUDY
11-4 x 10-4

PORCH

50-9

60-6

PLAN NO. 96513

Design by
Vaughn A. Lauban Designs

Refer to **Pricing Schedule B** on the order form for pricing information

A Modern Slant On A Country Theme

■ This plan features:

—Three bedrooms

—Two full and one half baths

■ Country styled front Porch highlighting exterior enhanced by dormer windows

■ Modern open floor plan for a more spacious feeling

■ Great Room accented by a quaint, corner fireplace and a ceiling fan

■ Dining Room flowing from the Great Room for easy entertaining

■ Kitchen graced by natural light from near by bay window and a convenient snackbar for meals on the go

■ Master Suite secluded in separate wing for total privacy

MAIN FLOOR — 1,648 SQ. FT.
GARAGE — 479 SQ. FT.

TOTAL LIVING AREA:
1,648 SQ. FT.

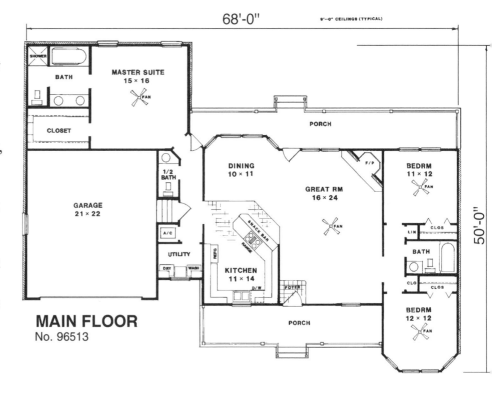

MAIN FLOOR
No. 96513

Design by
Landmark Designs, Inc.

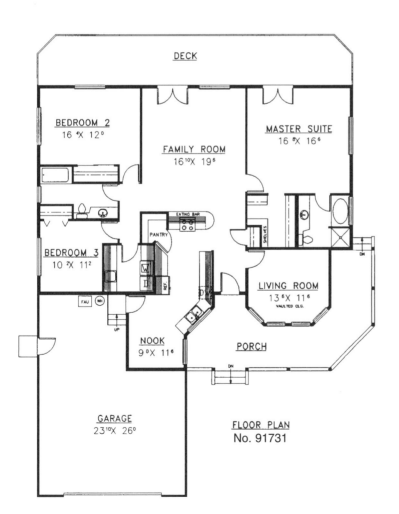

DECK

BEDROOM 2
16⁴X 12⁰

FAMILY ROOM
16¹⁰X 19⁶

MASTER SUITE
16⁶X 16⁶

EATING BAR

PANTRY

BEDROOM 3
10²X 11²

SHELVES

W
D

FAU

UP

NOOK
9⁰X 11⁶

PORCH

LIVING ROOM
13⁶X 11⁶
VAULTED CLG.

DN

GARAGE
23¹⁰X 26⁰

FLOOR PLAN
No. 91731

Country Style & Charm

◼ This plan features:

— Three bedrooms

— Two full baths

◼ Brick accents, front facing gable, and railed wrap-around covered Porch

◼ A built-in range and oven in a L-shaped Kitchen

◼ A Nook with Garage access for convenient unloading of groceries and other supplies

◼ A bay window wrapping around the front of the formal Living Room

◼ A Master Suite with French doors opening to the Deck

MAIN AREA — 1,857 SQ. FT.
GARAGE — 681 SQ. FT.
WIDTH — 51'-6"
DEPTH — 65'-0"

TOTAL LIVING AREA:
1,857 SQ. FT.

Design by
Frank Betz Associates, Inc.

Refer to **Pricing Schedule C** on the order form for pricing information

Small, Yet Lavishly Appointed

■ This plan features:

— Three bedrooms

— Two full and one half baths

■ The Dining Room, Living Room, Foyer and Master Bath all topped by high ceilings

■ Master Bedroom includes a decorative tray ceiling

■ Kitchen open to the Breakfast Room enhanced by a serving bar and a Pantry

■ Living Room with a large fireplace and a French door

■ An optional basement or crawl space foundation — please specify when ordering

MAIN FLOOR — 1,845 SQ. FT.
BONUS — 409 SQ. FT.
BASEMENT — 1,845 SQ. FT.
GARAGE — 529 SQ. FT.

TOTAL LIVING AREA:
1,845 SQ. FT.

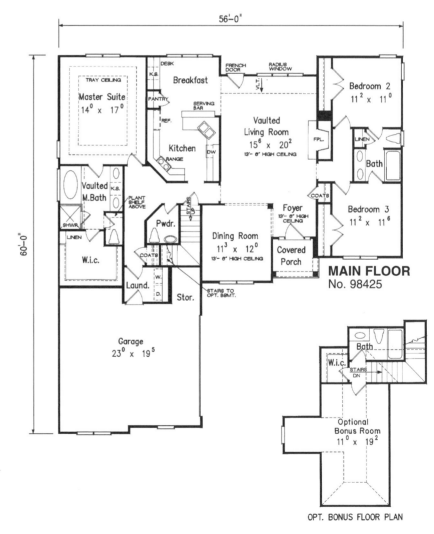

MAIN FLOOR
No. 98425

OPT. BONUS FLOOR PLAN

To order your Blueprints, call 1-800-235-5700

Refer to **Pricing Schedule D** on the order form for pricing information

Design by
Corley Plan Service

PLAN NO. 90454

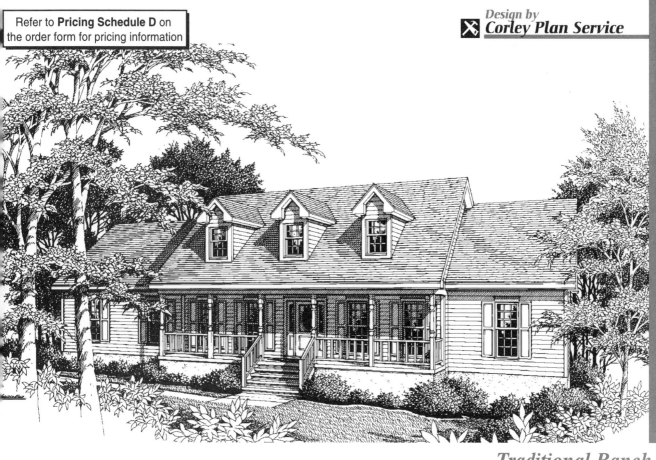

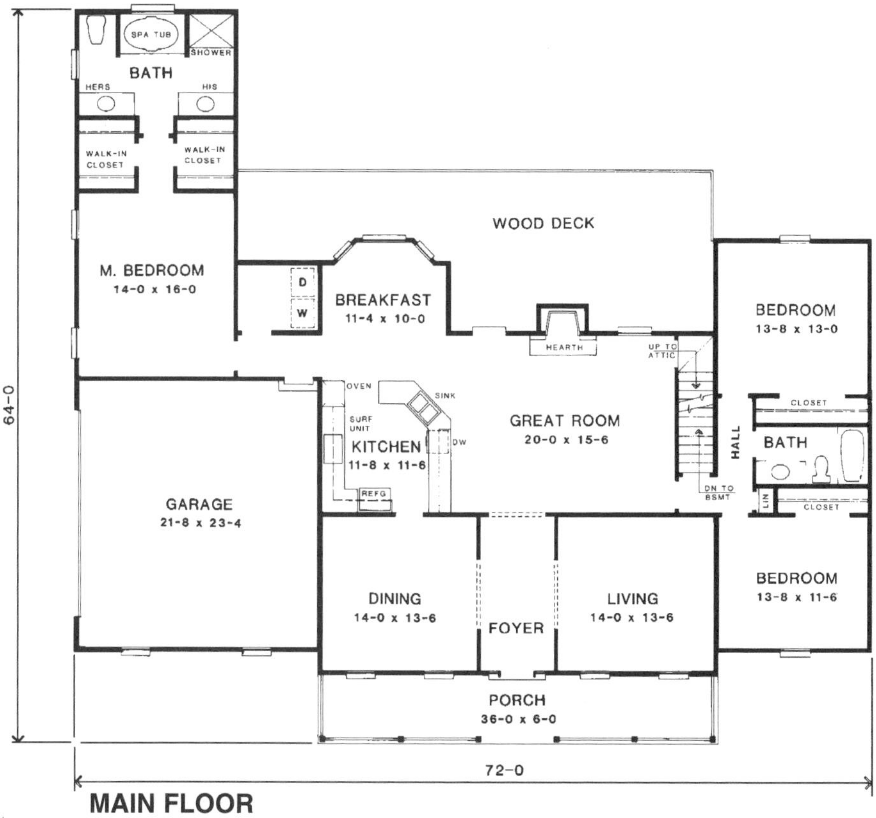

SPA TUB
SHOWER
BATH
HERS
HIS
WALK-IN CLOSET
WALK-IN CLOSET
WOOD DECK
M. BEDROOM
14-0 x 16-0
D
W
BREAKFAST
11-4 x 10-0
HEARTH
UP TO ATTIC
BEDROOM
13-8 x 13-0
CLOSET
OVEN
SINK
SURF UNIT
KITCHEN
11-8 x 11-6
DW
REFG
GREAT ROOM
20-0 x 15-6
HALL
BATH
DN TO BSMT
LIN
CLOSET
GARAGE
21-8 x 23-4
DINING
14-0 x 13-6
FOYER
LIVING
14-0 x 13-6
BEDROOM
13-8 x 11-6
PORCH
36-0 x 6-0
64-0
72-0

MAIN FLOOR
No. 90454

Traditional Ranch Plan

- This plan features:
- —Three bedrooms
- —Two full baths
- Large Foyer set between the formal Living and Dining Rooms
- Spacious Great Room adjacent to the open Kitchen /Breakfast Area
- Secluded Master Bedroom highlighted by the Master Bath with a garden tub, separate shower, and his-n-her vanity
- Bay window allows bountiful natural light into the Breakfast Area
- Two additional Bedrooms sharing a full Bath
- An optional basement or crawl space foundation — please specify when ordering

MAIN FLOOR — 2,218 SQ. FT.
BASEMENT — 1,658 SQ. FT.
GARAGE — 528 SQ. FT.

TOTAL LIVING AREA:
2,218 SQ. FT.

PLAN NO. 93171

Design by
Ahmann Design, Inc.

Refer to **Pricing Schedule B** on
the order form for pricing information

Keystones, Arches and Gables

■ This plan features:

— Three bedrooms

— Two full and one half baths

■ Tiled Entry opens to Living Room with focal point fireplace

■ U-shaped Kitchen with a built-in Pantry, eating bar and nearby Laundry/Garage entry

■ Comfortable Dining Room with bay window and French doors

■ Corner Master Bedroom offers a great walk-in closet and private Bath

■ No materials list is available for this plan

MAIN FLOOR — 1,642 SQ. FT.
BASEMENT — 1,642 SQ. FT.

TOTAL LIVING AREA:
1,642 SQ. FT.

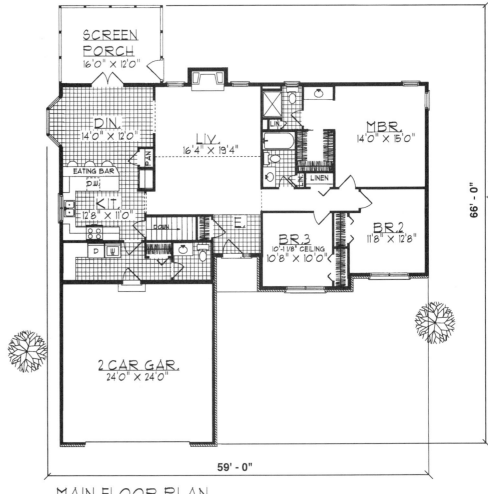

MAIN FLOOR PLAN
No. 93171

74

To order your Blueprints, call 1-800-235-5700

Design by
Vaughn A. Lauban Designs

MAIN FLOOR
No. 96505

Private Master Suite

■ This plan features:

— Three bedrooms

— Two full and one half bath

■ Secluded Master Bedroom suite tucked into the rear left corner of the home with a five-piece bath and two walk-in closets

■ Two additional Bedrooms at the opposite side of the home sharing the full Bath in the hall

■ Expansive Living Room highlighted by a corner fireplace and access to the rear Porch

■ Kitchen is sandwiched between the bright, bayed Nook and the formal Dining Room providing ease in serving

MAIN FLOOR — 2,069 SQ. FT.
GARAGE — 481 SQ. FT.

TOTAL LIVING AREA:
2,069 SQ. FT.

Design by
Donald A. Gardner Architects, Inc.

Refer to **Pricing Schedule D** on
the order form for pricing information

© 1997 Donald A Gardner Architects, Inc.

Country Style Home With Corner Porch

■ This plan features:

— Three bedrooms

— Two full baths

■ Dining Room has four floor to ceiling windows that overlook front Porch

■ Great Room topped by a cathedral ceiling, enhanced by a fireplace and sliding doors to the back Porch

■ Utility Room located near Kitchen and Breakfast Nook

■ Master Bedroom has a walk in closet and private Bath

■ A skylight Bonus Room over the two-car Garage

MAIN FLOOR — 1,815 SQ. FT.
GARAGE — 522 SQ. FT.
BONUS — 336 SQ. FT.

TOTAL LIVING AREA:
1,815 SQ. FT.

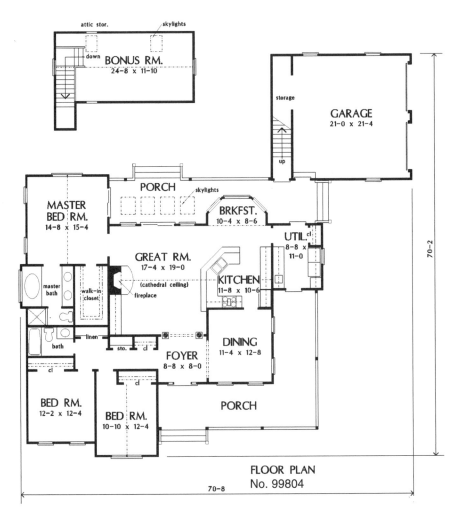

FLOOR PLAN
No. 99804

To order your Blueprints, call 1-800-235-5700

Design by
Donald A. Gardner Architects, Inc.

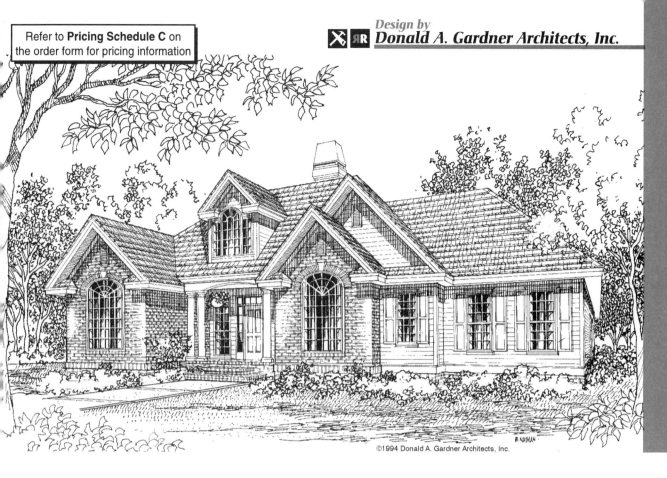

©1994 Donald A. Gardner Architects, Inc.

B. NATHAN

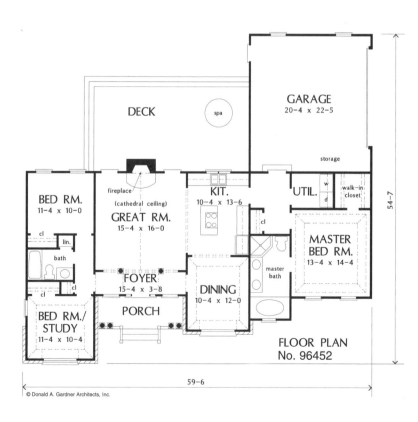

DECK

spa

GARAGE
20-4 x 22-5

storage

fireplace
(cathedral ceiling)

KIT.
10-4 x 13-6

UTIL.

w
d

walk-in
closet

BED RM.
11-4 x 10-0

GREAT RM.
15-4 x 16-0

cl

MASTER
BED RM.
13-4 x 14-4

54-7

cl

lin.

bath

cl

master
bath

FOYER
15-4 x 3-8

DINING
10-4 x 12-0

BED RM./
STUDY
11-4 x 10-4

PORCH

FLOOR PLAN
No. 96452

59-6

© Donald A. Gardner Architects, Inc.

Exciting Ceilings Add Appeal

■ This plan features:

— Three bedrooms

— Two full baths

■ Open design enhanced by cathedral and tray ceilings above arched windows

■ Foyer with columns defining Great Room with central fireplace and Deck access

■ Cooktop island in Kitchen provides great cooks with convenience and company

■ Ultimate Master Suite offers walk-in closet, tray ceiling, and whirlpool Bath

■ Front Bedroom/Study offers multiple uses with tray ceiling and arched window

MAIN FLOOR — 1,475 SQ. FT.
GARAGE & STORAGE — 478 SQ. FT.

TOTAL LIVING AREA:
1,475 SQ. FT.

Design by
Greg Marquis & Associates

Easy Living

- This plan features:
— Three bedrooms
— Two full baths
- The Family Room is enlarged by a vaulted ceiling and also has a fireplace
- The Kitchen is L-shaped and includes a center island
- The Dining Room is open to the Kitchen for maximum convenience
- The Master Bedroom has a private Bath, which has two building options
- Both of the secondary Bedrooms have walk-in closets
- No material list is available for this plan

MAIN FLOOR — 1,474 SQ. FT.
GARAGE — 454 SQ. FT.

TOTAL LIVING AREA:
1,474 SQ. FT.

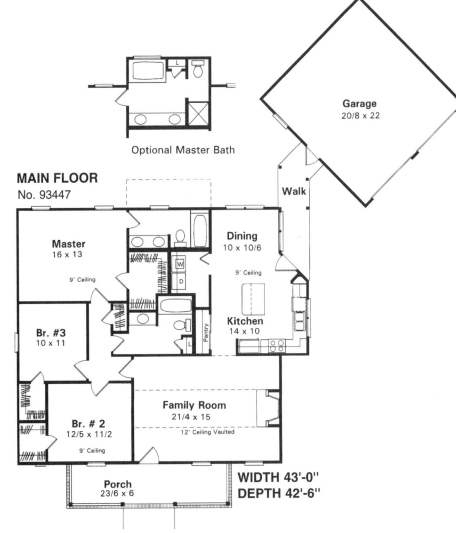

Optional Master Bath

Garage
20/8 x 22

MAIN FLOOR
No. 93447

Walk

Master
16 x 13

9' Ceiling

Dining
10 x 10/6

9' Ceiling

Br. #3
10 x 11

Pantry

Kitchen
14 x 10

Br. # 2
12/5 x 11/2

9' Ceiling

Family Room
21/4 x 15

12' Ceiling Vaulted

W
D

Porch
23/6 x 6

WIDTH 43'-0"
DEPTH 42'-6"

To order your Blueprints, call 1-800-235-5700

Design by
Rick Garner

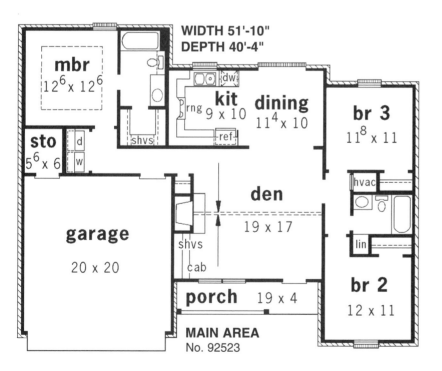

WIDTH 51'-10"
DEPTH 40'-4"

mbr
12^6 x 12^6

sto
5^6 x 6

d

w

garage
20 x 20

shvs

cab

porch 19 x 4

kit
9 x 10

rng

ref

shvs

dw

dining
11^4 x 10

den
19 x 17

br 3
11^8 x 11

hvac

lin

br 2
12 x 11

MAIN AREA
No. 92523

Private Master Suite

■ This plan features:

— Three bedrooms

— Two full baths

■ A spacious Great Room enhanced by a vaulted ceiling and fireplace

■ A well-equipped Kitchen with windowed double sink

■ A secluded Master Suite with decorative ceiling, private Master Bath, and walk-in closet

■ Two additional Bedrooms sharing hall Bath

■ An optional crawl space or slab foundation — please specify when ordering

MAIN FLOOR — 1,293 SQ. FT.
GARAGE — 433 SQ. FT.

TOTAL LIVING AREA:
1,293 SQ. FT.

Design by
Sater Design Group

Refer to **Pricing Schedule F** on
the order form for pricing information

Turret Study Creates Impact

■ This plan features:

—Three bedrooms

—Two full and one half baths

■ Entry doors opening into the formal Living Room focusing to the Lanai through sliding glass doors and a mitered glass corner

■ Double sided fireplace in the Living Room shared by the Master Suite

■ Leisure Room with fireplace wall having built-ins along the back wall

■ Spacious Master Suite including a fireplace, morning kitchen bar, and Lanai access

■ No materials list is available for this plan

MAIN FLOOR — 3,477 SQ. FT.
GARAGE — 771 SQ. FT.

TOTAL LIVING AREA:
3,477 SQ. FT.

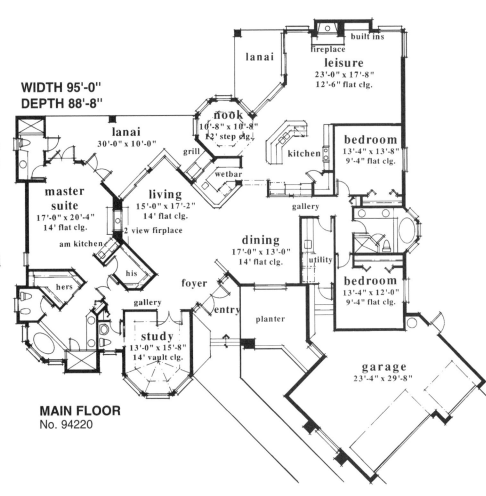

WIDTH 95'-0"
DEPTH 88'-8"

built ins
fireplace
lanai
leisure
23'-0" x 17'-8"
12'-6" flat clg.

lanai
30'-0" x 10'-0"
nook
10'-8" x 10'-8"
12' step clg.
grill
kitchen
bedroom
13'-4" x 13'-8"
9'-4" flat clg.

master suite
17'-0" x 20'-4"
14' flat clg.
living
15'-0" x 17'-2"
14' flat clg.
wetbar
gallery

am kitchen
2 view fireplace

his
dining
17'-0" x 13'-0"
14' flat clg.
utility

hers
foyer
bedroom
13'-4" x 12'-0"
9'-4" flat clg.

gallery
entry
planter

study
13'-0" x 15'-8"
14' vault clg.

garage
23'-4" x 29'-8"

MAIN FLOOR
No. 94220

To order your Blueprints, call 1-800-235-5700

Design by
Frank Betz Associates, Inc.

Main floor
No. 98430

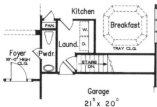

OPT. BASEMENT STAIRS LOCATION

With All the Amenities

- This plan features:
- — Three bedrooms
- — Two full and one half baths
- Sixteen foot high ceiling over the Foyer
- A fireplaced Great Room
- French door to the rear yard and decorative columns at its arched entrance
- Vaulted ceiling in Dining Room
- Expansive Kitchen features a center work island and a built-in Pantry and Breakfast Area
- Master Suite has a tray ceiling, lavish Bath and a walk-in closet
- An optional basement, slab or crawl space foundation — please specify when ordering

MAIN FLOOR — 1,884 SQ. FT.
BASEMENT — 1,908 SQ. FT.
GARAGE — 495 SQ. FT.

TOTAL LIVING AREA:
1,884 SQ. FT.

Design by
Donald A. Gardner Architects, Inc.

Refer to **Pricing Schedule C** on the order form for pricing information

© 1995 Donald A Gardner Architects, Inc.

Tremendous Curb Appeal

■ This plan features:

— Three bedrooms

— Two full baths

■ Wrap-around porch sheltering entry

■ Great Room topped by a cathedral ceiling and enhanced by a fireplace

■ Great Room, Dining Room and Kitchen open to each other for a feeling of spaciousness

■ Pantry, skylight and peninsula counter add to the comfort and efficiency of the Kitchen

■ Cathedral ceiling crowns the Master Suite; walk-in and linen closets, luxurious private Bath

MAIN FLOOR — 1,246 SQ. FT.
GARAGE — 420 SQ. FT.

TOTAL LIVING AREA:
1,246 SQ. FT.

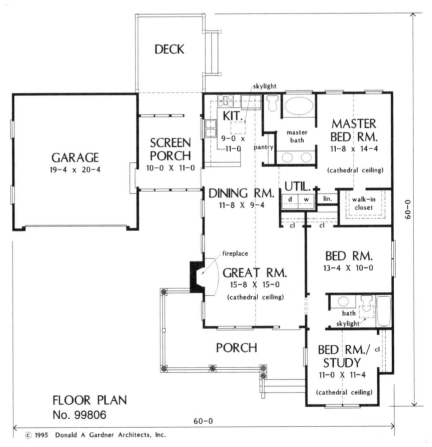

DECK

KIT.
9-0 x
11-0

skylight

GARAGE
19-4 x 20-4

SCREEN
PORCH
10-0 X 11-0

master
bath

pantry

MASTER
BED RM.
11-8 X 14-4

(cathedral ceiling)

DINING RM.
11-8 X 9-4

UTIL.
d   w   lin.

walk-in
closet

cl   cl

fireplace

GREAT RM.
15-8 X 15-0

(cathedral ceiling)

BED RM.
13-4 X 10-0

bath
skylight

PORCH

BED RM./
STUDY
11-0 X 11-4

(cathedral ceiling)

60-0

60-0

FLOOR PLAN
No. 99806

© 1995   Donald A Gardner Architects, Inc.

To order your Blueprints, call 1-800-235-5700

Refer to **Pricing Schedule A** on the order form for pricing information

Design by
The Garlinghouse Company

Gazebo Porch Creates Old-Fashioned Feel

■ This plan features:

— Three bedrooms

— Two full baths

■ An old-fashioned welcome is created by the covered Porch

■ The Breakfast Area overlooks the Porch and is separated from the Kitchen by an extended counter

■ The Dining Room and the Great Room are highlighted by a two sided fireplace, enhancing the temperature as well as the atmosphere

■ The roomy Master suite is enhanced by a whirlpool Bath with double vanity and a walk-in closet

■ No materials list is available for this plan

MAIN FLOOR — 1,452 SQ. FT.
GARAGE — 584 SQ. FT.

TOTAL LIVING AREA:
1,452 SQ. FT.

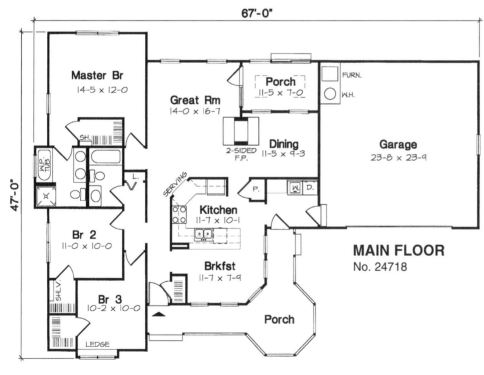

67'-0"

47'-0"

Master Br 14-5 x 12-0

Great Rm 14-0 x 16-7

Porch 11-5 x 7-0

FURN.

W.H.

2-SIDED F.P.

Dining 11-5 x 9-3

Garage 23-8 x 23-9

SERVING

SH.

W.P. TUB

L.

P.

W.

D.

Kitchen 11-7 x 10-1

Br 2 11-0 x 10-0

MAIN FLOOR
No. 24718

SHLV.

Brkfst 11-7 x 7-9

Br 3 10-2 x 10-0

LEDGE

Porch

Design by
Frank Betz Associates, Inc.

Refer to **Pricing Schedule C** on
the order form for pricing information

Spectacular Front Window

■ This plan features:

— Three bedrooms

— Two full baths

■ The Family Room has a vaulted ceiling and is accented by a fire-place

■ The Kitchen includes a walk-in Pantry

■ The Master Suite features a tray ceiling over the Bedroom and a vaulted ceiling over the Bath

■ An optional basement, crawl space or slab foundation — please specify when ordering

■ No materials list is available for this plan

MAIN FLOOR — 1,875 SQ. FT.
BASEMENT — 1,891 SQ. FT.
GARAGE — 475 SQ. FT.

TOTAL LIVING AREA:
1,875 SQ. FT.

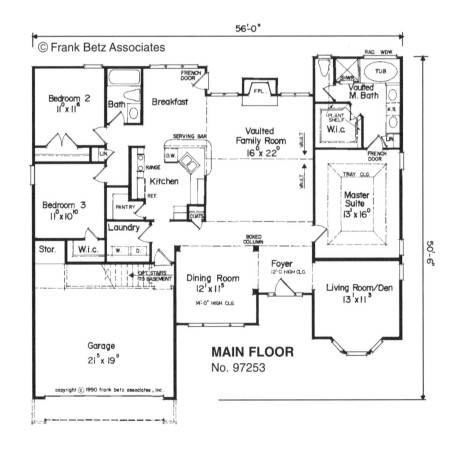

© Frank Betz Associates

56'-0"

Bedroom 2
11⁰ x 11⁶

Bath

Breakfast

FRENCH DOOR

FPL

RAD. WDW

SHWR

TUB

Vaulted M. Bath

K.S.

PLANT SHELF

W.i.c.

LIN.

FRENCH DOOR

SERVING BAR

D.W.

RANGE

Kitchen

REF.

Vaulted Family Room
16⁰ x 22⁰

VAULT

VAULT

TRAY CLG.

Bedroom 3
11⁰ x 10¹⁰

PANTRY

COATS

Master Suite
13³ x 16⁰

Laundry

Stor.

W.i.c.

W. D.

OPT. STAIRS TO BASEMENT

BOXED COLUMN

Foyer
12'-0" HIGH CLG.

Dining Room
12¹ x 11⁵
14'-0" HIGH CLG.

Living Room/Den
13¹ x 11³

Garage
21⁵ x 19⁹

copyright © 1990 frank betz associates, inc.

MAIN FLOOR
No. 97253

50'-6"

To order your Blueprints, call 1-800-235-5700

Design by
The Garlinghouse Company

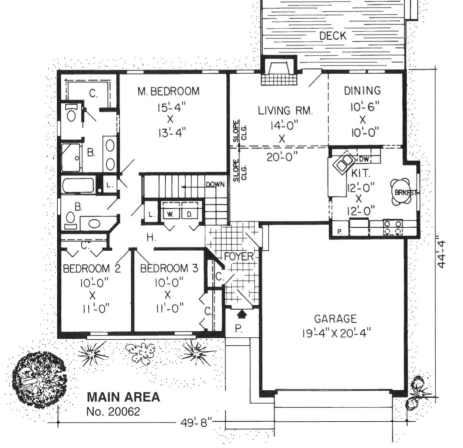

MAIN AREA
No. 20062

Inexpensive Ranch Design

■ This plan features:

— Three bedrooms

— Two full baths

■ A large picture window brightening the Breakfast Area

■ A well planned Kitchen

■ A Living Room which is accented by an open beam across the sloping ceiling and wood burning fireplace

■ A Master Bedroom with an extremely large Bath Area

MAIN AREA — 1,500 SQ. FT.
BASEMENT — 1,500 SQ. FT.
GARAGE — 482 SQ. FT.

TOTAL LIVING AREA:
1,500 SQ. FT.

Design by
The Garlinghouse Company

Home Sweet Home

■ This plan features:

— Three bedrooms

— Two full baths

■ Single-level format allows for
step-saving convenience

■ Large Living Room, highlighted
by a fireplace and built-in entertainment center, adjoins the
Dining Room

■ Skylights, a ceiling fan and room
defining columns accent the
Dining Room

■ A serving bar to the Dining
Room, and ample counter and
cabinet space in the Kitchen

■ Decorative ceiling treatment over
the Master Bedroom and a private Master Bath

■ No materials list is available for
this plan

MAIN FLOOR — 1,112 SQ. FT.
GARAGE — 563 SQ. FT.

TOTAL LIVING AREA:
1,112 SQ. FT.

MAIN FLOOR
No. 24723

To order your Blueprints, call 1-800-235-5700

Design by
X Vaughn A. Lauban Designs

51'

60'

GARAGE
22x24

MAIN FLOOR
No. 96522

MASTER SUITE
15x13

WHIRLPOOL

UTILITY

RANGE

KITCHEN
14x10

PORCH

BATH

DRY WASH REFG.

N/D

STAIR

SHOWER

BAR

BATH

EATING

LIN.

CLOSET

A/C

BEDRM.
13x12

CLOSET

CLOSET

BEDRM./STUDY
13x12

OPTIONAL DOOR

GREAT ROOM
22x22

FOYER

GAS
F/P

9' CEILINGS

PORCH

Cozy Three Bedroom

■ This plan features:

— Three bedrooms

— Two full baths

■ The triple arched front Porch adds to the curb appeal of the home

■ The expansive Great Room is accented by a cozy gas fireplace

■ The efficient Kitchen includes an eating bar that separates it from the Great Room

■ The Master Bedroom is highlighted by a walk-in closet and a whirlpool Bath

■ Two secondary bedrooms share use of the full hall Bath

■ The rear Porch extends dining to the outdoors

MAIN FLOOR — 1,515 SQ. FT.
GARAGE — 528 SQ. FT.

TOTAL LIVING AREA:
1,515 SQ. FT.

Design by
Donald A. Gardner Architects, Inc.

Refer to **Pricing Schedule E** on the order form for pricing information

© 1997 Donald A. Gardner Architects, Inc.

Relaxed Country Living

■ This plan features:

— Three bedrooms

— Two full baths

■ Comfortable country home with deluxe Master Suite, two Porches and dual-sided fireplace

■ Vaulted Great Room enjoys two clerestory dormers and a fireplace shared with the Breakfast Bay

■ Dining Room and front Bedroom/ Study have tray ceilings

■ Master Bedroom features a vaulted ceiling, back Porch access, and a super Bath

■ Skylit Bonus Room over Garage provides extra space

MAIN FLOOR — 2,027 SQ. FT.
BONUS ROOM — 340 SQ. FT.
GARAGE & STORAGE — 532 SQ. FT.

TOTAL LIVING AREA:
2,027 SQ. FT.

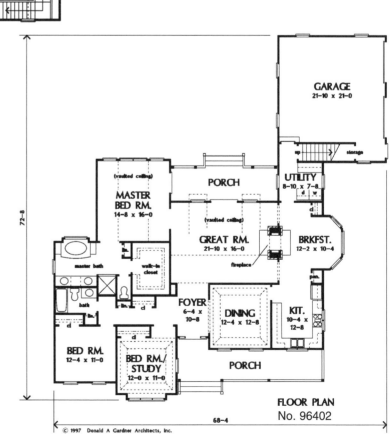

BONUS RM.
12–8 x 21–0

FLOOR PLAN
No. 96402

© 1997 Donald A Gardner Architects, Inc.

To order your Blueprints, call 1-800-235-5700

A Comfortable Informal Design

■ This plan features:

— Three bedrooms

— Two full baths

■ Warm, Country front Porch with wood details

■ Spacious Activity Room enhanced by a pre-fab fireplace

■ Open and efficient Kitchen/Dining Area highlighted by bay window, adjacent to Laundry and Garage entry

■ Corner Master Bedroom offers a pampering Bath with a garden tub and double vanity topped by a vaulted ceiling

■ An optional slab or crawl space foundation — please specify when ordering

MAIN FLOOR — 1,300 SQ. FT.
GARAGE — 576 SQ. FT.
PORCH — 166 SQ. FT.

TOTAL LIVING AREA:
1,300 SQ. FT.

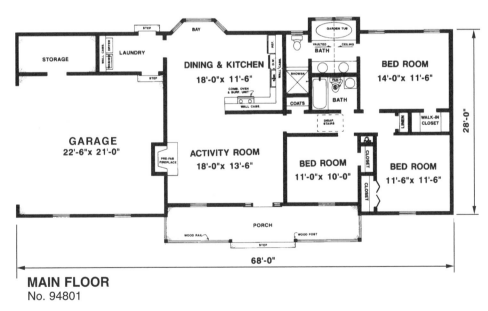

MAIN FLOOR
No. 94801

Design by
Corley Plan Service

Refer to **Pricing Schedule C** on the order form for pricing information

Split-Bedroom Ranch

■ This plan features:

— Three bedrooms

— Two full baths

■ The formal Foyer opens into the Great room which features a vaulted ceiling and a hearth fireplace

■ The U-shaped Kitchen is located between the Dining room and the Breakfast Nook

■ The secluded Master Bedroom is spacious and includes amenities such as walk-in closets and a full Bath

■ The covered front Porch and rear Deck provide additional space for entertaining

■ An optional basement, slab or a crawl space foundation — please specify when ordering

MAIN FLOOR — 1,804 SQ. FT.
BASEMENT — 1,804 SQ. FT.
GARAGE — 506 SQ. FT.

TOTAL LIVING AREA:
1,804 SQ. FT.

MAIN FLOOR
No. 90476

Design by
Fillmore Design Group

PLAN NO. 92238

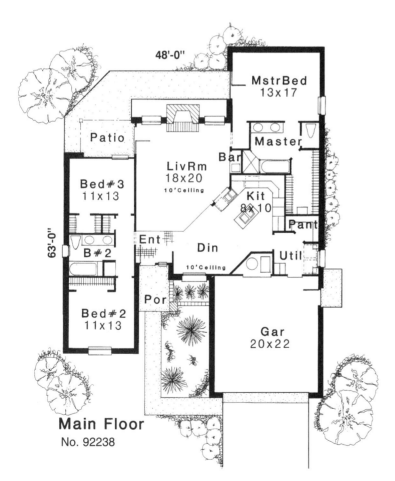

Main Floor
No. 92238

48'-0"

63'-0"

MstrBed
13x17

Patio

Master

LivRm
18x20
10'Ceiling

Bar

Kit
8x10

Bed#3
11x13

Pant

B#2

Ent

Din
10'Ceiling

Util

Por

Bed#2
11x13

Gar
20x22

Easy Everyday Living

- This plan features:
  — Three bedrooms
  — Two full baths

- Front entrance accented by segmented arches, sidelight and transom windows

- Open Living Room with focal point fireplace, wetbar and access to Patio

- Dining Area open to both the Living Room and Kitchen

- Efficient Kitchen with a cooktop island, walk-in Pantry and Utility Area with a Garage entry

- Large walk-in closet, double vanity bath and access to Patio featured in the Master Bedroom

- No materials list is available for this plan

MAIN FLOOR — 1,664 SQ. FT.
BASEMENT — 1,600 SQ. FT.
GARAGE — 440 SQ. FT

TOTAL LIVING AREA:
1,664 SQ. FT.

Design by
Larry E. Belk

Refer to **Pricing Schedule A** on the order form for pricing information

Quoin Accents Distinguish this Plan

■ This plan features:

— Three bedrooms

— Two full baths

■ A traditional brick elevation with quoin accents

■ A large Family Room with a corner fireplace and direct access to the outside

■ An arched opening leading to the Breakfast Area

■ A bay window illuminating the Breakfast Area with natural light

■ An efficiently designed, U-shaped Kitchen with ample cabinet and counter space

■ A Master Suite with a private master Bath

■ No materials list is available for this plan

MAIN FLOOR — 1,142 SQ. FT.
GARAGE — 428 SQ. FT.

TOTAL LIVING AREA:
1,142 SQ. FT.

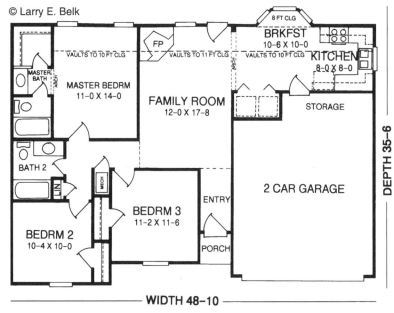

© Larry E. Belk

8 FT CLG
BRKFST
10-6 X 10-0
VAULTS TO 10 FT CLG
KITCHEN
8-0 X 8-0
FP
VAULTS TO 11 FT CLG
VAULTS TO 10 FT CLG
MASTER BATH
MASTER BEDRM
11-0 X 14-0
FAMILY ROOM
12-0 X 17-8
STORAGE
BATH 2
LIN
MECH
2 CAR GARAGE
BEDRM 3
11-2 X 11-6
ENTRY
DEPTH 35-6
BEDRM 2
10-4 X 10-0
PORCH

— WIDTH 48-10 —

MAIN FLOOR
No. 93017

To order your Blueprints, call 1-800-235-5700

Design by
Chatham Home Planning, Inc.

PLAN NO. 94641

Columns Accentuate Southern Flair

- This plan features:
- — Four bedrooms
- — Two full baths

- Four columns accentuating the warm Southern welcome alluded to by the front Porch

- Foyer leading to the Living Room and Dining Room

- Efficient Kitchen including a peninsula counter, plenty of counter and storage space and an easy flow into the Breakfast Room

- Master Bedroom topped by a decorative ceiling treatment and pampered by a compartmental master Bath with a whirlpool tub

- No materials list is available for this plan

MAIN FLOOR — 2,400 SQ. FT.
GARAGE — 534 SQ. FT.

TOTAL LIVING AREA:
2,400 SQ. FT.

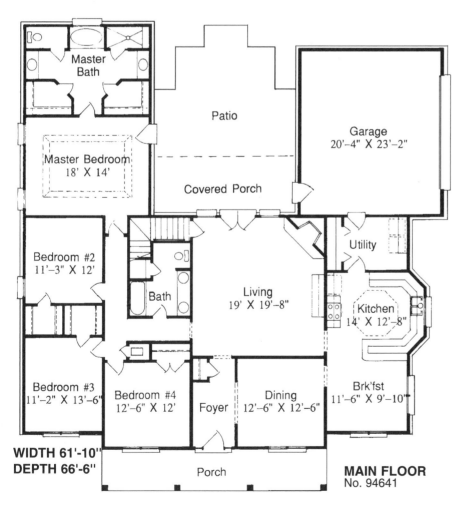

WIDTH 61'-10"
DEPTH 66'-6"

MAIN FLOOR
No. 94641

Design by
Frank Betz Associates, Inc.

Refer to **Pricing Schedule C** on the order form for pricing information

Split Bedroom Plan

■ This plan features:

— Three bedrooms

— Two full baths

■ Dining Room is crowned by a tray ceiling

■ Living Room/Den privatized by double doors at its entrance

■ The Kitchen includes a walk-in Pantry and a corner double sink

■ The vaulted Breakfast Room flows naturally from the Kitchen

■ The Master Suite is topped by a tray ceiling, and contains a compartmental Bath

■ An optional basement, slab or crawl space foundation — please specify when ordering

MAIN FLOOR — 2,051 SQ. FT.
BASEMENT — 2,051 SQ. FT.
GARAGE — 441 SQ. FT.

TOTAL LIVING AREA:
2,051 SQ. FT.

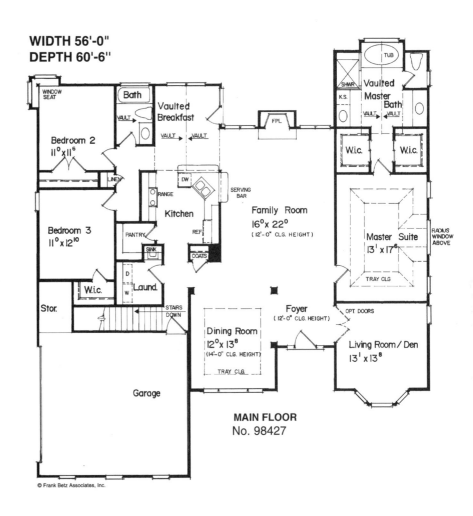

WIDTH 56'-0"
DEPTH 60'-6"

Window Seat

Bath

Vaulted Breakfast
VAULT

VAULT ← VAULT →

Bedroom 2
11⁰ x 11⁶

LINEN

DW

RANGE

Kitchen

SERVING BAR

FPL

Vaulted Master Bath

SHWR K.S.

VAULT VAULT

W.i.c. W.i.c.

RADIUS WINDOW ABOVE

Bedroom 3
11⁰ x 12¹⁰

PANTRY

SINK

REF

COATS

Family Room
16⁰ x 22⁰
(12'-0" CLG. HEIGHT)

Master Suite
13' x 17⁶

TRAY CLG

W.i.c.

D W

Laund.

Stor.

STAIRS DOWN

Foyer
(12'-0" CLG. HEIGHT)

OPT. DOORS

Dining Room
12⁰ x 13⁸
(14'-0" CLG. HEIGHT)

TRAY CLG

Living Room / Den
13' x 13⁸

Garage

MAIN FLOOR
No. 98427

© Frank Betz Associates, Inc.

To order your Blueprints, call 1-800-235-5700

Design by
Corley Plan Service

Expansive, Not Expensive

■ This plan features:

— Three bedrooms

— Two full baths

■ A Master Suite with his-n-her closets and a private Master Bath

■ Two additional Bedrooms that share a full hall closet

■ A pleasant Dining Room that overlooks a rear garden

■ A well-equipped Kitchen with a built-in planning corner and eat-in space

■ An optional basement, slab or crawl space foundation — please specify when ordering

MAIN FLOOR — 1,773 SQ. FT.

TOTAL LIVING AREA:
1,773 SQ. FT.

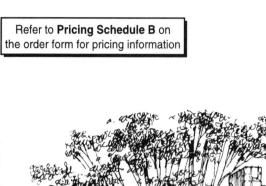

MAIN FLOOR
No. 90423

PATIO
16-0x10-0

DINING
12-0x13-4

KITCHEN
10x13

UTILITY

BEDROOM
11-0x13-4

M. BATH

CLOSET

CLOSET

STEP

SEAT

PANTRY

GARAGE
21-0x21-0

SCR. PORCH
12-0x20-4

M. BEDROOM
12-0x18-0

CLOSET

LIVING ROOM
15-6x17-8

DOWN

CLOSET

LINEN

DRESSING

LINEN

BEDROOM
12-0x11-4

COATS

FOYER

BATH

PORCH
26-0x6-0

43'-8"

88'-8"

PLAN NO. 94827

Design by
W. D. Farmer F.A.I.B.D.

Refer to **Pricing Schedule C** on the order form for pricing information

Luxury in One-story Plan

■ This plan features:

__ Three bedrooms

— Two full baths

■ Covered Stoop leads into dynamic Activity Room with fireplace, recessed ceiling, and adjacent Dining Room and Sun Deck

■ Open Kitchen/Breakfast Room offers loads of counter space and light with nearby Pantry, Laundry and Garage

■ Plush Bedroom Suite shows off a tray ceiling, walk-in closet, walk-in closet, and garden tub

■ An optional basement, slab or crawl space — please specify when ordering

MAIN FLOOR — 1,595 SQ. FT.
BASEMENT — 1,595 SQ. FT.
GARAGE — 491 SQ. FT.

TOTAL LIVING AREA:
1,595 SQ. FT.

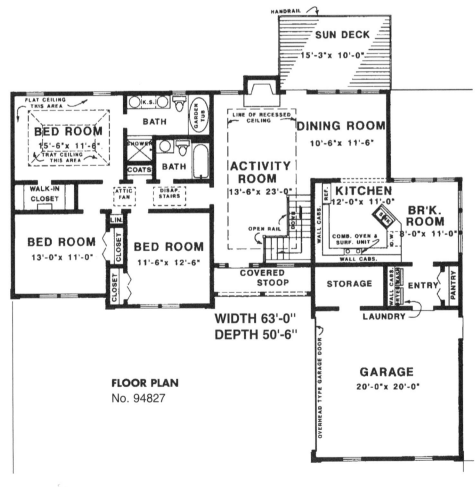

FLOOR PLAN
No. 94827

WIDTH 63'-0"
DEPTH 50'-6"

Design by
Frank Betz Associates, Inc.

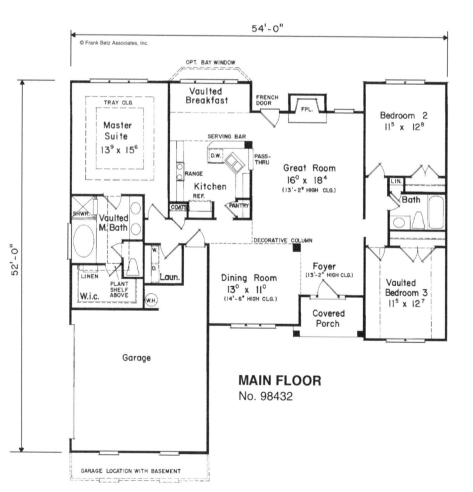

54'-0"

© Frank Betz Associates, Inc.

OPT. BAY WINDOW

Vaulted
Breakfast

FRENCH
DOOR

FPL.

TRAY CLG.

Master
Suite
13⁹ x 15⁶

SERVING BAR

D.W.

PASS-
THRU

Bedroom 2
11⁵ x 12⁸

RANGE

Kitchen

REF.

Great Room
16⁰ x 18⁴
(13'-2" HIGH CLG.)

COATS

PANTRY

LIN.

Bath

SHWR.

Vaulted
M. Bath

DECORATIVE COLUMN

W.
D.

LINEN

Laun.

PLANT
SHELF
ABOVE

W.i.c.

W.H.

Dining Room
13⁰ x 11⁰
(14'-6" HIGH CLG.)

Foyer
(13'-2" HIGH CLG.)

Vaulted
Bedroom 3
11⁵ x 12⁷

Covered
Porch

52'-0"

Garage

MAIN FLOOR
No. 98432

GARAGE LOCATION WITH BASEMENT

Keystone and Arched Windows

■ This plan features:

— Three bedrooms

— Two full baths

■ An arched window in the Dining Room offers eye-catching appeal

■ A fireplace and French door to the rear yard are in the Great Room

■ An efficient Kitchen includes a serving bar, Pantry and pass through to the Great Room

■ A plush Master Suite includes a private Bath and a walk-in closet

■ An optional basement, slab or crawl space foundation — please specify when ordering

MAIN FLOOR — 1,670 SQ. FT.
GARAGE — 240 SQ. FT.

TOTAL LIVING AREA:
1,670 SQ. FT.

Design by
Donald A. Gardner Architects, Inc.

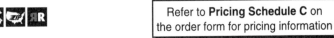

Refer to **Pricing Schedule C** on
the order form for pricing information

© 1995 Donald A Gardner Architects, Inc.

Cathedral Ceiling

■ This plan features:

— Three bedrooms

— Two full baths

■ Cathedral ceiling expanding the
Great room, Dining Room and
Kitchen

■ A versatile Bedroom or Study
topped by a cathedral ceiling
accented by double circle-top
windows

■ Master Suite complete with a
cathedral ceiling, including a bath
with a garden tub, linen closet
and a walk-in closet

MAIN FLOOR — 1,417 SQ. FT.
GARAGE — 441 SQ. FT.

TOTAL LIVING AREA:
1,417 SQ. FT.

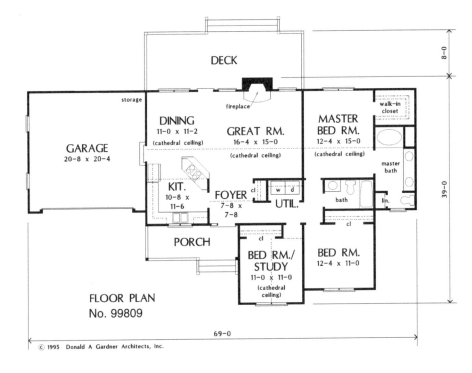

DECK

storage

DINING
11-0 x 11-2
(cathedral ceiling)

fireplace

GREAT RM.
16-4 x 15-0
(cathedral ceiling)

MASTER
BED RM.
12-4 x 15-0
(cathedral ceiling)

walk-in
closet

GARAGE
20-8 x 20-4

KIT.
10-8 x
11-6

FOYER
7-8 x
7-8

cl

w d

UTIL.

master
bath

bath

lin.

8-0

39-0

PORCH

cl

BED RM./
STUDY
11-0 x 11-0
(cathedral
ceiling)

cl

BED RM.
12-4 x 11-0

FLOOR PLAN
No. 99809

69-0

© 1995 Donald A Gardner Architects, Inc.

To order your Blueprints, call 1-800-235-5700

Design by
Rick Garner

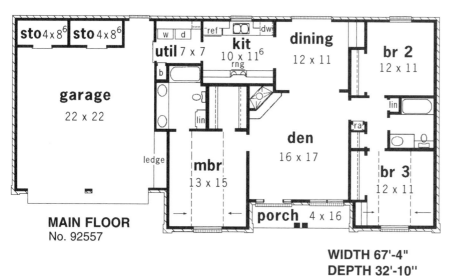

sto 4x8⁶	sto 4x8⁶

garage
22 x 22

util 7 x 7

kit
10 x 11⁶

dining
12 x 11

br 2
12 x 11

w | d ref dw

rng

b

lin

lin

ra

ledge

den
16 x 17

mbr
13 x 15

br 3
12 x 11

porch 4 x 16

MAIN FLOOR
No. 92557

WIDTH 67'-4"
DEPTH 32'-10"

Elegant Brick Exterior

■ This plan features:

—Three bedrooms

—Two full baths

■ Detailing and accenting columns highlighting the covered front Porch

■ Den is enhanced by a corner fireplace and adjoins Dining Room

■ Efficient Kitchen well-appointed and has easy access to the Utility/Laundry Room

■ Master Bedroom topped by a vaulted ceiling and has a private Bath and walk-in closet

■ An optional slab or crawl space foundation — please specify when ordering

MAIN FLOOR — 1,390 SQ. FT.
GARAGE — 590 SQ. FT.

TOTAL LIVING AREA:
1,390 SQ. FT.

Design by
Studer Residential Design, Inc.

Refer to **Pricing Schedule B** on
the order form for pricing information

Home For the Discriminating Buyer

■ This plan features:

— Three bedrooms

— Two full baths

■ A sloped ceiling and a corner fireplace enhancing the Great Room

■ A Kitchen with a garden window above the double sink

■ A peninsula counter joins the Kitchen and the Breakfast Room in an open layout

■ A Master Suite with a large walk-in closet, a private Bath with an oval corner tub, and a separate shower and double vanity

■ No materials list is available for this plan

MAIN AREA — 1,710 SQ. FT.
BASEMENT — 1,560 SQ. FT.
GARAGE — 455 SQ. FT.

TOTAL LIVING AREA:
1,710 SQ. FT.

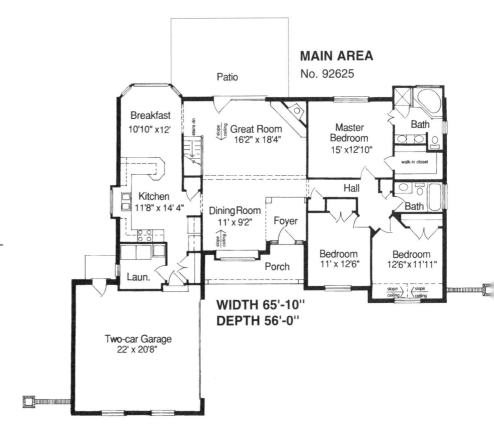

MAIN AREA
No. 92625

Patio

Breakfast
10'10" x12'

Great Room
16'2" x 18'4"

Master Bedroom
15' x12'10"

Bath

walk-in closet

Kitchen
11'8" x 14' 4"

Hall

Dining Room
11' x 9'2"

Foyer

Bath

Laun.

Porch

Bedroom
11' x 12'6"

Bedroom
12'6"x 11'11"

WIDTH 65'-10"
DEPTH 56'-0"

Two-car Garage
22' x 20'8"

slope ceiling

To order your Blueprints, call 1-800-235-5700

Design by
Design Basics, Inc.

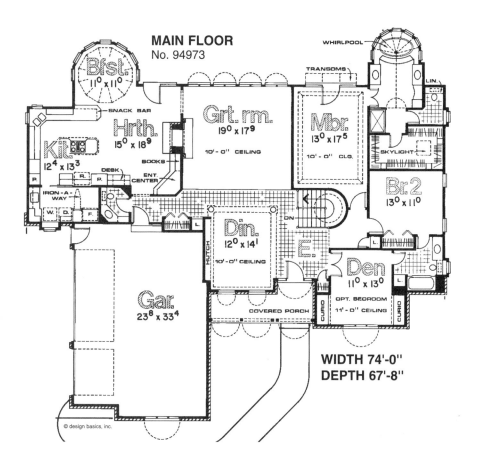

MAIN FLOOR
No. 94973

WIDTH 74'-0''
DEPTH 67'-8''

© design basics, inc.

Bricks and Arches Detail this Ranch

■ This plan features:

— Two bedrooms

— Two full and one half baths

■ A Master Bedroom with a vaulted ceiling, luxurious Bath, complimented by a skylit walk-in closet

■ A second bedroom that shares a full Bath with the Den/optional Bedroom which has built-in curio cabinets

■ A Great Room sharing a see-through fireplace with the Hearth Room, which also has a built-in entertainment center

■ A gazebo-shaped nook opening into the Kitchen with a center island, snack bar and desk

MAIN FLOOR — 2,512 SQ. FT.
GARAGE — 783 SQ. FT.

TOTAL LIVING AREA:
2,512 SQ. FT.

PLAN NO. 96418

Design by
Donald A. Gardner Architects, Inc.

Refer to **Pricing Schedule C** on the order form for pricing information

S. NATHAN

© 1990 Donald A. Gardner Architects, Inc.

Compact Three Bedroom

◼ This plan features:

— Three bedrooms

— Two full baths

◼ Dormers above the covered Porch light the foyer leading to the dramatic Great Room crowned in a cathedral ceiling and enhanced by a fireplace

◼ Great Room opens to the island Kitchen with Breakfast Area and access to a spacious rear Deck

◼ Tray ceilings adding interest to the Bedroom/Study, Dining Room and the Master Bedroom

◼ Luxurious Master Bedroom highlighted by a walk-in closet

MAIN FLOOR — 1,452 SQ. FT.
GARAGE AND STORAGE — 427 SQ. FT.

TOTAL LIVING AREA
1,452 SQ. FT.

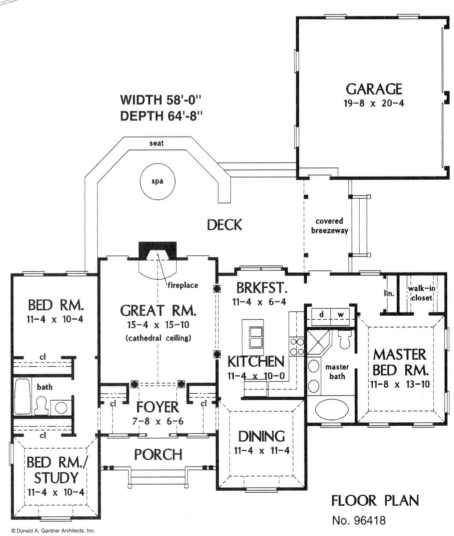

WIDTH 58'-0"
DEPTH 64'-8"

GARAGE
19-8 x 20-4

seat

spa

DECK

covered breezeway

fireplace

BED RM.
11-4 x 10-4

GREAT RM.
15-4 x 15-10
(cathedral ceiling)

BRKFST.
11-4 x 6-4

KITCHEN
11-4 x 10-0

lin.

walk-in closet

master bath

MASTER BED RM.
11-8 x 13-10

cl

bath

cl

cl

FOYER
7-8 x 6-6

cl

DINING
11-4 x 11-4

BED RM./ STUDY
11-4 x 10-4

PORCH

© Donald A. Gardner Architects, Inc.

FLOOR PLAN
No. 96418

102

To order your Blueprints, call 1-800-235-5700

Design by
Corley Plan Service

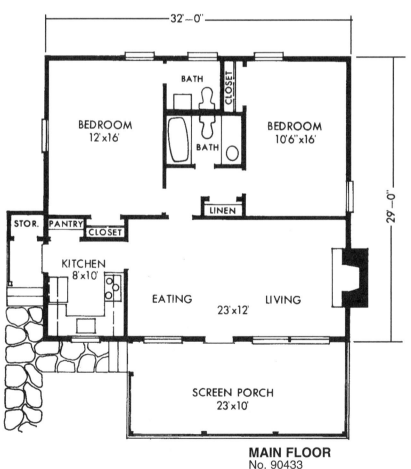

MAIN FLOOR
No. 90433

BEDROOM
12'x16'

BATH

CLOSET

BEDROOM
10'6"x16'

BATH

LINEN

STOR. PANTRY
CLOSET

KITCHEN
8'x10'

EATING   LIVING
23'x12'

SCREEN PORCH
23'x10'

32'–0"

29'–0"

Cabin in the Country

■ This plan features:

— Two bedrooms

— One full and one half baths

■ A Screened Porch for enjoyment of your outdoor surroundings

■ A combination Living and Dining Area with cozy fireplace for added warmth

■ An efficiently laid out Kitchen with a built-in Pantry

■ Two large Bedrooms located at the rear of the home

■ An optional slab or crawl space foundation — please specify when ordering

MAIN FLOOR — 928 SQ. FT.
SCREENED PORCH — 230 SQ. FT.
STORAGE — 14 SQ. FT.

TOTAL LIVING AREA:
928 SQ. FT.

Design by
Jannis Vann & Associates, Inc.

Refer to **Pricing Schedule A** on the order form for pricing information

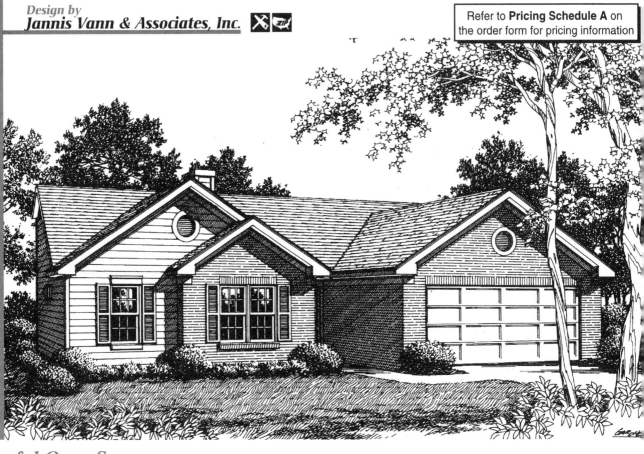

Wonderful Open Spaces

■ This plan features:

— Three bedrooms

— Two full baths

■ A Family Room, Kitchen and Breakfast Area that all connect to form a great space

■ A central fireplace adds warmth and atmosphere to the Family Room, Kitchen and the Breakfast Area

■ An efficient Kitchen that is high-lighted by a peninsula counter and doubles as a snack bar

■ The Master Suite has a walk-in closet and a double vanity

■ A wooden Deck that can be accessed from the Breakfast Area

■ An optional crawl space or slab foundation — please specify when ordering

MAIN FLOOR — 1,388 SQ. FT.
GARAGE — 400 SQ. FT.

TOTAL LIVING AREA:
1,388 SQ. FT.

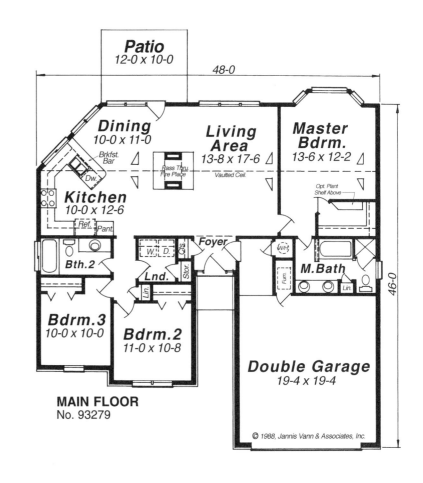

MAIN FLOOR
No. 93279

© 1988, Jannis Vann & Associates, Inc.

Design by
Donald A. Gardner Architects, Inc.

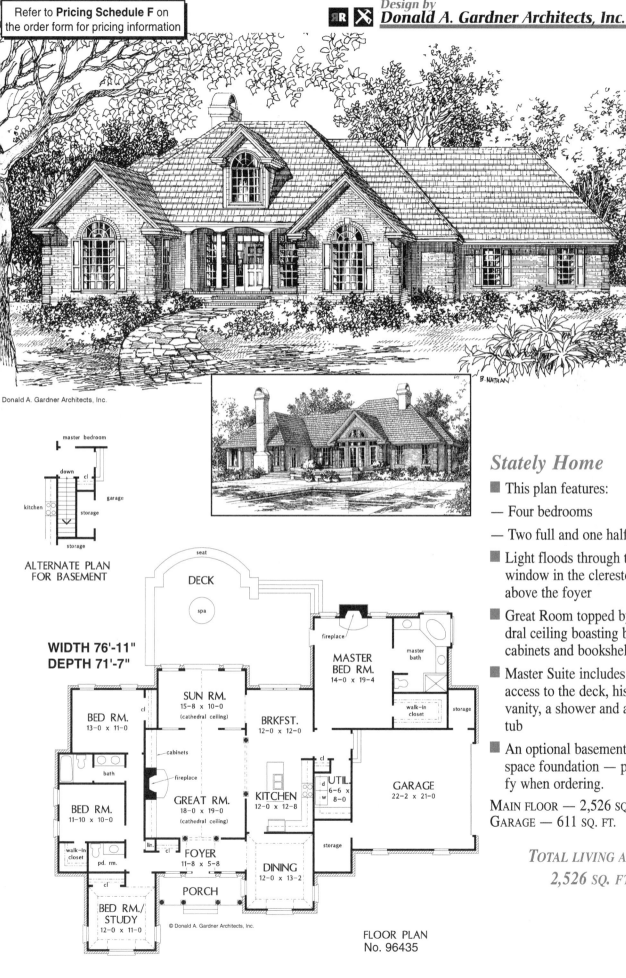

Donald A. Gardner Architects, Inc.

B. NATHAN

ALTERNATE PLAN
FOR BASEMENT

master bedroom

down   cl

garage

kitchen   storage

storage

seat

DECK

spa

WIDTH 76'-11"
DEPTH 71'-7"

SUN RM.
15-8 x 10-0
(cathedral ceiling)

BRKFST.
12-0 x 12-0

fireplace

MASTER
BED RM.
14-0 x 19-4

master
bath

walk-in
closet

storage

BED RM.
13-0 x 11-0

cl

cabinets

bath

fireplace

GREAT RM.
18-0 x 19-0
(cathedral ceiling)

KITCHEN
12-0 x 12-8

cl

d
w

UTIL
6-6 x
8-0

GARAGE
22-2 x 21-0

BED RM.
11-10 x 10-0

lin.

cl

walk-in
closet

pd. rm.

FOYER
11-8 x 5-8

DINING
12-0 x 13-2

storage

cl

BED RM./
STUDY
12-0 x 11-0

PORCH

© Donald A. Gardner Architects, Inc.

FLOOR PLAN
No. 96435

Stately Home

■ This plan features:

— Four bedrooms

— Two full and one half baths

■ Light floods through the arched window in the clerestory dormer above the foyer

■ Great Room topped by a cathedral ceiling boasting built-in cabinets and bookshelves

■ Master Suite includes a fireplace, access to the deck, his and her vanity, a shower and a whirlpool tub

■ An optional basement or crawl space foundation — please specify when ordering.

MAIN FLOOR — 2,526 SQ. FT.
GARAGE — 611 SQ. FT.

TOTAL LIVING AREA:
2,526 SQ. FT.

Design by
Landmark Designs, Inc.

Refer to **Pricing Schedule A** on the order form for pricing information

Country Ranch

- This plan features:
- — Three bedrooms
- — Two full baths
- A railed and covered wrap-around Porch, adding charm to this Country-styled home
- A high vaulted ceiling in the Living Room
- A smaller Kitchen with ample cupboard and counter space, that is augmented by a large Pantry
- An informal Family Room with access to the wood Deck
- A private Master Suite with a spa tub and a walk-in closet
- A Shop and Storage Area in the two-car Garage

MAIN AREA — 1,485 SQ. FT.
GARAGE — 701 SQ. FT.

TOTAL LIVING AREA:
1,485 SQ. FT.

51'-6"

63'-0"

FLOOR PLAN
No. 91797

To order your Blueprints, call 1-800-235-5700

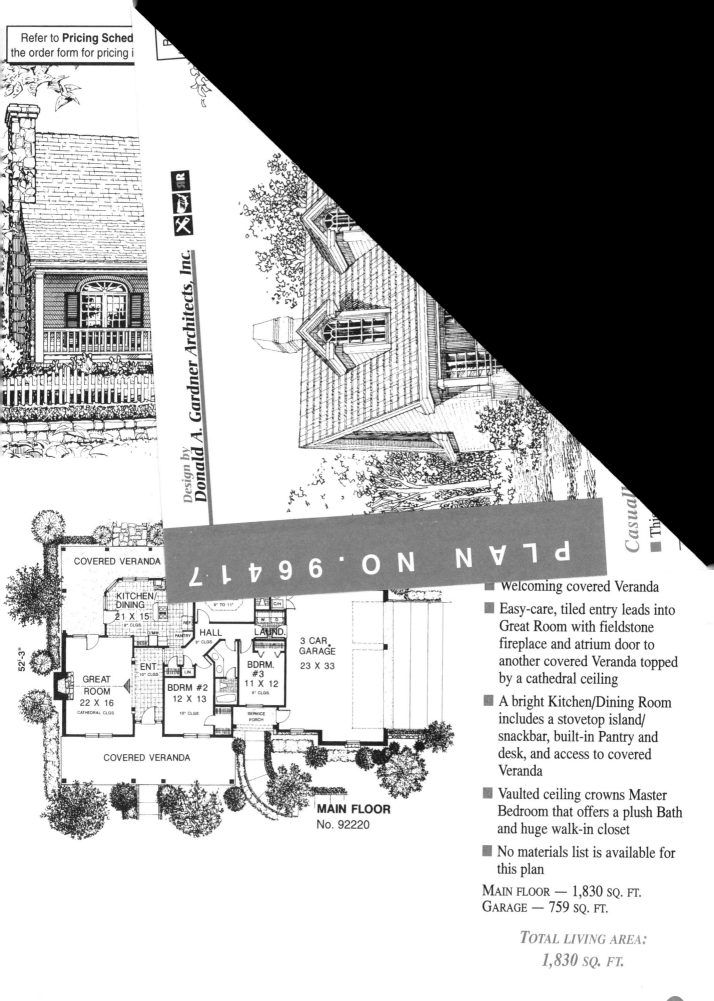

Design by
Donald A. Gardner Architects, Inc.

Casual
■ This

PLAN NO. 96417

COVERED VERANDA

KITCHEN/ DINING
21 X 15

HALL

LAUND.

3 CAR GARAGE
23 X 33

GREAT ROOM
22 X 16
CATHEDRAL CLGS.

ENT.

BDRM #2
12 X 13

BDRM. #3
11 X 12

52'-3"

COVERED VERANDA

SERVICE PORCH

MAIN FLOOR
No. 92220

■ Welcoming covered Veranda

■ Easy-care, tiled entry leads into Great Room with fieldstone fireplace and atrium door to another covered Veranda topped by a cathedral ceiling

■ A bright Kitchen/Dining Room includes a stovetop island/ snackbar, built-in Pantry and desk, and access to covered Veranda

■ Vaulted ceiling crowns Master Bedroom that offers a plush Bath and huge walk-in closet

■ No materials list is available for this plan

MAIN FLOOR — 1,830 SQ. FT.
GARAGE — 759 SQ. FT.

TOTAL LIVING AREA:
1,830 SQ. FT.

Refer to **Pricing Schedule D** on the order form for pricing information

© 1995 Donald A. Gardner Architects, Inc.

...ly Elegant

...s plan features:

— Three bedrooms

— Two full baths

■ Arched windows, dormers and charming front and back Porches with columns creating Country flavoring

■ Central Great Room topped by a cathedral ceiling, a fireplace and a clerestory window

■ Breakfast Bay for casual dining is open to the Kitchen

■ Columns accenting the entryway into the formal Dining Room

■ Cathedral ceiling crowning the Master Bedroom

■ Master Bath with skylights, whirlpool tub, shower, and a double vanity

MAIN FLOOR — 1,561 SQ. FT.
GARAGE & STORAGE — 346 SQ. FT.

TOTAL LIVING AREA:
1,561 SQ. FT.

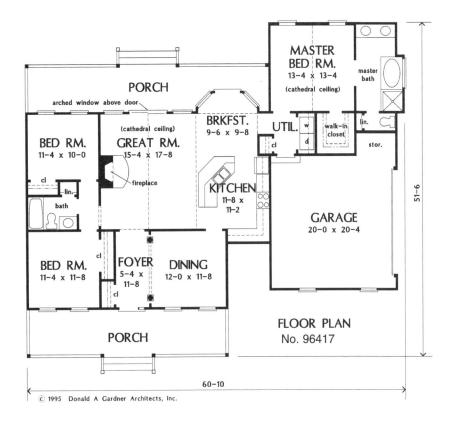

© 1995 Donald A Gardner Architects, Inc.

FLOOR PLAN
No. 96417

To order your Blueprints, call 1-800-235-5700

Design by
Donald A. Gardner Architects, Inc.

©1995 Donald A. Gardner Architects, Inc.

P L A N   N O . 9 6 4 5 8

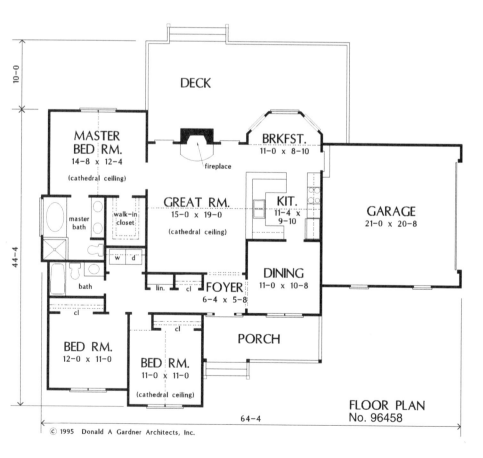

FLOOR PLAN
No. 96458

© 1995 Donald A Gardner Architects, Inc.

Country Charm and Convenience

■ This plan features:

— Three bedrooms

— Two full baths

■ The open design pulls the Great Room, Kitchen and Breakfast Bay into one common area

■ Cathedral ceilings in the Great Room , Master Bedroom and a secondary Bedroom

■ The rear Deck expands the living and entertaining space

■ The Dining Room provides a quiet place for relaxed family dinners

■ Two additional Bedrooms share a full Bath

MAIN FLOOR — 1,512 SQ. FT.
GARAGE & STORAGE — 455 SQ. FT.

TOTAL LIVING AREA:
1,512 SQ. FT.

Design by
Donald A. Gardner Architects, Inc.

Refer to **Pricing Schedule D** on the order form for pricing information

©1995 Donald A. Gardner Architects, Inc.

B. NATHAN

Your Family Will Grow In Style

■ This plan features:

— Three bedrooms

— Two full baths

■ Open Great Room and Kitchen enlarged by a cathedral ceiling

■ Wooden rear Deck expand entertaining to the outdoors

■ Cathedral ceiling adding volume and drama to the Master Suite

■ Flexible Bedroom/Study includes a cathedral ceiling and a double window with an arched top

■ Second floor Bonus Space may be finished with two more Bedrooms

MAIN FLOOR — 1,633 SQ. FT.
GARAGE & STORAGE — 512 SQ. FT.
BONUS — 595 SQ. FT.

TOTAL LIVING AREA:
1,633 SQ. FT.

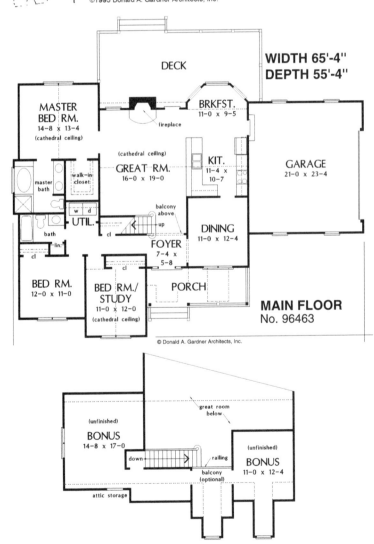

WIDTH 65'-4"
DEPTH 55'-4"

DECK

MASTER BED RM.
14-8 x 13-4
(cathedral ceiling)

BRKFST.
11-0 x 9-5

fireplace

GARAGE
21-0 x 23-4

(cathedral ceiling)

KIT.
11-4 x 10-7

GREAT RM.
16-0 x 19-0

master bath

walk-in closet

w d

UTIL.

bath

balcony above
up

DINING
11-0 x 12-4

FOYER
7-4 x 5-8

cl

lin.

cl

cl

BED RM.
12-0 x 11-0

BED RM./ STUDY
11-0 x 12-0
(cathedral ceiling)

PORCH

MAIN FLOOR
No. 96463

© Donald A. Gardner Architects, Inc.

great room below

(unfinished)

BONUS
14-8 x 17-0

down

railing

(unfinished)

BONUS
11-0 x 12-4

balcony (optional)

attic storage

110

To order your Blueprints, call 1-800-235-5700

Design by
Donald A. Gardner Architects, Inc.

PLAN NO. 96483

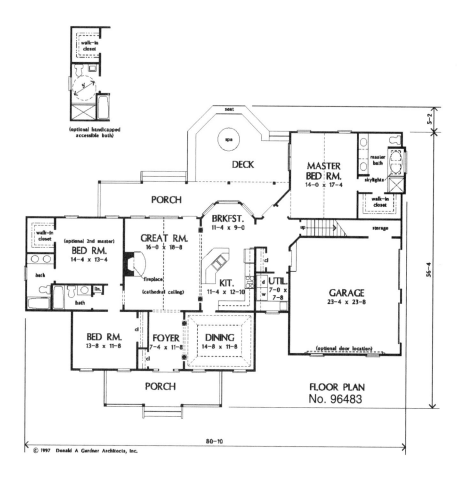

(optional handicapped accessible bath)

FLOOR PLAN No. 96483

© 1997 Donald A Gardner Architects, Inc.

Grace and Style

■ This plan features:

— Three bedrooms

— Three full baths

■ Foyer accented by columns gives entry into the formal Dining Room

■ Angled island Kitchen is open to the Breakfast Bay

■ Great Room topped by a cathedral ceiling and enhanced by a fireplace

■ Secluded Master Suite with a skylit Bath

■ Two secondary bedrooms, one with a private Bath

■ Bonus room may create a terrific fourth Bedroom and Bath

MAIN FLOOR — 2,057 SQ. FT.
GARAGE & STORAGE — 622 SQ. FT.
BONUS ROOM — 444 SQ. FT.

TOTAL LIVING AREA:
2,057 SQ. FT.

Design by
Rick Garner

Refer to **Pricing Schedule C** on the order form for pricing information

Secluded Master Suite

■ This plan features:

— Three bedrooms

— Two full baths

■ A convenient one-level design with an open floor plan between the Kitchen, Breakfast Area and Great Room

■ A vaulted ceiling and a large cozy fireplace in the Great Room

■ A well-equipped Kitchen using a peninsula counter as an eating bar

■ A Master Suite with a luxurious Master Bath

■ Two additional Bedrooms having use of a full hall Bath

■ An optional crawl space or slab foundation — please specify when ordering

MAIN AREA — 1,680 SQ. FT.
GARAGE — 538 SQ. FT.

TOTAL LIVING AREA:
1,680 SQ. FT.

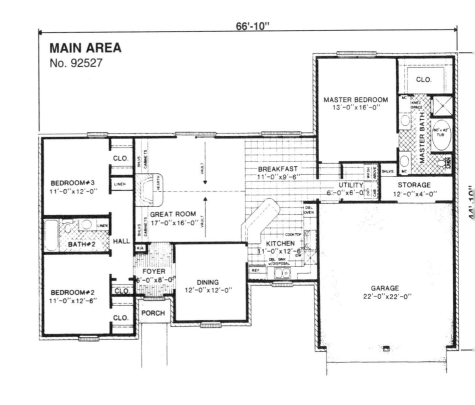

MAIN AREA
No. 92527

66'-10"

MASTER BEDROOM
13'-0" x 16'-0"

CLO.

MASTER BATH

CLO.

BEDROOM #3
11'-0" x 12'-0"

LINEN

BREAKFAST
11'-0" x 9'-6"

UTILITY
6'-0" x 6'-0"

STORAGE
12'-0" x 4'-0"

GREAT ROOM
17'-0" x 16'-0"

VAULT

BATH #2

HALL

KITCHEN
11'-0" x 12'-6"

FOYER
6'-0" x 8'-0"

BEDROOM #2
11'-0" x 12'-6"

CLO.

DINING
12'-0" x 12'-0"

GARAGE
22'-0" x 22'-0"

CLO.

PORCH

To order your Blueprints, call 1-800-235-5700

Design by
Vaughn A. Lauban Designs

PLAN NO. 96519

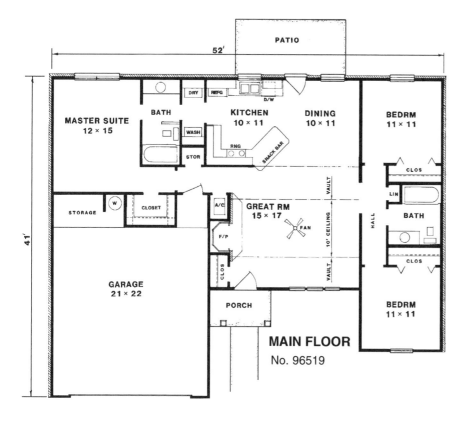

MAIN FLOOR
No. 96519

Labels within floor plan:
52'
41'
PATIO
MASTER SUITE 12 × 15
BATH
KITCHEN 10 × 11
DINING 10 × 11
BEDRM 11 × 11
DRY
REFG
D/W
WASH
RNG
STOR
SNACK BAR
CLOS
LIN
BATH
STORAGE
W
CLOSET
A/C
GREAT RM 15 × 17
FAN
10' CEILING
VAULT
F/P
CLOS
HALL
CLOS
GARAGE 21 × 22
PORCH
BEDRM 11 × 11

Split-Bedroom Floor Plan

■ This plan features:

— Three bedrooms

— Two full baths

■ A split-bedroom floor plan gives the Master Bedroom ultimate privacy

■ A snack bar peninsula counter is one of the many conveniences of the Kitchen

■ The Patio is accessed from the Dining Room and expands dining to the outdoors

■ No materials list is available for this plan

■ An optional crawl space or slab foundation — please specify when ordering

MAIN FLOOR — 1,243 SQ. FT.
GARAGE — 523 SQ. FT.

TOTAL LIVING AREA:
1,243 SQ. FT.

Design by
Landmark Designs, Inc.

Refer to **Pricing Schedule B** on the order form for pricing information

Economy at It's Best

■ This plan features:

— Three bedrooms

— Two full and one three-quarter bath

■ Attractive Pßorch adds to the curb appeal of this economical to build home

■ A vaulted ceiling topping the Entry, Living and Dining Rooms

■ A lovely bay window, adding sophistication to the Living Room,

■ A Master Suite with a walk-in closet, and a private compartmented Bath with an oversized shower

■ A walk-in Pantry adds to the storage space of the cooktop island Kitchen, which is equipped with a double sink with a window above

MAIN AREA — 1,717 SQ. FT.
GARAGE — 782 SQ. FT.
WIDTH — 80'-0"
DEPTH — 42'-0"

TOTAL LIVING AREA:
1,717 SQ. FT.

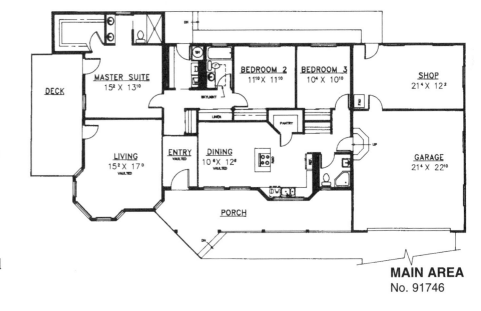

MAIN AREA
No. 91746

Design by
Donald A. Gardner Architects, Inc.

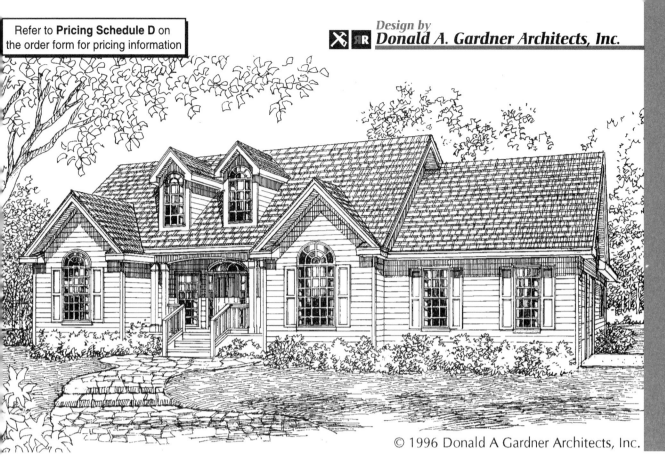

© 1996 Donald A Gardner Architects, Inc.

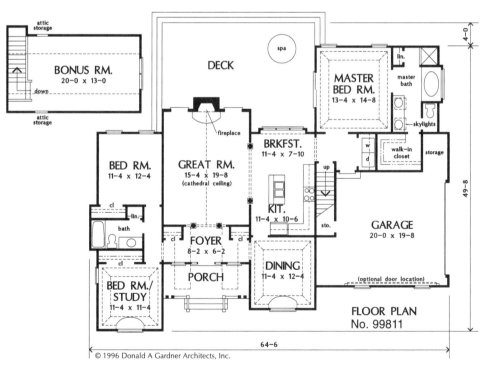

© 1996 Donald A Gardner Architects, Inc.

Cathedral Ceiling Enlarges Great Room

■ This plan features:

— Three bedrooms

— Two full baths

■ Two dormers add volume to the Foyer

■ Great Room, topped by a cathedral ceiling, is open to the Kitchen and Breakfast area

■ Accent columns define the Foyer, Great Room, Kitchen and Breakfast Area

■ Private Master Suite crowned in a tray ceiling and highlighted by a skylit Bath

■ Front Bedroom topped by a tray ceiling

MAIN FLOOR — 1,699 SQ. FT.
GARAGE — 498 SQ. FT.
BONUS — 336 SQ. FT.

TOTAL LIVING AREA:
1,699 SQ. FT.

Design by
Marshall Associates

Refer to **Pricing Schedule A** on the order form for pricing information

Easy Maintenance

■ This plan features:

— Two bedroom

— Two three quarter baths

■ Abundant glass and a wrap-around Deck to enjoy the outdoors

■ A tiled entrance into a large Great Room with a fieldstone fireplace and Dining Area under a sloped ceiling

■ A compact tiled Kitchen open to Great Room and adjacent to the Utility Area

■ Two Bedrooms, one with a private Bath, offer ample closet space

■ No materials list is available for this plan

MAIN AREA — 786 SQ. FT.
DECK — 580 SQ. FT.

TOTAL LIVING AREA:
786 SQ. FT.

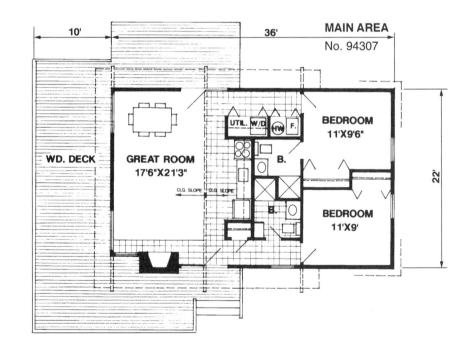

To order your Blueprints, call 1-800-235-5700

Design by
DDI Architecture

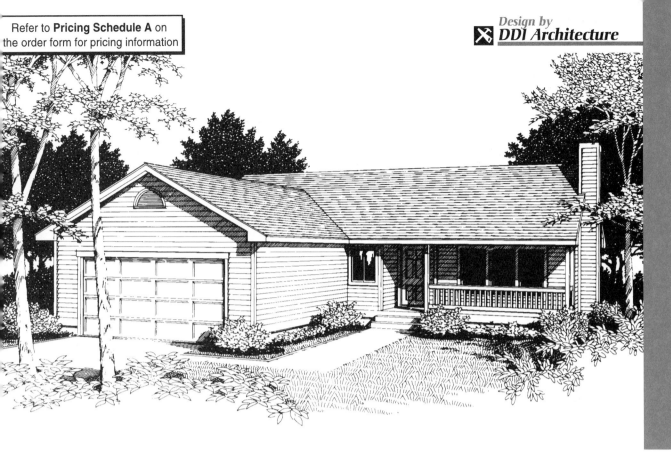

47'-0"

54'-0"

PATIO

BDRM-2
11/0 x 10/10

BDRM-3
11/0 x 10/10

KIT.
10/4 x 10/10

VAULTED
DINING RM.
10/8 x 11/2

PANT

LINEN

TUB

VAULTED
LIVING RM.
15/10 x 20/8

HEARTH

MASTER
12/10 x 15/2

COVERED PORCH

GARAGE
21/4 x 21/8

MAIN AREA
No. 91807

An Affordable, Stylish Floor Plan

■ This plan features:

— Three bedrooms

— One full and one three quarter baths

■ A covered Porch entry

■ An old-fashioned hearth fireplace in the vaulted ceiling Living Room

■ A handy Kitchen with U-shaped counter that is accessible from the Dining Room

■ A Master Bedroom with a large walk-in closet and private Bath

■ An optional crawl space or slab foundation — please specify when ordering

MAIN AREA0 — 1,410 SQ. FT.
GARAGE — 484 SQ. FT.

TOTAL LIVING AREA:
1,410 SQ. FT.

Design by
The Garlinghouse Company

Refer to **Pricing Schedule B** on the order form for pricing information

Traditional Ranch

▪ This plan features:

— Three bedrooms

— Two full baths

▪ A large front palladium window gives this home curb appeal, and allows a view of the front yard from the Living Room

▪ A vaulted ceiling in the Living Room, adds to the architectural interest and the spacious feel of the room

▪ Sliding glass doors in the Dining Room lead to a wood Deck

▪ A built-in Pantry, double sink and breakfast bar in the efficient Kitchen

▪ The Master Suite includes a walk-in closet and a private Bath with a double vanity

MAIN AREA —1,568 SQ. FT.
BASEMENT — 1,568 SQ. FT.
GARAGE — 509 SQ. FT.

TOTAL LIVING AREA:
1,568 SQ. FT.

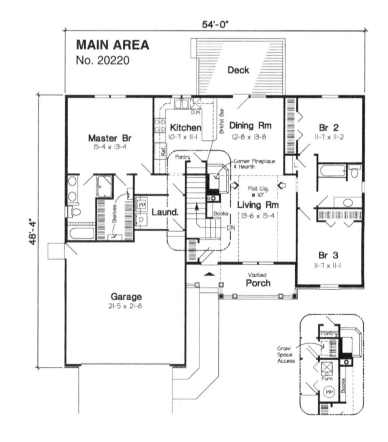

To order your Blueprints, call 1-800-235-5700

Design by
Vaughn A. Lauban Designs

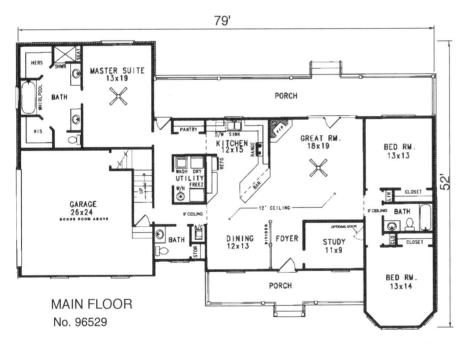

MAIN FLOOR
No. 96529

Porches Expands Living Space

- This plan features:

— Three bedrooms

— Two full and one half baths

- Porches on the front and the rear of this home expand the living space to the outdoors

- The spacious Great Room is enhanced by a twelve foot ceiling and a fireplace

- The well-appointed kitchen has an extended counter/eating bar

- The Master Suite is enhanced by his and her walk-in closets

- There is a Bonus Room for the future expansion

MAIN FLOOR — 2,089 SQ. FT.
BONUS ROOM — 497 SQ. FT.
GARAGE — 541 SQ. FT.

TOTAL LIVING AREA:
2,089 SQ. FT.

Design by
The Garlinghouse Company

Refer to **Pricing Schedule C** on the order form for pricing information

Attractive Combination of Brick and Siding

■ This plan features:

— Three Bedrooms

— Two full Baths

■ A Great Room with sunny bayed area, fireplace and built-in entertainment center

■ A private Master Bedroom with luxurious Master Bath and walk-in closet

■ Dining Room has a Butler Pantry

■ Two additional Bedrooms have use of hall full Bath

MAIN LEVEL — 2,010 SQ. FT.
BASEMENT — 2,010 SQ. FT.

TOTAL LIVING AREA:
2,010 SQ. FT.

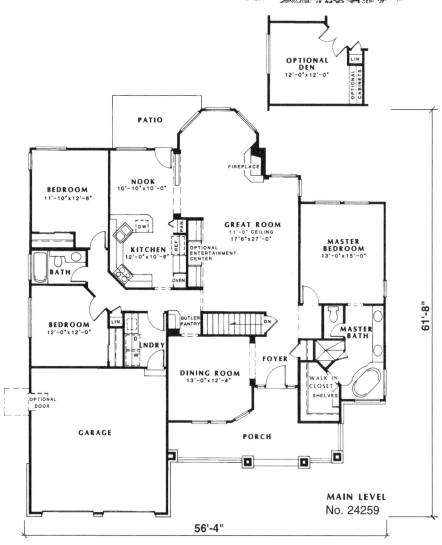

OPTIONAL DEN
12'-0" x 12'-0"

PATIO

BEDROOM
11'-10" x 12'-6"

NOOK
10'-10" x 10'-0"

FIREPLACE

KITCHEN
12'-0" x 10'-6"

GREAT ROOM
11'-0" CEILING
17'6" x 27'-0"

OPTIONAL ENTERTAINMENT CENTER

OVEN

MASTER BEDROOM
13'-0" x 15'-0"

BATH

BEDROOM
12'-0" x 12'-0"

LIN.

LNDRY

BUTLER PANTRY

DN

MASTER BATH

FOYER

WALK IN CLOSET
SHELVES

OPTIONAL DOOR

GARAGE

DINING ROOM
13'-0" x 12'-4"

PORCH

61'-8"

56'-4"

MAIN LEVEL
No. 24259

To order your Blueprints, call 1-800-235-5700

Design by
Studer Residential Design, Inc.

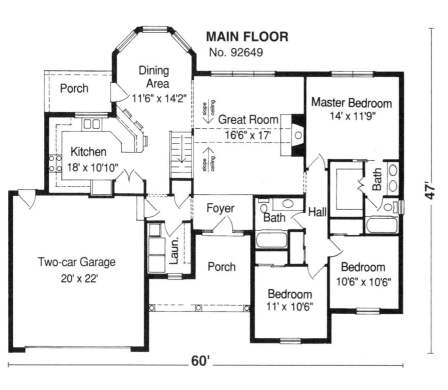

MAIN FLOOR
No. 92649

Dining Area 11'6" x 14'2"

Porch

Great Room 16'6" x 17'
slope ceiling
slope ceiling

Master Bedroom 14' x 11'9"

Kitchen 18' x 10'10"

Bath

Foyer

Bath

Hall

Laun.

Two-car Garage 20' x 22'

Porch

Bedroom 11' x 10'6"

Bedroom 10'6" x 10'6"

60'

47'

Multiple Gables Galore

■ This plan features:

— Three bedrooms

— Two full baths

■ Multiple gables and a cozy front Porch

■ Cheery Great Room capped by a sloped ceiling and a fireplace

■ The Dining Area includes double hung windows and angles adding light and dimension to the room

■ A functional Kitchen providing an abundance of counter space and a breakfast bar

■ A Master Bedroom Suite including a walk-in closet and private Bath

■ No materials list is available for this plan

MAIN FLOOR — 1,508 SQ. FT.
BASEMENT — 1,439 SQ. FT.
GARAGE — 440 SQ. FT.

TOTAL LIVING AREA:
1,508 SQ. FT.

Design by
The Garlinghouse Company

Refer to **Pricing Schedule A** on
the order form for pricing information

Champagne Style on a Soda-Pop Budget

■ This plan features:

— Three bedrooms

— One full and one three quarter baths

■ Multiple gables, circle-top windows, and a unique exterior setting this delightful Ranch apart in any neighborhood

■ Living and Dining Rooms flowing together to create a very roomy feeling

■ Sliding doors leading from the Dining Room to a covered patio

■ A Master Bedroom with a private Bath

MAIN AREA — 988 SQ. FT.
BASEMENT — 988 SQ. FT.
GARAGE — 280 SQ. FT
OPTIONAL 2-CAR GARAGE — 384 SQ. FT.

TOTAL LIVING AREA:
988 SQ. FT.

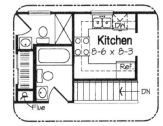

Optional Basement Plan

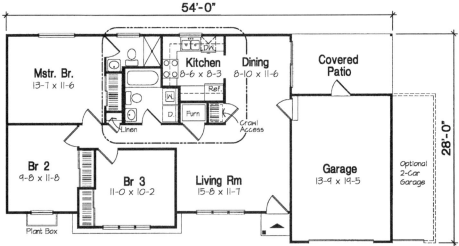

Main Floor
No. 24302

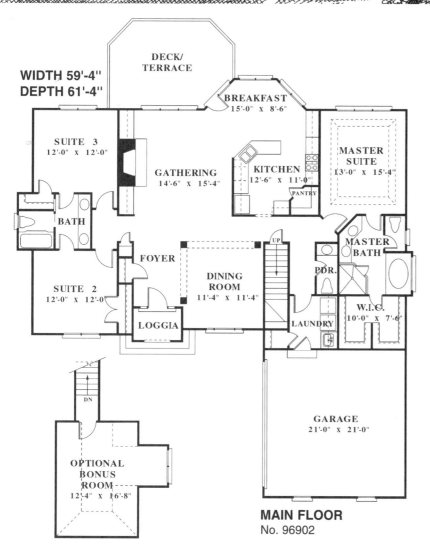

WIDTH 59'-4"
DEPTH 61'-4"

DECK/ TERRACE

BREAKFAST
15'-0" x 8'-6"

SUITE 3
12'-0" x 12'-0"

GATHERING
14'-6" x 15'-4"

KITCHEN
12'-6" x 11'-0"

MASTER SUITE
13'-0" x 15'-4"

PANTRY

BATH

FOYER

MASTER BATH

UP

PDR.

SUITE 2
12'-0" x 12'-0"

DINING ROOM
11'-4" x 11'-4"

W.I.C.
10'-0" x 7'-6"

LOGGIA

LAUNDRY

DN

OPTIONAL BONUS ROOM
12'-4" x 16'-8"

GARAGE
21'-0" x 21'-0"

MAIN FLOOR
No. 96902

Step-Saving Floor Plan

■ This plan features:

— Three bedrooms

— Two full and one half baths

■ Recessed entrance leads into Foyer, Dining Room defined by columns, and Gathering Room beyond

■ Expansive Gathering Room with an inviting fireplace, opens to Deck/Terrace and Breakfast/ Kitchen Area for comfortable gatherings

■ Corner Master Suite offers privacy, a decorative ceiling, wall of windows, plush Bath and double, walk-in closet

■ No materials list is available for this plan

MAIN FLOOR — 1,950 SQ. FT.
BASEMENT — 1,287 SQ. FT.
GARAGE — 466 SQ. FT.
BONUS — 255 SQ. FT.

TOTAL LIVING AREA:
1,950 SQ. FT.

Design by
Frank Betz Associates, Inc.

Expansive Living Room

■ This plan features:
— Three bedrooms
— Two full baths

■ Vaulted ceiling crowns spacious Living Room highlighted by a fireplace

■ Built-in Pantry and direct access from the garage adding to the conveniences of the Kitchen

■ Walk-in closet and a private five- piece Bath topped by a vaulted ceiling in the Master Bedroom

■ An optional basement, crawl space or slab foundation — please specify when ordering

MAIN FLOOR — 1,346 SQ. FT.
GARAGE — 395 SQ. FT.
BASEMENT — 1358 SQ. FT.

TOTAL LIVING AREA:
1,346 SQ. FT.

MAIN FLOOR
No. 98434

Design by
Ahmann Design, Inc.

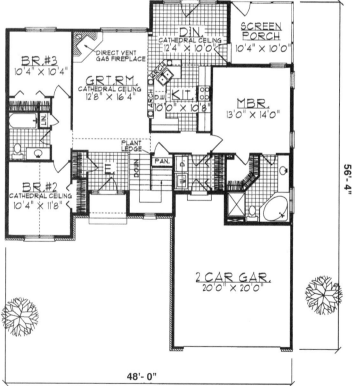

MAIN FLOOR PLAN
No. 93165

48'- 0"

56'- 4"

BR. #3
10'4" X 10'4"

GRT. RM.
CATHEDRAL CEILING
12'8" X 16'4"

DIRECT VENT
GAS FIREPLACE

DIN.
CATHEDRAL CEILING
12'4" X 10'0"

SCREEN
PORCH
10'4" X 10'0"

KIT.
10'0" X 10'8"

MBR.
13'0" X 14'0"

PLANT
LEDGE

PAN.

BR. #2
CATHEDRAL CEILING
10'4" X 11'8"

2 CAR GAR.
20'0" X 20'0"

Brick Details Add Class

■ This plan features:

— Three bedrooms

— Two full baths

■ Keystone entrance leads into an easy care, tiled Entry with plant ledge and convenient closet

■ Expansive Great Room with cathedral ceiling, triple window and a corner gas fireplace

■ Hub Kitchen accented by arches and columns serves Great Room and Dining Area

■ Private Master Bedroom suite with a walk-in closet and plush bath with corner whirlpool tub

■ This plan is not to be built within a 20 mile radius of Iowa City, IA

■ No materials list is available for this plan

MAIN FLOOR — 1,472 SQ. FT.
BASEMENT — 1,472 SQ. FT.
GARAGE — 424 SQ. FT.

TOTAL LIVING AREA:
1,472 SQ. FT.

Design by
Donald A. Gardner Architects, Inc.

Refer to **Pricing Schedule D** on the order form for pricing information

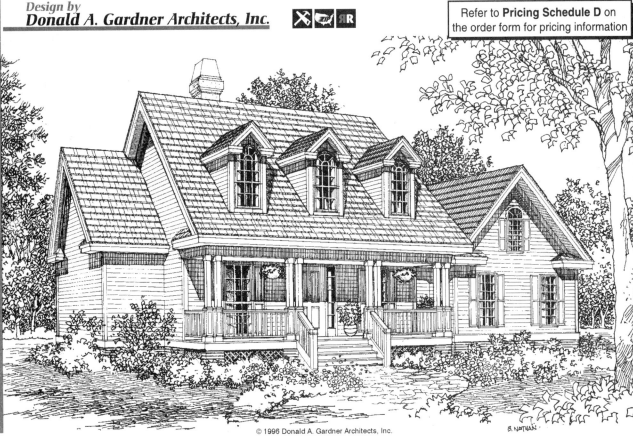

© 1996 Donald A. Gardner Architects, Inc.

B. NATHAN

Dramatic Dormers

■ This plan features:
— Three bedrooms
— Two full baths

■ A Foyer open to the dramatic dormer, defined by columns

■ A Dining Room augmented by a tray ceiling

■ A Great Room expands into the Kitchen and Breakfast Room

■ A privately located Master Suite is topped by a tray ceiling

■ Two additional Bedrooms, located at the opposite side share a full Bath and linen closet

MAIN FLOOR — 1,685 SQ. FT.
GARAGE & STORAGE — 536 SQ. FT.
BONUS — 331 SQ. FT.

TOTAL LIVING AREA:
1,685 SQ. FT.

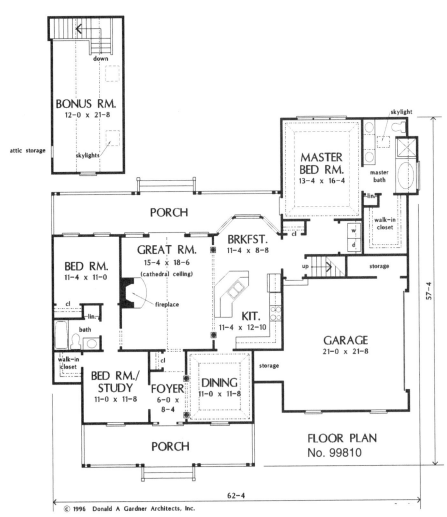

BONUS RM.
12-0 x 21-8

attic storage

skylights

down

PORCH

BED RM.
11-4 x 11-0

GREAT RM.
15-4 x 18-6
(cathedral ceiling)

fireplace

BRKFST.
11-4 x 8-8

MASTER BED RM.
13-4 x 16-4

skylight

master bath

walk-in closet

KIT.
11-4 x 12-10

storage

up

GARAGE
21-0 x 21-8

cl

lin.

bath

walk-in closet

BED RM./ STUDY
11-0 x 11-8

FOYER
6-0 x 8-4

DINING
11-0 x 11-8

storage

PORCH

FLOOR PLAN
No. 99810

57-4

62-4

© 1996 Donald A Gardner Architects, Inc.

To order your Blueprints, call 1-800-235-5700

Refer to **Pricing Schedule B** on the order form for pricing information

Design by
Rick Garner

PLAN NO. 92503

Charming Southern Traditional

■ This plan features:

— Three bedrooms

— Two full baths

■ A covered front Porch with striking columns, brick quoins, and dentil molding

■ A spacious Great Room with vaulted ceilings, a fireplace, and built-in cabinets

■ A Utility Room adjacent to the Kitchen which leads to the two-car Garage and Storage Rooms

■ A Master Bedroom including a large walk-in closet and a compartmentalized Bath

■ An optional crawl space or slab foundation — please specify when ordering

MAIN AREA — 1,271 SQ. FT.
GARAGE — 506 SQ. FT.

TOTAL LIVING AREA:
1,271 SQ. FT.

garage
21 x 21

kit 12 x 9

ref · dw

rng

b

d
w

cab

shvs

util

sto

dining
11 x 11

mbr
14 x 12

shvs

living
15⁶ x 16

vault

vault

ra

br 2
11 x 11

br 3
11 x 11

shvs

porch 20¹⁰ x 5

shvs

WIDTH 63'-10"
DEPTH 38'-10"

MAIN AREA
No. 92503

Design by
Donald A. Gardner Architects, Inc.

Refer to **Pricing Schedule C** on
the order form for pricing information

© 1997 Donald A. Gardner Architects, Inc.

Illusion of Spaciousness

- This plan features:
- — Three bedrooms
- — Two full baths
- Open living spaces and vaulted ceilings create an illusion of spaciousness
- Cathedral ceilings maximize space in Great Room and Dining Room
- Kitchen features skylight and Breakfast Bar
- Well equipped Master Suite in rear for privacy
- Two additional Bedrooms in front share a full Bath

MAIN FLOOR — 1,246 SQ. FT.
GARAGE — 420 SQ. FT.

TOTAL LIVING AREA:
1,246 SQ. FT.

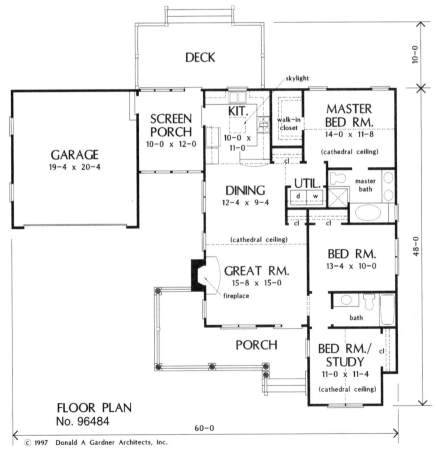

FLOOR PLAN
No. 96484

© 1997 Donald A Gardner Architects, Inc.

To order your Blueprints, call 1-800-235-5700

Design by
Living Concepts

WIDTH 63'-10"
DEPTH 80'-4"

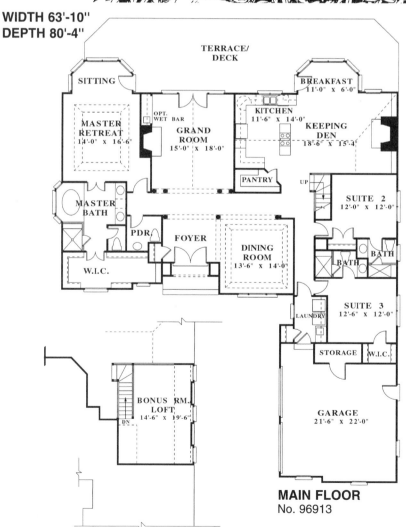

TERRACE/DECK

SITTING

BREAKFAST
11'-0" x 6'-0"

MASTER RETREAT
14'-0" x 16'-6"

OPT. WET BAR

GRAND ROOM
15'-0" x 18'-0"

KITCHEN
11'-6" x 14'-0"

KEEPING DEN
18'-6" x 15'-4"

PANTRY

MASTER BATH

UP

SUITE 2
12'-0" x 12'-0"

PDR.

FOYER

W.I.C.

DINING ROOM
13'-6" x 14'-0"

BATH

BATH

SUITE 3
12'-6" x 12'-0"

LAUNDRY

STORAGE

W.I.C.

BONUS RM. LOFT
14'-6" x 19'-6"

DN

GARAGE
21'-6" x 22'-0"

MAIN FLOOR
No. 96913

Outstanding Elevation

■ This plan features:

— Three bedrooms

— One full, two three-quarter and one half baths

■ Grand double door entrance into Foyer and formal Dining Room and Grand Room defined by columns

■ Cozy fireplace and French doors to Terrace/Deck enhance Grand Room

■ Efficient Kitchen with Pantry and cooktop island easily serves Breakfast Area, Deck and Keeping Den

■ No materials list is available for this plan

MAIN FLOOR — 2,677 SQ. FT.
GARAGE — 543 SQ. FT.
BONUS — 319 SQ. FT.

TOTAL LIVING AREA:
2,677 SQ. FT.

Design by
Corley Plan Service ✕

Refer to **Pricing Schedule C** on
the order form for pricing information

Moderate Ranch Has Features of Much Larger Plan

■ This plan features:

— Three bedrooms

— Two full baths

■ A large Great Room with a vaulted ceiling and a stone fireplace with bookshelves on either side

■ A spacious Kitchen with ample cabinet space conveniently located next to the large Dining Room

■ A Master Suite having a large bath with a garden tub, double vanity and a walk-in closet

■ An optional basement, slab or crawl space foundation — please specify when ordering

MAIN FLOOR — 1,811 SQ. FT.
BASEMENT — 1,811 SQ. FT.
GARAGE — 484 SQ. FT.

TOTAL LIVING AREA:
1,811 SQ. FT.

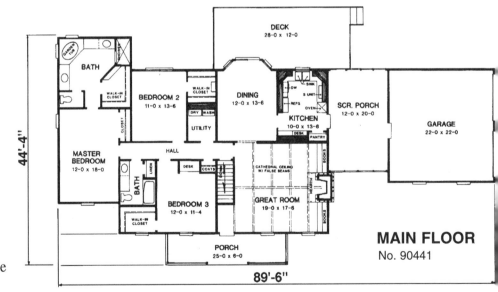

MAIN FLOOR
No. 90441

To order your Blueprints, call 1-800-235-5700

Design by
Donald A. Gardner Architects, Inc.

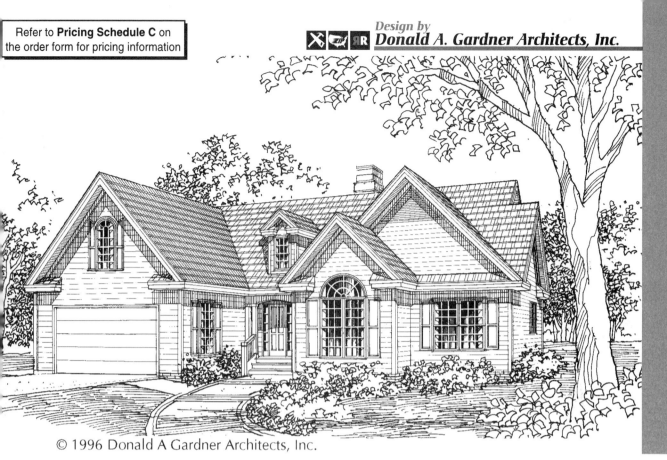

© 1996 Donald A Gardner Architects, Inc.

Sunny Dormer Brightens Foyer

- This plan features:
  —Three bedrooms
  —Two full baths
- Today's comforts with cost effective construction
- Open Great room, Dining Room, and Kitchen topped by a cathedral ceiling emphasizing spaciousness
- Adjoining Deck providing extra living or entertaining room
- Front bedroom crowned in cathedral ceiling and pampered by a private Bath with garden tub, dual vanity and a walk-in closet
- Skylit Bonus Room above the garage offering flexibility and opportunity for growth

MAIN FLOOR — 1,386 SQ. FT.
GARAGE — 517 SQ. FT.
BONUS ROOM — 314 SQ. FT.

TOTAL LIVING AREA:
1,386 SQ. FT.

FLOOR PLAN
No. 99812

DECK

DINING
9–10 x 11–0
(cathedral ceiling)

GREAT RM.
15–10 x 16–10
(cathedral ceiling)
fireplace

MASTER
BED RM.
12–4 x 13–6
(cathedral ceiling)

walk-in closet

master bath

bath

KIT.
9–10 x 11–8

d
w

FOYER
9–6 x 5–6

cl

cl

BED RM.
11–0 x 11–0

storage

up

PORCH

BED RM.
11–0 x 11–0
(cathedral ceiling)

GARAGE
22–0 x 20–8

10–0

48–0

54–10

© 1996 Donald A Gardner Architects, Inc.

Design by
Ahmann Design, Inc.

A Must See Design

■ This plan features:

— Three bedrooms

— Two full baths

■ Attractive, arched entrance leads
into Great Room with a wall of
windows and expansive cathedral
ceiling above a cozy fireplace

■ Convenient Kitchen easily
accesses Nook and Dining areas,
Laundry and Garage

■ Corner Master Bedroom
enhanced by two large, walk-in
closets, cathedral ceiling and private, double vanity Bath

■ Two secondary Bedrooms with
large closets share a double vanity Bath

■ No materials list is available for
this plan

MAIN FLOOR — 2,229 SQ. FT.
BASEMENT — 2,229 SQ. FT.
GARAGE — 551 SQ. FT.

TOTAL LIVING AREA:
2,229 SQ. FT.

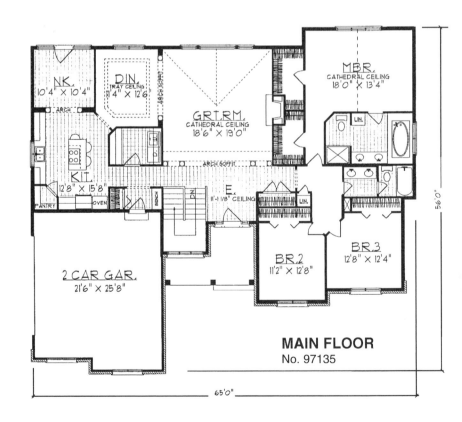

MAIN FLOOR
No. 97135

To order your Blueprints, call 1-800-235-5700

Varied Roof Heights Create Interesting Lines

■ This plan features:

— Three bedrooms

— Two full and one half baths

■ A spacious Family Room with a heat-circulating fireplace, which is visible from the Foyer

■ A large Kitchen with a cooktop island, opening into the Dinette Bay

■ A Master Suite with his-n-her closets and a private Master Bath

■ Two additional Bedrooms which share a full hall Bath

■ Formal Dining and Living Rooms, flowing into each other for easy entertaining

MAIN AREA — 1,613 SQ. FT.
BASEMENT — 1,060 SQ. FT.
GARAGE — 461 SQ. FT.

TOTAL LIVING AREA:
1,613 SQ. FT.

MAIN AREA
No. 90601

PATIO
83'-8"

27'-4"

LAV

mud rm laund.

DINETTE 7'-8"×12'-4"

KIT 8'-6"×13'

island cook top

dw s

sl. gl. dr.

fireplace

wd bin

BATH

BATH

MASTER BED RM 14'-6"×13'-0"

cl

cl

HALL

lin

pantry

ref

DINING RM 11'-0"×12'-0"

LIVING RM 17'-6"×13'-4"

FAMILY RM 15'-8"×13'-0"

BED RM 10'-0"×10'-0"

BED RM 10'-0"×13'-4"

cl

cl

cl

FOYER

up

dn

TWO CAR GARAGE 22'-0"×20'-0"

COVERED PORCH

Keystone Arches and Decorative Windows

■ This plan features:

— Three bedrooms

— One full and one three quarter baths

■ Brick and stucco enhance the dramatic front elevation

■ Inviting Entry leads into expansive Great Room with hearth fireplace framed by transom windows

■ The Dining Room is topped by decorative ceiling and is convenient to the Great Room and the Kitchen/Breakfast Area

■ Corner Master Suite enjoys a tray ceiling, roomy walk-in closet and a plush Bath with a double vanity and whirlpool window tub

MAIN FLOOR — 1,666 SQ. FT.
BASEMENT — 1,666 SQ. FT.
GARAGE — 496 SQ. FT.

TOTAL LIVING AREA:
1,666 SQ. FT.

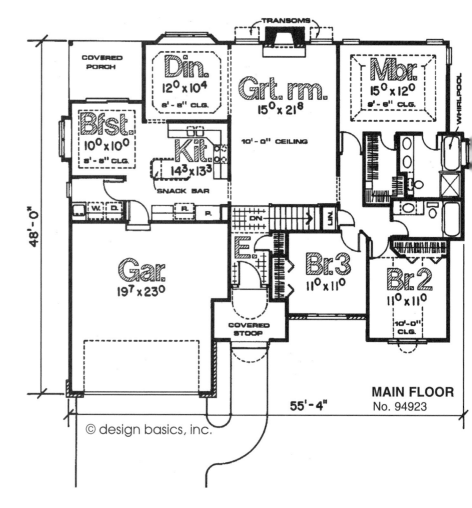

MAIN FLOOR
No. 94923

© design basics, inc.

Crawl Space Access

Deck
(Optional)

Great Room
22-7 x 12-10

Screened Porch
10-0 x 10-0

Mbr 1
11-9 x 16-11

Dining
12-2 x 9-10

Snack Bar

Kitchen
11-0 x 8-11

Foyer

Br 2
11-10 x 11-3

Cabinets

Breakfast
11-0 x 6-6

Air Lock

Covered Porch

Garage
19-9 x 28-0

Den
15-5 x 10-2

Window Seat

50'-0

54'-0"

MAIN FLOOR
No. 24714

Energy Efficient Air-Lock Entry

- This plan features:
— Two bedrooms
— Two full baths

- The attractive covered Porch highlights the curb appeal of this charming home

- A window seat and a vaulted ceiling enhance the private Den

- The sunken Great Room is accented by a fireplace that is nestled between windows

- A screened Porch, accessed from the Dining Room, extends the living space to the outdoors

- The Master Bath features a garden tub, separate shower, his-n-her walk-in closets and a skylight

- No materials list is available for this plan

MAIN FLOOR — 1,771 SQ. FT.
BASEMENT — 1,194 SQ. FT.
GARAGE — 517 SQ. FT.

TOTAL LIVING AREA:
1,771 SQ. FT.

Design by
Atlanta Plan Source

Refer to **Pricing Schedule D** on the order form for pricing information

Traditional Ranch

■ This plan features:

— Three bedrooms

— Two full baths

■ A tray ceiling over Master Suite which is equipped with his-n-her walk-in closets and a private Master Bath with a cathedral ceiling

■ A formal Living Room with a cathedral ceiling

■ A decorative tray ceiling in the elegant formal Dining Room

■ A spacious Family Room with a vaulted ceiling and a fireplace

■ A modern, well-appointed Kitchen with snack bar and bayed Breakfast Area

MAIN AREA — 2,275 SQ. FT.
BASEMENT — 2,207 SQ. FT.
GARAGE — 512 SQ. FT.

TOTAL LIVING AREA:
2,275 SQ. FT.

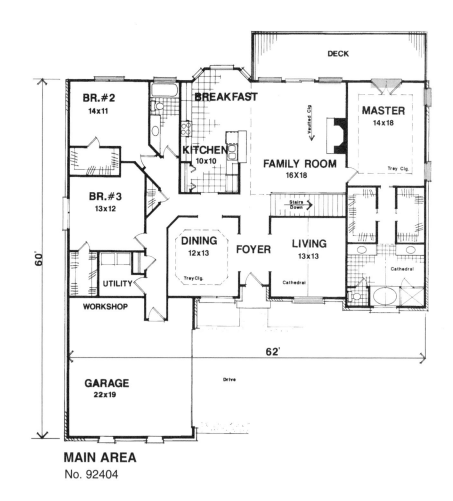

BR.#2
14x11

BREAKFAST

KITCHEN
10x10

MASTER
14x18

Trey Clg.

FAMILY ROOM
16X18

Vaulted Clg

DECK

BR.#3
13x12

Stairs Down

60'

DINING
12x13

Trey Clg.

FOYER

LIVING
13x13

Cathedral

Cathedral

UTILITY

WORKSHOP

62'

GARAGE
22x19

Drive

MAIN AREA
No. 92404

To order your Blueprints, call 1-800-235-5700

Design by
Ahmann Design, Inc.

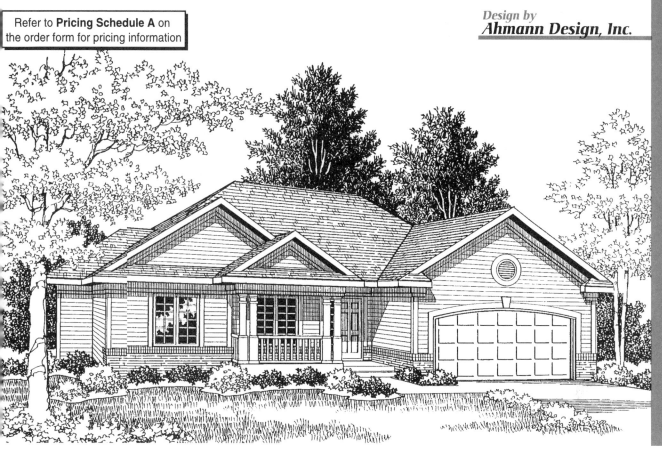

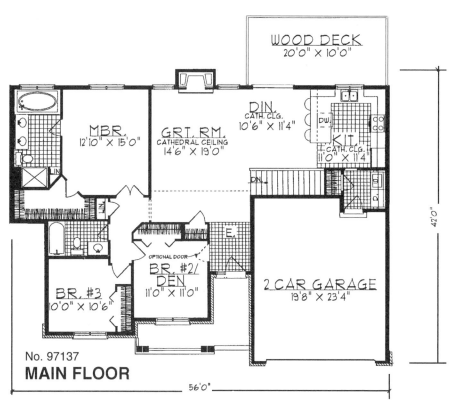

WOOD DECK
20'0" X 10'0"

MBR.
12'10" X 15'0"

GRT. RM.
CATHEDRAL CEILING
14'6" X 19'0"

DIN.
CATH. CLG.
10'6" X 11'4"

KIT.
CATH. CLG.
11'0" X 11'4"

DN.

DN.

OPTIONAL DOOR

BR. #2/
DEN
11'0" X 11'0"

BR. #3
10'0" X 10'6"

2 CAR GARAGE
19'8" X 23'4"

42'0"

56'0"

No. 97137
MAIN FLOOR

Country Flair

■ This plan features:
— Three bedrooms
— Two full baths

■ An inviting front Porch leads into a tiled Entry and Great Room with focal point fireplace

■ Open layout of Great Room, Dining Area, Wood Deck and Kitchen easily accommodates a busy family

■ Master Bedroom set in a quiet corner, offers a huge walk-in closet and double vanity Bath

■ Two additional Bedrooms, one an optional Den, share a full hall Bath

■ No materials list is available for this plan

MAIN FLOOR — 1,461 SQ. FT.
BASEMENT — 1,461 SQ. FT.
GARAGE — 458 SQ. FT.

TOTAL LIVING AREA:
1,461 SQ. FT.

Design by
Donald A. Gardner Architects, Inc.

Refer to **Pricing Schedule D** on the order form for pricing information

©1997 Donald A. Gardner Architects, Inc.

Pretty as a Picture

■ This plan features:

— Three bedrooms

— Two full baths

■ The wrapping front Porch is beautiful and functional

■ Inside the Great Room has a cathedral ceiling and a fireplace

■ The Dining Room has a tray ceiling and windows that overlook the front Porch

■ The Kitchen has a convenient layout with a work triangle

■ The Master Bedroom is isolated and features a galley Bath that leads into the walk-in closet

■ There is a bonus room over the Garage

MAIN FLOOR — 1,911 SQ. FT.
BONUS — 406 SQ. FT.
GARAGE — 551 SQ. FT.

TOTAL LIVING AREA:
1,911 SQ. FT.

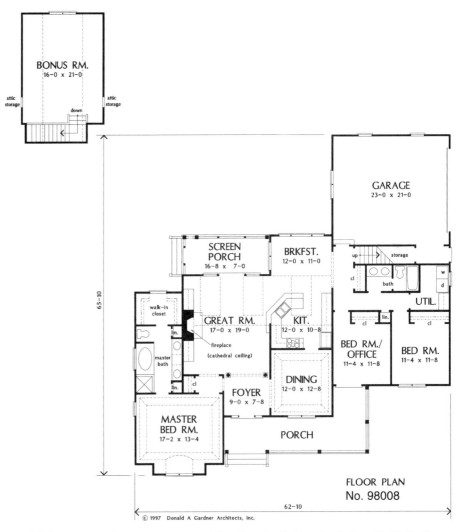

© 1997 Donald A Gardner Architects, Inc.

To order your Blueprints, call 1-800-235-5700

Design by
Frank Betz Associates, Inc.

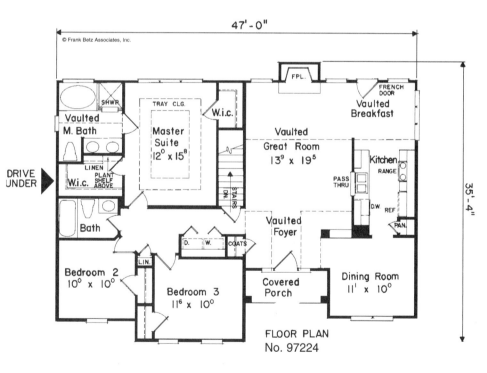

© Frank Betz Associates, Inc.

47' - 0"

35' - 4"

FPL.

FRENCH DOOR

Vaulted Breakfast

SHWR

TRAY CLG.

W.i.c.

Vaulted M. Bath

Master Suite 12⁰ x 15⁸

Vaulted Great Room 13⁹ x 19⁵

Kitchen RANGE

PASS THRU

LINEN PLANT SHELF ABOVE

D.W. REF

DRIVE UNDER

Wi.c.

STAIRS DN

PAN.

Bath

Vaulted Foyer

LIN.

D. W. COATS

Bedroom 2 10⁰ x 10⁰

Bedroom 3 11⁶ x 10⁰

Covered Porch

Dining Room 11' x 10⁰

FLOOR PLAN
No. 97224

Vaulted Ceilings Create Spacious Feelings

■ This plan features:

— Three bedrooms

— Two full baths

■ Open layout with vaulted ceilings in Foyer, Great Room and Breakfast Area

■ Kitchen with pass thru and Pantry, efficiently serves bright Breakfast Area, Great Room and formal Dining Room

■ Luxurious Master Suite offers a tray ceiling, two walk-in closets and a double vanity Bath with vaulted ceiling

■ No materials list is available for this plan

MAIN FLOOR — 1,363 SQ. FT.
BASEMENT — 715 SQ. FT.
GARAGE — 677 SQ. FT.

TOTAL LIVING AREA:
1,363 SQ. FT.

Design by
Frank Betz Associates, Inc.

Refer to **Pricing Schedule B** on the order form for pricing information

© Frank Betz Associates

Easy Living

■ This plan features:

— Three bedrooms

— Two full baths

■ Arched windows, keystones, and shutters highlight the exterior

■ The Kitchen has a space saving Pantry and plenty of counter space

■ Both secondary Bedrooms have spectacular front wall windows

■ The Master Suite is enormous and features a glass walled sitting Area

■ A walk in closet, a dual vanity and a whirlpool tub highlights the Master Bath

■ No materials list is available for this plan

MAIN FLOOR — 1,743 SQ. FT.
BASEMENT — 998 SQ. FT.
GARAGE — 763 SQ. FT.

TOTAL LIVING AREA:
1,743 SQ. FT.

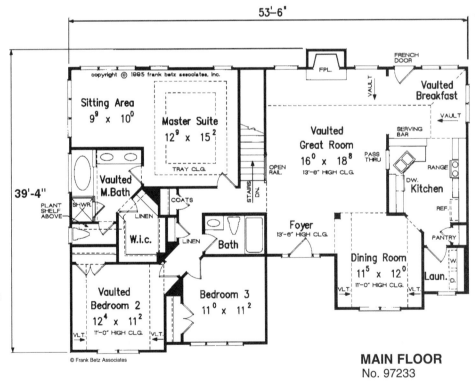

MAIN FLOOR
No. 97233

To order your Blueprints, call 1-800-235-5700

Design by
Donald A. Gardner Architects, Inc.

© 1996 Donald A. Gardner Architects, Inc.

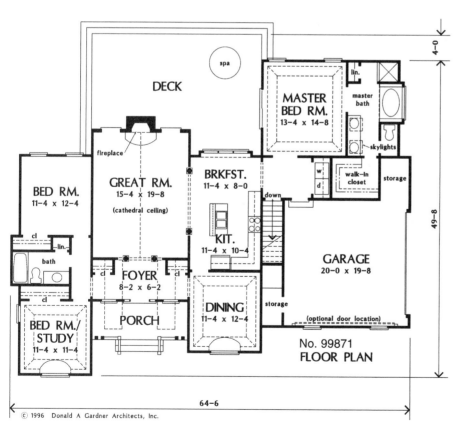

No. 99871
FLOOR PLAN

© 1996 Donald A Gardner Architects, Inc.

Charm and Personality

■ This plan features:

— Three bedrooms

— Two full baths

■ Interior columns dramatically open the Foyer and Kitchen to the spacious Great Room

■ The Great Room has a cathedral ceiling and a fireplace

■ Master Suite with a tray ceiling combines privacy with access to the rear Deck with spa

■ Tray ceilings with round-top picture windows bring a special elegance to the Dining Room and the front Swing Room

■ An optional basement or crawl space foundation — please specify when ordering

MAIN FLOOR — 1,655 SQ. FT.
GARAGE — 434 SQ. FT.

TOTAL LIVING AREA:
1,655 SQ. FT.

Design by
Frank Betz Associates, Inc.

Refer to **Pricing Schedule D** on
the order form for pricing information

Those Fabulous Details

■ This plan features:

— Four bedrooms

— Two full and one half baths

■ Hub of home is Vaulted Family
Room with French door

■ Vaulted Breakfast Area expands
efficient Kitchen

■ Spacious Master Suite boasts a
Sitting Area with fireplace

■ Plan offers optional expansion to
second floor Bonus Room and
Bath

■ An optional basement or crawl
space foundation — please specify when ordering

■ No materials list is available for
this plan

MAIN FLOOR — 2,311 SQ. FT.
BONUS — 425 SQ. FT.
BASEMENT — 2,311 SQ. FT.
GARAGE — 500 SQ. FT.

TOTAL LIVING AREA:
2,311 SQ. FT.

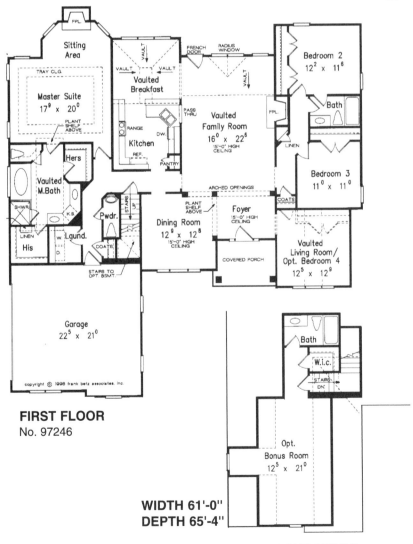

FIRST FLOOR
No. 97246

WIDTH 61'-0"
DEPTH 65'-4"

OPT. BONUS FLOOR PLAN

To order your Blueprints, call 1-800-235-5700

Design by
Frank Betz Associates, Inc.

© Frank Betz Associates, Inc.

51'-0"

50'-6"

SHWR.

RADIUS WINDOW

FRENCH DOOR

FPL.

PANTRY

Breakfast

SERVING BAR

Bedroom 3
10⁰ x 10⁰

Vaulted M.Bath

PLANT SHELF ABOVE

LINEN

W.i.c.

Vaulted Great Room
14⁰ x 17⁰
14'-7" HIGH CLG.

PASS THRU

RANGE

Kitchen

DW.

REF.

LINEN

Bath

TRAY CLG.

Master Suite
12⁰ x 15⁰

DECORATIVE COLUMNS

Foyer
14'-7" HIGH CLG.

PLANT SHELF ABOVE

Dining Room
11⁰ x 11⁵
14'-7" HIGH CLG.

Laund.

W.

D.

Bedroom 2
10² x 10¹⁰

Vaulted Sitting Room

VAULT   VAULT

Covered Porch

COATS

Storage

Garage
19⁵ x 19⁹

No. 98441
FLOOR PLAN

REF.

COATS

Laund.

W.
D.

Bedroom 2
10² x 12⁰

STAIRS DN.

GARAGE LOCATION W/ BASEMENT

OPT. BASEMENT STAIR LOCATION

High Ceilings and Arched Windows

- This plan features:
- — Three bedrooms
- — Two full baths
- Kitchen with a serving bar for the Breakfast Room
- Great Room topped by a vaulted ceiling accented by a fireplace
- Tray ceiling in the Master Suite and a vaulted ceiling over the Sitting Room and the Master Bath
- No materials list is available for this plan
- An optional basement or crawl space foundation — please specify when ordering

MAIN FLOOR — 1,502 SQ. FT.
GARAGE — 448 SQ. FT.
BASEMENT — 1,555 SQ. FT.

TOTAL LIVING AREA:
1,502 SQ. FT.

Design by
Frank Betz Associates, Inc.

Refer to **Pricing Schedule B** on
the order form for pricing information

Elegant Ceiling Treatments

■ This plan features:

— Three Bedrooms

— Two full baths

■ A cozy wrapping front Porch sheltering entrance

■ Dining Room defined by columns at the entrances

■ Kitchen highlighted by a peninsula counter/serving bar

■ Breakfast Room flowing from the Kitchen

■ An optional basement or crawl space foundation — please specify when ordering

■ No materials list is available for this plan

MAIN FLOOR — 1,692 SQ. FT.
BONUS ROOM — 358 SQ. FT.
BASEMENT — 1,705 SQ. FT.
GARAGE — 472 SQ. FT.

TOTAL LIVING AREA:
1,692 SQ. FT.

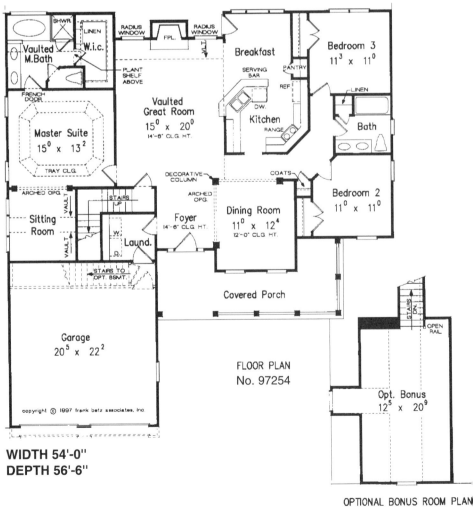

WIDTH 54'-0"
DEPTH 56'-6"

FLOOR PLAN
No. 97254

OPTIONAL BONUS ROOM PLAN

To order your Blueprints, call 1-800-235-5700

Design by
Sater Design Group

PLAN NO. 94242

A Custom Look

■ This plan features:

— Three bedrooms

— Two full, one half, and one three quarter baths

■ Exterior highlighted by triple arched glass in entry Porch

■ Triple arches lead into Formal Living and Dining rooms, Verandah and beyond

■ Kitchen, Nook, and Leisure Room easily flow together

■ Owners' wing has a Master Suite with glass alcove to rear yard, a lavish Bath and a Study

■ Two additional Bedrooms with corner windows and over-sized closets access a full Bath

■ No materials list is available for this plan

MAIN FLOOR — 2,978 SQ. FT.
GARAGE — 702 SQ. FT.

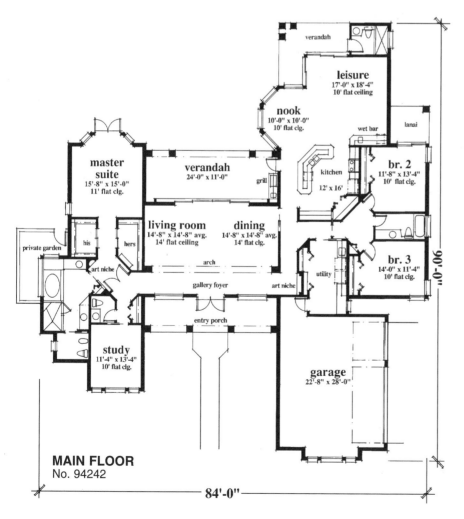

MAIN FLOOR
No. 94242

84'-0"

TOTAL LIVING AREA:
2,978 SQ. FT.

Design by
Rick Garner

Refer to **Pricing Schedule D** on the order form for pricing information

European Styling with a Georgian Flair

■ This plan features:

— Four bedrooms

— Two full baths

■ Arched windows, quoins and shutters on the exterior, a columned covered front and a rear Porch

■ Formal Foyer gives access to the Dining Room to the left and spacious Den straight ahead

■ Kitchen flows into the informal Eating Area

■ An optional crawl space or slab foundation — please specify when ordering

MAIN FLOOR — 1,873 SQ. FT.
GARAGE — 613 SQ. FT.
BONUS — 145 SQ. FT.

TOTAL LIVING AREA:
1,873 SQ. FT.

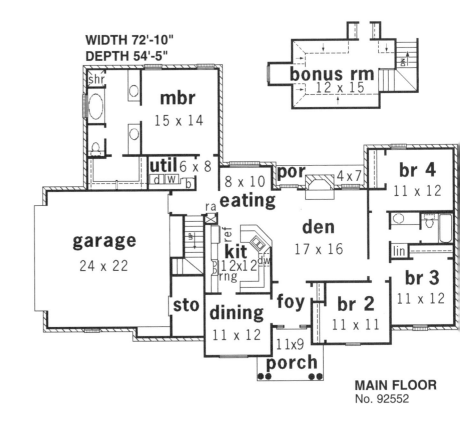

WIDTH 72'-10"
DEPTH 54'-5"

bonus rm
12 x 15

mbr
15 x 14

util 6 x 8

por 4 x 7

br 4
11 x 12

eating

garage
24 x 22

kit
12x12

den
17 x 16

br 3
11 x 12

sto

dining
11 x 12

foy

br 2
11 x 11

porch
11x9

MAIN FLOOR
No. 92552

To order your Blueprints, call 1-800-235-5700

Design by
Frank Betz Associates, Inc.

LOWER FLOOR

Vaulted
Family Room
15⁰ x 16⁹
14'-0" HIGH CLG.

REF.
Kitchen
PANTRY
W. D.

Garage
18¹¹ x 19⁴

STAIRS DN.

WIDTH 40'-0"
DEPTH 49'-2"

RAD. WDW.

W.i.c.
LINEN
SHWR.
Vaulted
M.Bath

PLANT SHELF ABOVE

FRENCH DOOR
FPL.
VAULT

Breakfast

SERVING BAR

Kitchen
RANGE
PASS THRU
DW.
REF.
PANTRY
W. D.

Vaulted
Family Room
15⁰ x 16⁹
14'-0" HIGH CLG.

Master Suite
15⁴ x 11¹⁰

VAULT

Bath

Bedroom 3
10⁰ x 10⁰

PLANT SHELF ABOVE

Foyer
11'-0" HIGH CLG.

COATS
LIN.

Garage
18¹¹ x 19⁴

Bedroom 2
10⁰ x 11⁰

Covered Porch

copyright © 1996 frank betz associates, inc.

FIRST FLOOR
No. 97259

Charming Three-Bedroom

■ This plan features:

— Three bedrooms

— Two full baths

■ Covered Porch leads into Foyer with plant shelves and Vaulted Family Room beyond

■ Efficient Kitchen with Pantry, Laundry and pass thru opens to bright Breakfast Area

■ Private Master Suite offers a vaulted ceiling, walk-in closet and vaulted Master Bath

■ An optional basement or crawl space foundation — please specify when ordering

■ No materials list is available for this plan

MAIN FLOOR — 1,222 SQ. FT.
BASEMENT — 1,218 SQ. FT.
GARAGE — 410 SQ. FT.

TOTAL LIVING AREA:
1,222 SQ. FT.

Design by
Studer Residential Design, Inc.

Definitely Detailed

■ This plan features:

— Three bedrooms

— Two full baths

■ An artistically detailed brick exterior adds to the appeal of this home

■ The Great Room has a wall of windows and a warming fireplace

■ The Kitchen is arranged in a U-shape and features a center island plus a walk-in Pantry

■ The Bedrooms are all on one side of the home for privacy

■ An optional plan for the basement includes a Recreation Room, an Exercise Room, and a Bath

■ No materials list is available for this plan

MAIN FLOOR — 1,963 SQ. FT.

LOWER LEVEL — 1,963 SQ. FT.

TOTAL LIVING AREA:
1,963 SQ. FT.

WIDTH 58'-10''
DEPTH 48'-8''

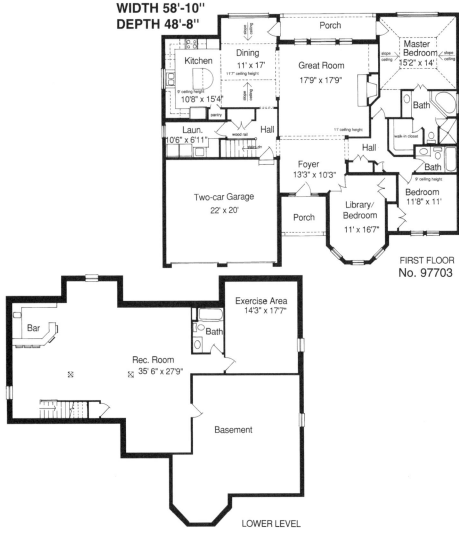

FIRST FLOOR
No. 97703

LOWER LEVEL

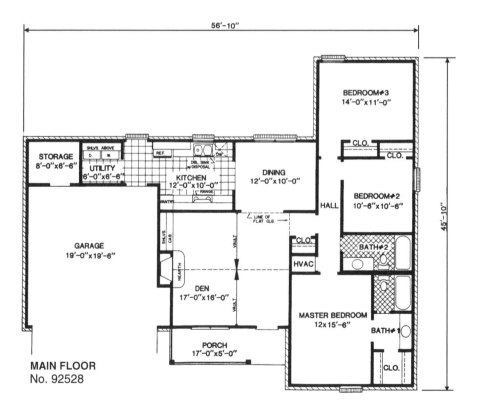

56'-10"

BEDROOM#3
14'-0"x11'-0"

STORAGE
8'-0"x6'-6"

SHLVS. ABOVE

REF.

D.   W.

UTILITY
6'-0"x6'-6"

DBL SINK
w/ DISPOSAL

DINING
12'-0"x10'-0"

CLO.

CLO.

KITCHEN
12'-0"x10'-0"

RANGE

PANTRY

BEDROOM#2
10'-6"x10'-6"

HALL

45'-10"

SHLVS
CAB

LINE OF
FLAT CLG.

CLO.

BATH#2

GARAGE
19'-0"x19'-6"

HEARTH

VAULT

HVAC

DEN
17'-0"x16'-0"

VAULT

MASTER BEDROOM
12x15'-6"

BATH#1

PORCH
17'-0"x5'-0"

CLO.

MAIN FLOOR
No. 92528

Warm and Inviting

■ This plan features:

— Three bedrooms

— Two full baths

■ A Den with a cozy fireplace and vaulted ceiling

■ A well-equipped Kitchen that contains a double sink and built-in Pantry

■ A spacious Master Bedroom with a private Master Bath and walk-in closet

■ Additional Bedrooms sharing full hall Bath

■ An optional crawl space or slab foundation — please specify when ordering

MAIN FLOOR — 1,363 SQ. FT.
GARAGE — 434 SQ. FT.

TOTAL LIVING AREA:
1,363 SQ. FT.

Design by
Frank Betz Associates, Inc.

Refer to **Pricing Schedule A** on the order form for pricing information

Striking Style

■ This plan features:

— Three bedrooms

— Two full baths

■ The Foyer has a 12-foot ceiling

■ The Dining Room has a front window wall and arched openings

■ The secondary Bedrooms are in their own wing and share a Bath

■ The Breakfast Bay is open to the galley Kitchen

■ The Master Suite features a tray ceiling, a walk-in closet and a private Bath

■ An optional basement or crawl space foundation — please specify when ordering

MAIN FLOOR — 1,432 SQ. FT.
BASEMENT — 1,454 SQ. FT.
GARAGE — 440 SQ. FT.

TOTAL LIVING AREA:
1,432 SQ. FT.

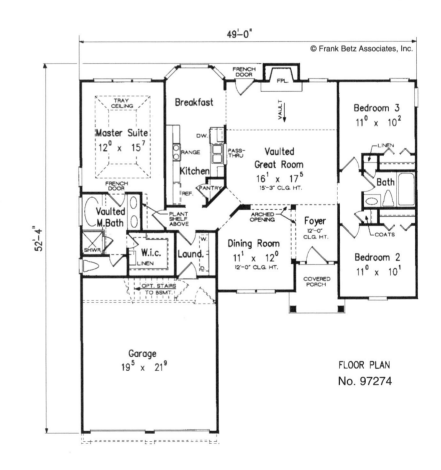

© Frank Betz Associates, Inc.

FLOOR PLAN
No. 97274

To order your Blueprints, call 1-800-235-5700

Design by
Alan Mascord Design Associates, Inc.

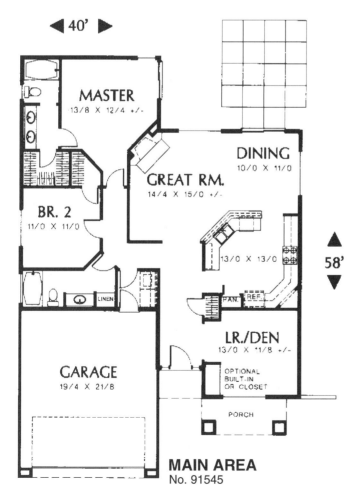

◄ **40'** ►

MASTER
13/8 X 12/4 +/-

DINING
10/0 X 11/0

GREAT RM.
14/4 X 15/0 +/-

BR. 2
11/0 X 11/0

13/0 X 13/0

▲
58'
▼

LINEN

PAN. REF.

LR./DEN
13/0 X 11/8 +/-

GARAGE
19/4 X 21/8

OPTIONAL
BUILT-IN
OR CLOSET

PORCH

MAIN AREA
No. 91545

Great Starter or Empty Nester

■ This plan features:

— Two bedrooms

— Two full baths

■ Formal Living Room or a cozy Den; the front room to the right of the Entry Hall adapts to your lifestyle

■ An efficient Kitchen with ample counter and storage space

■ A formal Dining Room situated next to the Kitchen and flowing from the Great Room

■ A corner fireplace highlighting the Great Room

■ A walk-in closet and a private double vanity Bath in the Master Suite

■ An additional Bedroom that easily accesses the full Bath in the hall

MAIN AREA — 1,420 SQ. FT.

TOTAL LIVING AREA:
1,420 SQ. FT.

PLAN NO. 98435

Design by
Frank Betz Associates, Inc.

Refer to **Pricing Schedule C** on the order form for pricing information

Outstanding Four Bedroom

■ This plan features:

— Four bedrooms

— Two full baths

■ Radius window highlights exterior and formal Dining Room

■ Vaulted ceiling enhances the Great Room accented by a fireplace framed by windows

■ Arched opening to the Kitchen from the Great Room

■ Tray ceiling and a five-piece compartmental Bath provides luxury in the Master Suite

■ An optional basement or crawl space foundation — please specify when ordering

MAIN FLOOR — 1,945 SQ. FT.

TOTAL LIVING AREA:
1,945 SQ. FT.

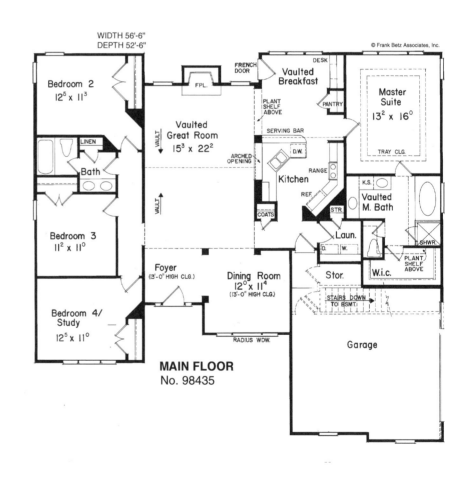

MAIN FLOOR
No. 98435

152 To order your Blueprints, call 1-800-235-5700

Design by
Filmore Design Group

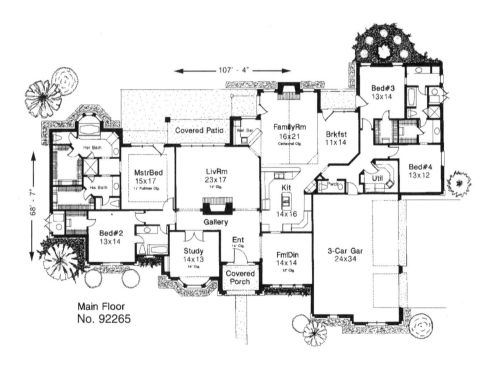

Main Floor
No. 92265

Luxurious Masterpiece

■ This plan features:

— Four bedrooms

— Three full and one half baths

■ Expansive formal Living Room with a fourteen foot ceiling and a raised hearth fireplace

■ Informal Family Room offers another fireplace, wetbar, cathedral ceiling and access to the covered Patio

■ Hub Kitchen with a cooktop island, peninsula counter/snack-bar, and a bright Breakfast Area

■ French doors lead into a quiet Study offering many uses

■ Private Master Bedroom enhanced by pullman ceiling and lavish his-n-her Baths

■ No materials list is available for this plan

MAIN FLOOR — 3,818 SQ. FT.
GARAGE — 816 SQ. FT.

TOTAL LIVING AREA:
3,818 SQ. FT.

Design by
Perfect Plan 🔨

Refer to **Pricing Schedule A** on
the order form for pricing information

Inviting Porch Adorns Affordable Home

◼ This plan features:

— Three bedrooms

— Two full baths

◼ A large and spacious Living Room that adjoins the Dining Room for ease in entertaining

◼ A private bedroom wing offering a quiet atmosphere

◼ A Master Bedroom with his-n-her closets and a private Bath

◼ An efficient Kitchen with a walk-in Pantry

MAIN AREA — 1,243 SQ. FT.
BASEMENT — 1,103 SQ. FT.
GARAGE — 490 SQ. FT.

TOTAL LIVING AREA:
1,243 SQ. FT.

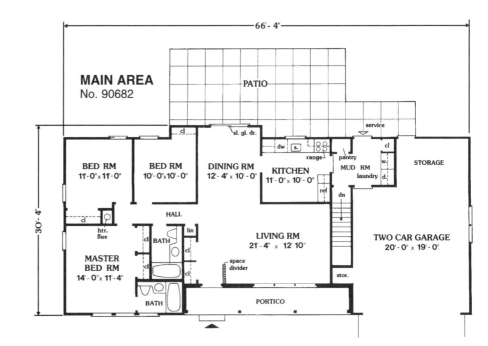

Design by
Donald A. Gardner Architects, Inc.

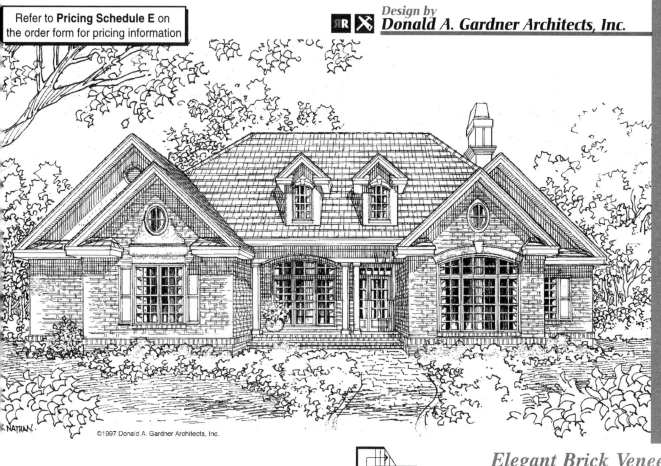

©1997 Donald A. Gardner Architects, Inc.

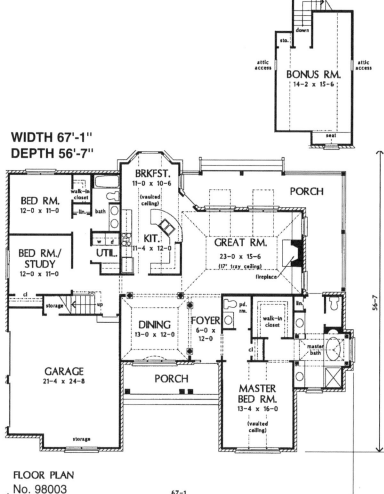

WIDTH 67'-1"
DEPTH 56'-7"

FLOOR PLAN
No. 98003
© 1997 Donald A Gardner Architects, Inc.

Elegant Brick Veneer

■ This plan features:

— Three bedrooms

— Two full and one half baths

■ Arched and oval windows enhance the elegance of this home

■ Open, formal Dining Room defined by columns and topped with tray ceiling

■ Expansive Great Room offers a tray ceiling, and a cozy fireplace

■ Curved serving counter, vaulted ceiling and bright Breakfast Area highlight Kitchen

■ Separate Master Bedroom accented by a vaulted ceiling, roomy walk-in closet and lavish Bath

MAIN FLOOR — 2,198 SQ. FT.
BONUS ROOM — 325 SQ. FT.
GARAGE — 588 SQ. FT.

TOTAL LIVING AREA:
2,198 SQ. FT.

Design by
Donald A. Gardner Architects, Inc.

© 1996 Donald A Gardner Architects, Inc.

Great As A Mountain Retreat

■ This plan features:

— Three bedrooms

— Two full baths

■ Board and batten siding, stone, and stucco combine to give this popular plan a casual feel

■ User friendly Kitchen with huge Pantry for ample Storage and island counter

■ Casual family meals in sunny Breakfast bay; formal gatherings in the columned Dining Area

■ Master Suite is topped by a deep tray ceiling, has a large walk-in closet, an extravagant private Bath and direct access to back Porch

MAIN FLOOR — 1,912 SQ. FT.
GARAGE — 580 SQ. FT.
BONUS — 398 SQ. FT.

TOTAL LIVING AREA:
1,912 SQ. FT.

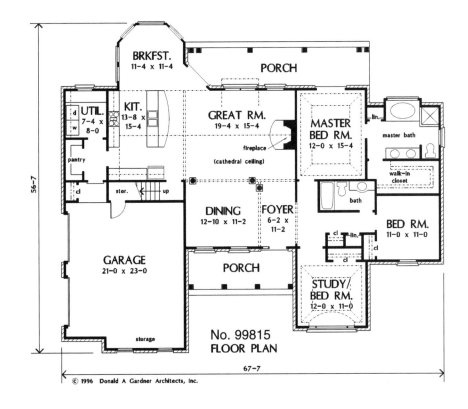

No. 99815
FLOOR PLAN

© 1996 Donald A Gardner Architects, Inc.

To order your Blueprints, call 1-800-235-5700

Design by
Donald A. Gardner Architects, Inc.

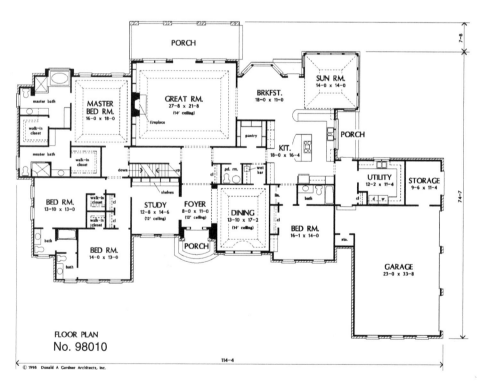

FLOOR PLAN
No. 98010

© 1998 Donald A Gardner Architects, Inc.

114-4

Always in Style

■ This plan features:
— Four bedrooms
— Four full and two half baths

■ Brick, gables and a traditional hip roof always seem to be in style

■ Inside find dramatic spaces that include the Dining Room and the Great Room both with 14′ ceilings

■ The Study features a wall of built in bookshelves

■ The Kitchen has a center island with a cooktop

■ The Master Sedroom is opulent with dual Baths and closets

■ Storage space abounds with a walk-in Pantry, numerous closets

■ This plan is not to be built in Greenville County, SC

MAIN FLOOR — 4,523 SQ. FT.
GARAGE — 1,029 SQ. FT.

TOTAL LIVING AREA:
4,523 SQ. FT.

©1997 Donald A. Gardner Architects, Inc.

Compact Country Home

■ This plan features:

— Three bedrooms

— Two full baths

■ Economical squared off design stylish with gables and arches

■ Welcoming front Porch leads into Foyer, Great Room and Deck beyond

■ Comfortable gathering area created by open layout of Great Room, Dining Area and Kitchen

■ Master Suite provides privacy, an elegant tray ceiling, walk-in closet and lavish Bath

■ Two more Bedrooms, with ample closets

MAIN FLOOR — 1,517 SQ. FT.
BONUS ROOM — 287 SQ. FT.
GARAGE — 447 SQ. FT.

TOTAL LIVING AREA:
1,517 SQ. FT.

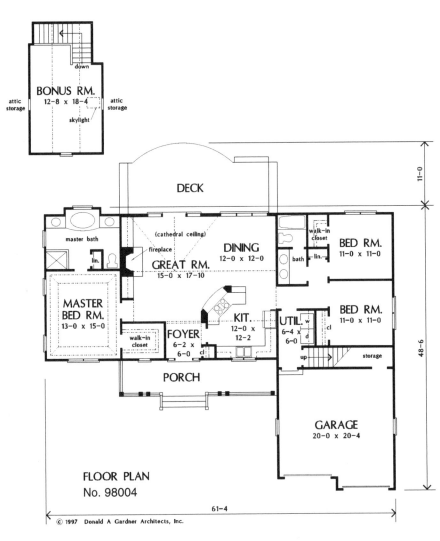

BONUS RM. 12-8 x 18-4

FLOOR PLAN
No. 98004

© 1997 Donald A Gardner Architects, Inc.

To order your Blueprints, call 1-800-235-5700

Design by
Atlanta Plan Source

PLAN NO. 92400

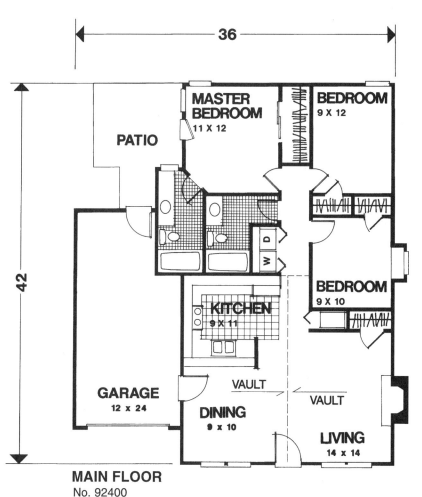

36

42

PATIO

MASTER BEDROOM
11 X 12

BEDROOM
9 X 12

KITCHEN
9 X 11

BEDROOM
9 X 10

W D

GARAGE
12 X 24

VAULT

VAULT

DINING
9 X 10

LIVING
14 X 14

MAIN FLOOR
No. 92400

Quaint Starter Home

■ This plan features:

— Three bedrooms

— Two full baths

■ A vaulted ceiling giving an airy feeling to the Dining and Living Rooms

■ A streamlined Kitchen with a comfortable work area, a double sink and ample cabinet space

■ A cozy fireplace in the Living Room

■ A Master Suite with a large closet, French doors leading to the Patio and a private Bath

■ Two additional Bedrooms sharing a full Bath

■ No materials list is available for this plan

MAIN AREA — 1,050 SQ. FT.
GARAGE — 261 SQ. FT.

TOTAL LIVING AREA:
1,050 SQ. FT.

Design by
Donald A. Gardner Architects, Inc.

Refer to **Pricing Schedule C** on
the order form for pricing information

© 1998 Donald A. Gardner, Inc.

Efficient Design

■ This plan features:

— Three bedrooms

— Two full baths

■ Foyer introduces a wonderful Great Room with cathedral ceiling, inviting fireplace with built-in cabinets, and rear Porch access

■ Comfortable family gatherings created by open layout of Great Room, Dining Area and Kitchen

■ Compact Kitchen easy to work in with Pantry and angled breakfast bar

■ Secluded Master Bedroom features a lavish Bath

■ Expansion and attic storage provided by bonus room over Garage

MAIN FLOOR — 1,476 SQ. FT.
BONUS ROOM — 340 SQ. FT.
GARAGE & STORAGE — 567 SQ. FT.

TOTAL LIVING AREA:
1,476 SQ. FT.

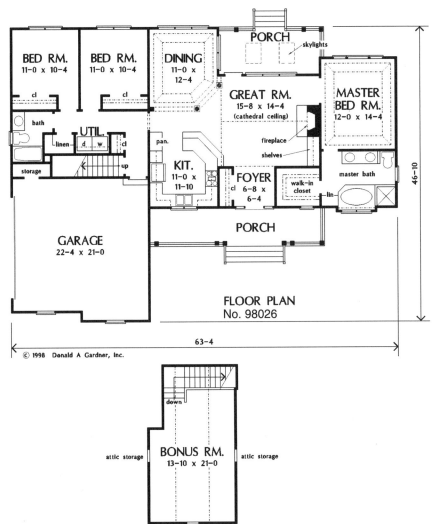

© 1998 Donald A Gardner, Inc.

To order your Blueprints, call 1-800-235-5700

Design by
Fillmore Design Group

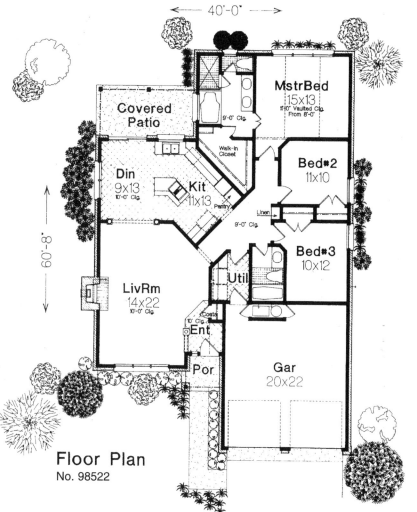

40'-0"

60'-8"

Covered Patio

Din
9x13
10'-0" Clg.

Kit
11x13
Pantry

MstrBed
15x13
11'-0" Vaulted Clg.
From 8'-0"

9'-0" Clg.

Walk-In Closet

Bed#2
11x10

Linen

9'-0" Clg.

Bed#3
10x12

Util

LivRm
14x22
10'-0" Clg.

Coats
10" Clg.

Ent

Por

Gar
20x22

Floor Plan
No. 98522

Brick Abounds

■ This plan features:

— Three bedrooms

— Two full baths

■ The covered front Porch opens into the entry that has a 10-foot ceiling and a coat closet

■ The Living Room is distinguished by a fireplace

■ The Dining Room features a 10-foot ceiling and access to the Patio

■ The Kitchen is angled and has a Pantry and a cooktop island

■ The Master Bedroom is located in the rear for privacy and boasts a triangular walk-in closet

■ No materials list is available for this plan

MAIN FLOOR — 1,528 SQ. FT.
GARAGE — 440 SQ. FT.

TOTAL LIVING AREA:
1,528 SQ. FT.

Design by
Donald A. Gardner Architects, Inc.

Refer to **Pricing Schedule C** on the order form for pricing information

© 1996 Donald A. Gardner Architects, I

Compact Plan

◼ This plan features:

— Three bedrooms

— Two full baths

◼ A Great Room topped by a cathedral ceiling adjoins the Dining Room and Kitchen to create a spacious living area

◼ A bay window enlarging the Dining Room and a palladian window allowing ample light into the Great Room

◼ An efficient U-shaped Kitchen leading directly to the garage, convenient for unloading groceries

◼ A Master Suite highlighted by ample closet space and a private skylit bath enhanced by a dual vanity and a separate tub and shower

MAIN FLOOR — 1,372 SQ. FT.
GARAGE & STORAGE — 537 SQ. FT.

TOTAL LIVING AREA:
1,372 SQ. FT.

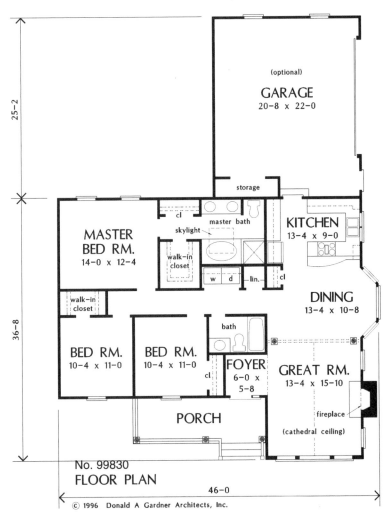

No. 99830
FLOOR PLAN

© 1996 Donald A Gardner Architects, Inc.

To order your Blueprints, call 1-800-235-5700

Design by
Donald A. Gardner Architects, Inc.

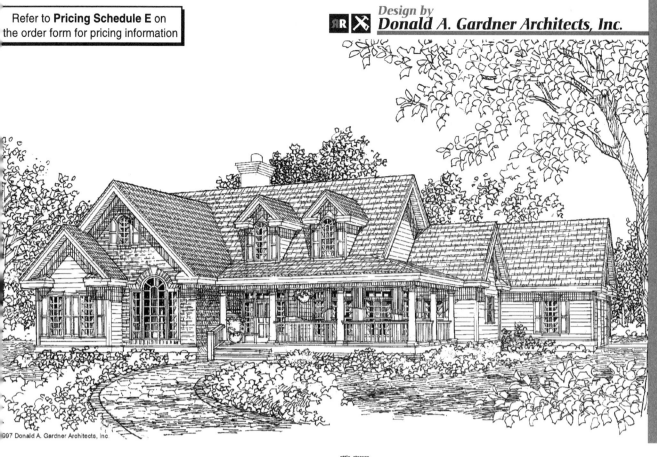

997 Donald A. Gardner Architects, inc.

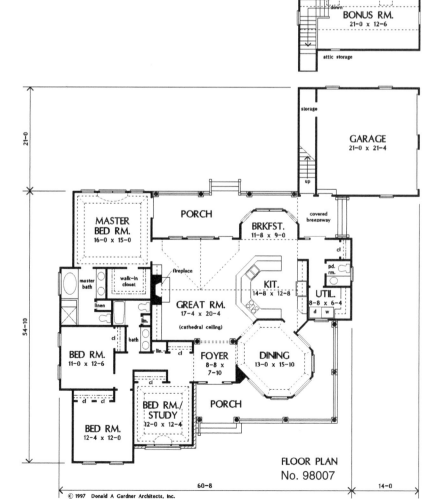

attic storage

skylights

down

BONUS RM.
21-0 x 12-6

attic storage

storage

GARAGE
21-0 x 21-4

up

21-0

54-10

MASTER BED RM.
16-0 x 15-0

master bath

walk-in closet

linen

PORCH

fireplace

GREAT RM.
17-4 x 20-4
(cathedral ceiling)

BRKFST.
11-8 x 9-0

covered breezeway

cl

KIT.
14-8 x 12-8

pd. rm.

UTIL.
8-8 x 6-4

d   w

lin.

bath

lin.

cl

cl

BED RM.
11-0 x 12-6

FOYER
8-8 x 7-10

DINING
13-0 x 15-10

BED RM./ STUDY
12-0 x 12-4

PORCH

BED RM.
12-4 x 12-0

cl   cl

cl

FLOOR PLAN
No. 98007

© 1997 Donald A Gardner Architects, Inc.

60-8   14-0

An Exciting Mixture

■ This plan features:

— Four bedrooms

— Two full and one half baths

■ The exterior is an exciting mixture of brick, and siding

■ The Dining Room has five windows that view the Porch

■ A fireplace with built-ins set between it adds character to the Great Room

■ The U-shaped Kitchen is the ultimate for cooking convenience

■ The walk in closet in the Master Bedroom is a clothes hounds delight

■ There is a bonus room over the Garage awaiting your finishing touches

MAIN FLOOR — 2,273 SQ. FT.
BONUS — 342 SQ. FT.
GARAGE — 528 SQ. FT.

TOTAL LIVING AREA:
2,273 SQ. FT.

Design by
Filmore Design Group

Refer to **Pricing Schedule E** on the order form for pricing information

One Floor Convenience

- ■ This plan features:

— Four bedrooms

— Three full baths

- ■ A distinguished brick exterior adds curb appeal

- ■ Formal Entry/Gallery opens to large Living Room with hearth fireplace set between windows overlooking Patio and rear yard

- ■ Efficient Kitchen with angled counters and serving bar easily serves Breakfast Room, Patio and formal Dining Room

- ■ Corner Master Bedroom enhanced by a vaulted ceiling and pampering Bath with a large walk-in closet

- ■ No materials list is available for this plan

MAIN FLOOR —2,675 SQ. FT.
GARAGE — 638 SQ. FT.

TOTAL LIVING AREA:
2,675 SQ. FT.

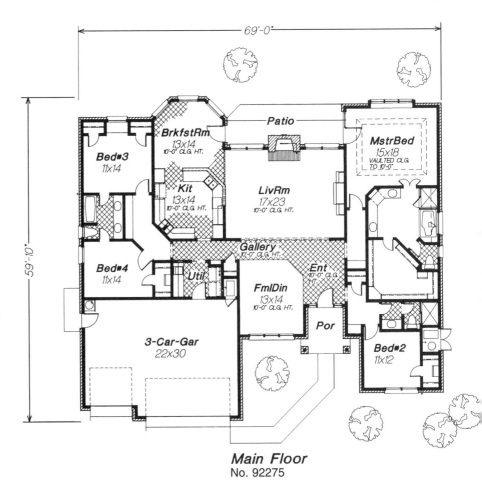

Main Floor
No. 92275

To order your Blueprints, call 1-800-235-5700

Refer to **Pricing Schedule B** on the order form for pricing information

Design by
Corley Plan Service

PLAN NO. 90409

Rocking Chair Living

■ This plan features:

— Three bedrooms

— Two full baths

■ A massive fireplace separating Living and Dining Rooms

■ An isolated Master Suite with a walk-in closet and a helpful compartmentalized Bath

■ A galley-type Kitchen between the Breakfast Room and Dining Room

■ An optional basement, slab or crawl space foundation — please specify when ordering

MAIN AREA — 1,670 SQ. FT.
BASEMENT — 1,670 SQ. FT.
GARAGE — 427 SQ. FT.

TOTAL LIVING AREA:
1,670 SQ. FT.

MAIN AREA
No. 90409

STORAGE
8'-4"x7'-6"

UTILITY
8'-2"x7'-6"

W. D.

BREAKFAST
10'-0"x9'-6"

KITCHEN
9'-8"x8'-8"

PAN.

DRESS.

BATH

CL.

GARAGE
21'-2"x20'-2"

M. BEDROOM
15'-8"x13'-10"

PATIO
14'-0"x10'-0"

DINING RM.
19'-8"x11'-2"

BEDROOM
12'-10"x12'-0"

CL.

CL.

LIN.

BATH

CATHEDRAL CLG.

GREAT RM.
19'-8"x18'-2"

BEDROOM
13'-0"x11'-0"

CL.

CL.

PORCH
21'-0"x6'-0"

30'-0"

73'-8"

Design by
The Garlinghouse Company

Refer to **Pricing Schedule A** on the order form for pricing information

Delightful, Compact Home

◼ This plan features:

— Three bedrooms

— Two full baths

◼ A fireplaced Living Room further enhanced by a wonderful picture window

◼ A counter island featuring double sinks separating the Kitchen and Dining areas

◼ A Master Bedroom that includes a private Master Bath and double closets

◼ Two additional Bedrooms with ample closet space that share a full Bath

MAIN AREA — 1,146 SQ. FT.

TOTAL LIVING AREA:
1,146 SQ. FT.

slab/crawlspace option

Floor Plan
No. 34003

To order your Blueprints, call 1-800-235-5700

Design by
Frank Betz Associates, Inc.

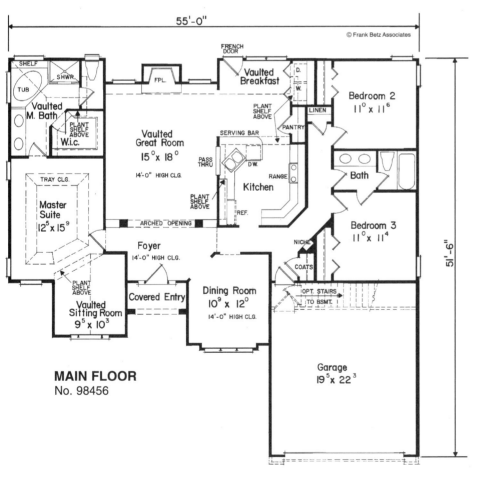

55'-0"

© Frank Betz Associates

FRENCH DOOR

Vaulted Breakfast

FPL.

D.

W.

Bedroom 2
11⁰ x 11⁶

SHELF

SHWR.

TUB

Vaulted M. Bath

PLANT SHELF ABOVE

W.I.C.

PLANT SHELF ABOVE

PANTRY

LINEN

SERVING BAR

Vaulted Great Room
15⁰ x 18⁰
14'-0" HIGH CLG.

PASS THRU

D.W.

Kitchen

RANGE

Bath

TRAY CLG.

Master Suite
12⁵ x 15⁹

PLANT SHELF ABOVE

REF.

ARCHED OPENING

Foyer
14'-0" HIGH CLG.

Bedroom 3
11⁰ x 11⁴

NICHE

COATS

PLANT SHELF ABOVE

Vaulted Sitting Room
9⁵ x 10³

Covered Entry

Dining Room
10⁹ x 12⁰
14'-0" HIGH CLG.

OPT. STAIRS TO BSMT.

51'-6"

MAIN FLOOR
No. 98456

Garage
19⁵ x 22³

High Ceilings Add Volume

■ This plan features:

— Three bedrooms

— Two full baths

■ A covered entry gives way to a 14-foot high ceiling in the Foyer

■ An arched opening greets you in the Great Room

■ The Dining Room is brightened by triple windows with transoms

■ The Kitchen is a gourmet's delight

■ The Master Suite is sweet with a tray ceiling, vaulted Sitting Area and private Bath

■ An optional basement, slab or crawl space foundation — please specify when ordering

MAIN FLOOR — 1,715 SQ. FT.
BASEMENT — 1,715 SQ. FT.
GARAGE — 450 SQ. FT.

TOTAL LIVING AREA:
1,715 SQ. FT.

Design by
The Garlinghouse Company

Refer to **Pricing Schedule B** on the order form for pricing information

Arches are Appealing

■ This plan features:

— Three bedrooms

— Two full baths

■ Welcoming front Porch enhanced by graceful columns and curved windows

■ Expansive Great Room accented by a corner fireplace and outdoor access

■ Open and convenient Kitchen with a work island, angled, peninsula counter/eating bar, and nearby Laundry and Garage entry

■ Secluded Master Bedroom with a large walk-in closet and luxurious Bath with a dressing table

■ No materials list is available for this plan

MAIN FLOOR — 1,642 SQ. FT.
BASEMENT — 1,642 SQ. FT.
GARAGE — 420 SQ. FT.

TOTAL LIVING AREA:
1,642 SQ. FT.

Optional Basement Stairs

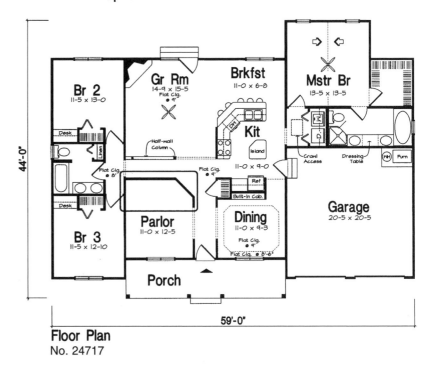

Floor Plan
No. 24717

To order your Blueprints, call 1-800-235-5700

Design by
Frank Betz Associates, Inc.

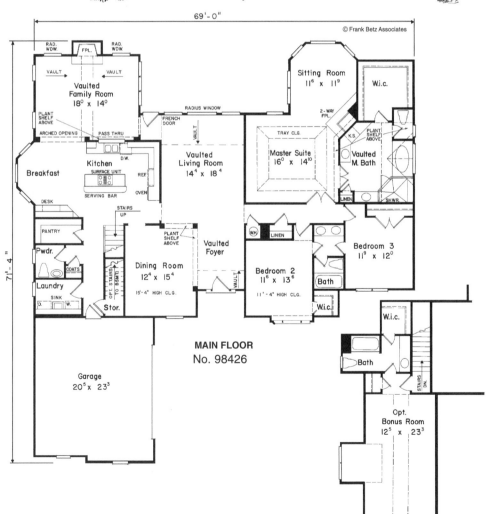

MAIN FLOOR
No. 98426

69'-0"

71'-4"

© Frank Betz Associates

- Vaulted Family Room 18⁰ x 14⁰
- Breakfast
- Kitchen
- Sitting Room 11⁶ x 11⁹
- W.i.c.
- Vaulted Living Room 14⁴ x 18⁴
- Master Suite 16⁰ x 14¹⁰
- Vaulted M. Bath
- Bedroom 3 11⁹ x 12⁰
- Vaulted Foyer
- Dining Room 12⁴ x 15⁴
- Bedroom 2 11⁶ x 13⁶
- Pantry
- Pwdr.
- Laundry
- Stor.
- Garage 20⁵ x 23³
- Bath
- W.i.c.
- Opt. Bonus Room 12⁵ x 23³

OPT. BONUS ROOM

Delightful Detailing

■ This plan features:

— Three bedrooms

— Two full and one half baths

■ The vaulted ceiling extends from the Foyer into the Living Room

■ Dining Room is delineated by columns with a plant shelf above

■ Family Room has a vaulted ceiling, and a fireplace

■ The Kitchen has an island serving bar

■ The Master Suite is highlighted by a Sitting Room, a walk-in closet and a private Bath with a vaulted ceiling

■ An optional basement or a crawl space foundation — please specify when ordering

MAIN FLOOR — 2,622 SQ. FT.
BONUS ROOM — 478 SQ. FT.
BASEMENT — 2,622 SQ. FT.
GARAGE — 506 SQ. FT.

TOTAL LIVING AREA:
2,622 SQ. FT.

To order your Blueprints, call 1-800-235-5700

©1998 Donald A. Gardner Architects, Inc.

Country French Home

■ This plan features:

— Three bedrooms

— Two full and one half baths

■ Unique Court leads to Porch and into Foyer opeing to curved Dining Area and Great Room defined by columns

■ An inviting fireplace nestled between shelves and a wall of glass with Deck access enhance the Great Room

■ Country Kitchen with cooktop island, curved Breakfast Area and easy access to Porch and Deck

■ Comfortable Master Bedroom offers tray ceiling, tow walk-in closets and Master Bath with two vanities and a garden window tub

MAIN FLOOR — 2,250 SQ. FT.
GARAGE — 565 SQ. FT.

TOTAL LIVING AREA:
2,250 SQ. FT.

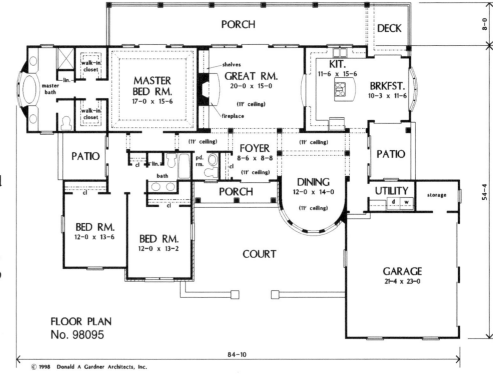

FLOOR PLAN
No. 98095

© 1998 Donald A Gardner Architects, Inc.

Refer to **Pricing Schedule A** on the order form for pricing information

Design by
Frank Betz Associates, Inc.

PLAN NO. 98443

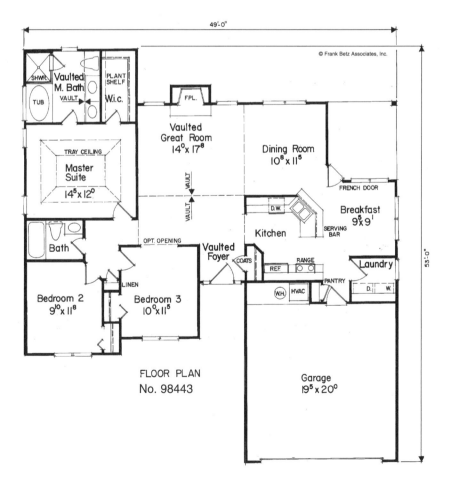

© Frank Betz Associates, Inc.

49'-0"

SHWR. | Vaulted M. Bath | PLANT SHELF
TUB | VAULT | Wi.c.

TRAY CEILING
Master Suite
14⁵ x 12⁰

FPL.

Vaulted Great Room
14⁰ x 17⁸

Dining Room
10⁸ x 11⁵

VAULT VAULT

VAULT VAULT

Bath

D.W.

Breakfast
9⁵ x 9¹

SERVING BAR

OPT. OPENING

Vaulted Foyer

Kitchen

COATS

LINEN

REF. RANGE

Bedroom 2
9¹⁰ x 11⁸

Bedroom 3
10⁰ x 11⁵

W.H. HVAC

PANTRY

Laundry

D. W.

53'-0"

FLOOR PLAN
No. 98443

Garage
19⁵ x 20⁰

One Floor Convenience

■ This plan features:

— Three bedrooms

— Two full baths

■ Vaulted Foyer and vaulted Great Room create a larger feeling to the home

■ Dining Room opens into the Great Room

■ Kitchen including a serving bar and easy flow into the Breakfast Room

■ Master Suite topped by a decorative tray ceiling and a vaulted ceiling in the Master Bath

■ An optional crawl space or slab foundation — please specify when ordering

■ No materials list is available for this plan

MAIN FLOOR — 1,359 SQ. FT.
GARAGE — 439 SQ. FT.

TOTAL LIVING AREA:
1,359 SQ. FT.

Design by
Donald A. Gardner Architects, Inc.

Refer to **Pricing Schedule C** on the order form for pricing information

Perfect for Family Gatherings

■ This plan features:
— Three bedrooms
— Two full baths
■ An open layout between the Great Room, Kitchen, and Breakfast Bay sharing a cathedral ceiling and a fireplace
■ Master Bedroom with a soaring cathedral ceiling, direct access to the deck and a well appointed Bath with a large walk-in closet
■ Additional Bedrooms sharing a full Bath in the hall
■ Centrally located utility and storage spaces

MAIN FLOOR — 1,346 SQ. FT.
GARAGE AND STORAGE — 462 SQ. FT.

TOTAL LIVING AREA:
1,346 SQ. FT.

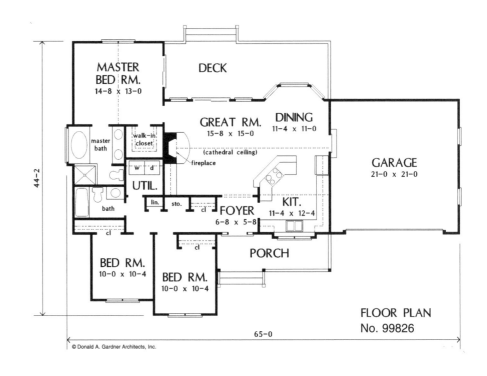

To order your Blueprints, call 1-800-235-5700

Design by
Donald A. Gardner Architects, Inc.

© 1998 Donald A. Gardner, Inc.

PLAN NO. 98029

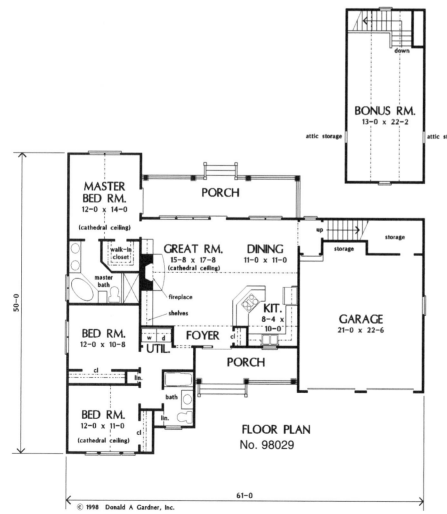

BONUS RM.
13-0 x 22-2

attic storage   attic storage

down

MASTER BED RM.
12-0 x 14-0
(cathedral ceiling)

PORCH

walk-in closet

GREAT RM.
15-8 x 17-8
(cathedral ceiling)

DINING
11-0 x 11-0

master bath

fireplace

shelves

KIT.
8-4 x 10-0

GARAGE
21-0 x 22-6

up

storage

storage

BED RM.
12-0 x 10-8

w   d

UTIL.

FOYER

cl

PORCH

BED RM.
12-0 x 11-0
(cathedral ceiling)

cl

lin.

bath

lin.

cl

50-0

61-0

FLOOR PLAN
No. 98029

© 1998 Donald A Gardner, Inc.

Multiple Gables and Double Dormer

■ This plan features:

— Three bedrooms

— Two full baths

■ Distinguished details inside and out make this modest home very appealing

■ Cathedral ceiling, cozy fireplace, built-in shelves and a wall of windows with Porch access enhance the Great Room, Dining area and open Kitchen

■ Quiet corner Master Bedroom features a cathedral ceiling, walk-in closet and and plush Bath

■ Bonus Room over Garage provides options for growing family

MAIN FLOOR — 1,377 SQ. FT.
BONUS ROOM — 383 SQ. FT.
GARAGE & STORAGE — 597 SQ. FT.

TOTAL LIVING AREA:
1,377 SQ. FT.

Design by
Fillmore Design Group

Refer to **Pricing Schedule D** on the order form for pricing information

For The Busy Family

■ This plan features:

— Four Bedrooms

— Three full baths

■ Porch shelters entry into Gallery, Formal Dining Area, and Living Room with cozy fireplace between book shelves and a wall of windows

■ Open and efficient Kitchen easily serves Breakfast Alcove, Patio, and Dining Area

■ Corner Master Bedroom provides a huge walk-in closet and lavish Bath

■ Two Bedrooms, one with two closets and a window seat, share a full Bath, while fourth Bedroom has separate Bath

■ No materials list is available for this plan

MAIN FLOOR — 2,233 SQ. FT.
GARAGE — 635 SQ. FT.

TOTAL LIVING AREA:
2,233 SQ. FT.

WIDTH 64'10"
DEPTH 56'-10"

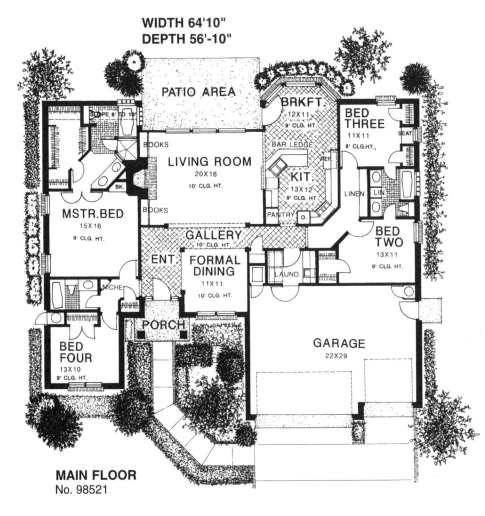

MAIN FLOOR
No. 98521

To order your Blueprints, call 1-800-235-5700

Design by
Donald A. Gardner Architects, Inc.

© 1996 Donald A Gardner Architects, Inc.

European Sophistication

- This plan features:
- — Three bedrooms
- — Two full baths

- Keystone arches, gables, and stucco give the exterior European sophistication

- Large Great Room with fireplace, and U-shaped Kitchen

- Octagonal tray ceiling dresses up the Dining Room

- Special ceiling treatments include a cathedral ceiling in the Great Room and tray ceilings in both the Master and front Bedrooms

- Indulgent Master Bath with a separate toilet area and a garden tub, shower, and dual vanity

MAIN FLOOR — 1,699 SQ. FT.
GARAGE — 637 SQ. FT.
BONUS — 386 SQ. FT.

TOTAL LIVING AREA:
1,699 SQ. FT.

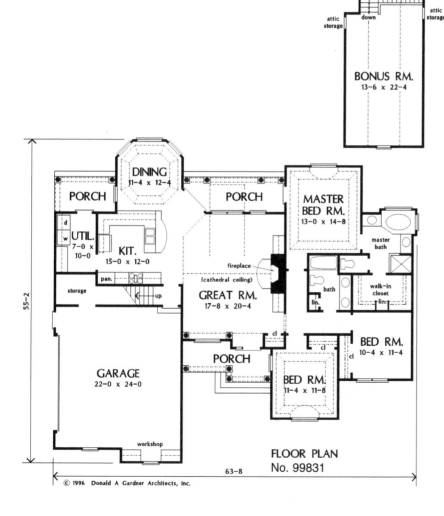

FLOOR PLAN
No. 99831

© 1996 Donald A Gardner Architects, Inc.

Design by
Rick Garner

Refer to **Pricing Schedule C** on the order form for pricing information

Enhanced by a Columned Porch

■ This plan features:

— Three bedrooms

— Two full baths

■ A Great Room with a fireplace and decorative ceiling

■ A large efficient Kitchen with Breakfast Area

■ A Master Bedroom with a private Master Bath and walk-in closet

■ A formal Dining Room located near the Kitchen

■ Two additional Bedrooms with walk-in closets and use of full hall Bath

■ An optional crawl space or slab foundation — please specify when ordering

MAIN FLOOR — 1,754 SQ. FT.
GARAGE — 552 SQ. FT.

TOTAL LIVING AREA:
1,754 SQ. FT.

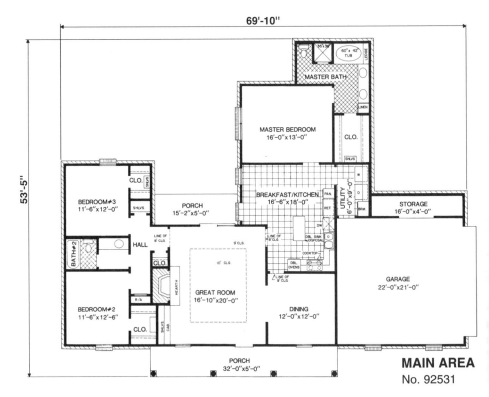

MAIN AREA
No. 92531

Design by
Vaughn A. Lauban Designs

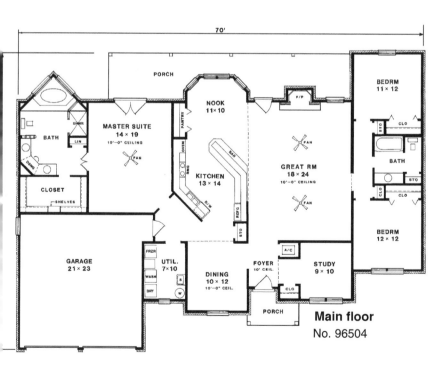

Main floor
No. 96504

Outstanding Family Home

■ This plan features:

— Three bedrooms

— Two full baths

■ Split bedroom layout, perfect floor plan for a family with older children

■ Great Room features a cozy fireplace, access to the rear Porch, and an open layout with the Nook and Kitchen

■ Extended counter in the Kitchen for snack bar, meals or snacks

■ Formal Dining Room directly accessing the Kitchen

■ Bright Nook with built-in Pantry

■ Master Suite contains access to rear porch and a pampering Bath and walk-in closet

MAIN FLOOR — 2,162 SQ. FT.
GARAGE — 498 SQ. FT.

TOTAL LIVING AREA:
2,162 SQ. FT.

Design by
The Garlinghouse Company

Refer to **Pricing Schedule B** on the order form for pricing information

Skylight Brightens Master Bedroom

■ This plan features:

— Three bedrooms

— Two full baths

■ A covered Porch entry

■ A foyer separating the Dining Room from the Breakfast Area and Kitchen

■ A Living Room enhanced by a vaulted beam ceiling and a fireplace

■ A Master Bedroom with a decorative ceiling and a skylight in the private Bath

■ An optional Deck accessible through sliding doors off the Master Bedroom

MAIN FLOOR — 1,686 SQ. FT.
BASEMENT — 1,676 SQ. FT.
GARAGE — 484 SQ. FT.

TOTAL LIVING AREA:
1,686 SQ. FT.

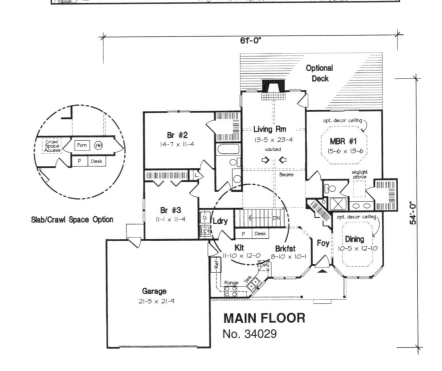

61'-0"

Optional Deck

Br #2
14-7 x 11-4

Living Rm
13-5 x 23-4
vaulted

opt. decor ceiling

MBR #1
15-6 x 13-6

skylight above

Beams

Crawl Space Access
Furn
HW
P
Desk

Slab/Crawl Space Option

Br #3
11-1 x 11-4

Ldry

P   Desk   DN

opt. decor ceiling

54'-0"

Kit
11-10 x 12-0

Brkfst
8-10 x 10-1

Foy

Dining
10-5 x 12-10

Range   Sink
DW

Garage
21-5 x 21-4

MAIN FLOOR
No. 34029

Design by
Donald A. Gardner Architects, Inc.

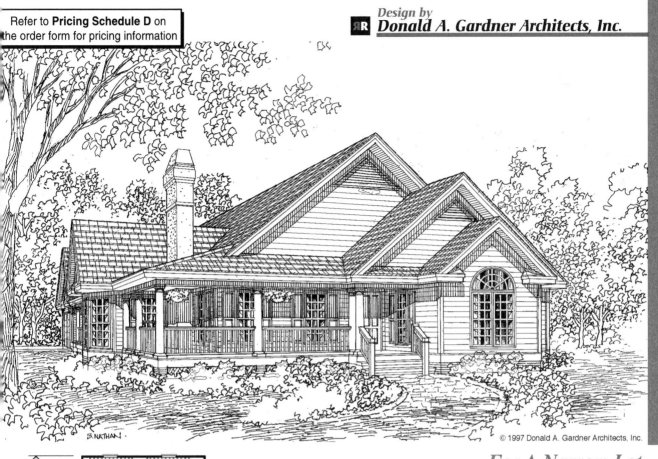

B. NATHAN

© 1997 Donald A. Gardner Architects, Inc.

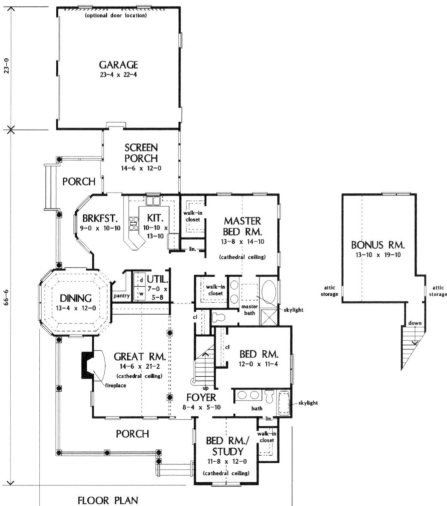

GARAGE
23-4 x 22-4

(optional door location)

23-0

66-9

SCREEN PORCH
14-6 x 12-0

PORCH

BRKFST.
9-0 x 10-10

KIT.
10-10 x 13-10

walk-in closet

lin.

MASTER BED RM.
13-8 x 14-10
(cathedral ceiling)

UTIL.
7-0 x 5-8

d
w

pantry

walk-in closet

cl

master bath

skylight

DINING
13-4 x 12-0

GREAT RM.
14-6 x 21-2
(cathedral ceiling)

fireplace

cl

BED RM.
12-0 x 11-4

up

FOYER
8-4 x 5-10

bath

skylight

PORCH

BED RM./ STUDY
11-8 x 12-0
(cathedral ceiling)

lin.

walk-in closet

BONUS RM.
13-10 x 19-10

attic storage

attic storage

down

FLOOR PLAN
No. 98034   48-8

© 1997 Donald A Gardner Architects, Inc.

For A Narrow Lot

■ This plan features:

— Three bedrooms

— Two full baths

■ A wrap-around front Porch, triple gable and arched window add to this charming home

■ Columns, a vaulted ceiling and inviting fireplace accent the Great Room

■ Unusual octagon Dining Area with Porch access

■ Open Kitchen easily serves Dining area, Breakfast alcove and screen Porch

■ Master Bedroom offers walk-in closets and skylit Bath

■ No materials list is available for this plan

MAIN FLOOR — 1,918 SQ. FT.
BONUS ROOM — 307 SQ. FT.
GARAGE — 552 SQ. FT.

TOTAL LIVING AREA:
1,918 SQ. FT.

Design by
Fillmore Design Group

Attractive Exterior

■ This plan features:

— Three bedrooms

— Two full baths

■ In the gallery columns separate space into the Great Room and the Dining Room

■ Access to backyard covered Patio from bayed Breakfast Nook

■ The large Kitchen is a chef's dream with lots of counter space and a Pantry

■ The Master Bedroom is removed from traffic areas and contains a luxurious Master Bath

■ A hall connects the two secondary Bedrooms which share a full skylit Bath

■ No materials list is available for this plan

MAIN FLOOR — 2,167 SQ. FT.
GARAGE — 690 SQ. FT.

TOTAL LIVING AREA:
2,167 SQ. FT.

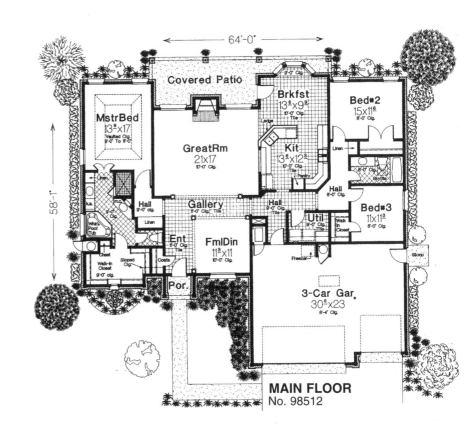

MAIN FLOOR
No. 98512

Design by
National Home Planning Service

MAIN FLOOR
No. 99081

BEDROOM
11' x 10'-8"

CLOSET

BATH

LINEN

CLOSET

CLOSET

BEDROOM
11' x 10'-8"

FOYER

GREAT ROOM
15' x 18'

UP

DINING ROOM
11' x 10'

DINETTE
11' x 8'

KITCHEN
11' x 10'

WALK-IN CLOSET

MASTER BATH

MASTER BEDROOM
15' 8 x 13' 4

2-CAR GARAGE
22' x 23'

53'-8"

80'-8"

Easy Living Ranch

■ This plan features:

— Three bedrooms

— Two full baths

■ Distinct exterior features, including vinyl siding, a series of gables, an arched window and a front door with sidelights

■ Dining Room with a 14-foot ceiling

■ Directly behind the Dining Room is the Kitchen with a serving bar

■ Breakfast Area with easy access to the Great Room

■ Master Bedroom crowned in a tray ceiling

■ Master Bath including a large walk-in closet

■ No material list is available for this plan

MAIN FLOOR — 1,590 SQ. FT.
BASEMENT — 1,590 SQ. FT.
GARAGE — 560 SQ. FT.

TOTAL LIVING AREA:
1,590 SQ. FT.

Design by
Fillmore Design Group

Refer to **Pricing Schedule F** on the order form for pricing information

Exceptional Family Living

■ This plan features:

— Four bedrooms

— Three full and one half baths

■ A decorative dormer, a bay window and an eyebrow arched window provide for a pleasing Country farmhouse facade

■ The cozy Study has its own fireplace and a bay window

■ The large formal Living Room has a fireplace and built-in bookcases

■ The huge island Kitchen is open to the Breakfast Bay and the Family Room

■ The Master Suite includes a large Bath with a unique closet

■ No materials list is available for this plan

MAIN FLOOR — 4,082 SQ. FT.
GARAGE — 720 SQ. FT.

TOTAL LIVING AREA:
4,082 SQ. FT.

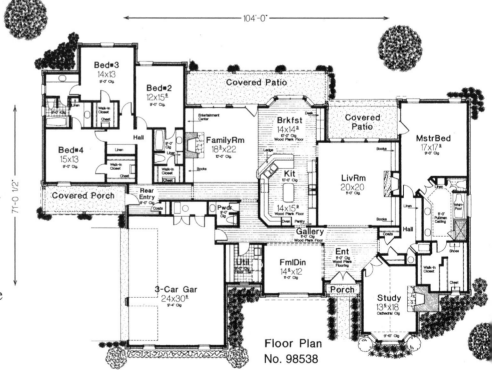

Floor Plan
No. 98538

To order your Blueprints, call 1-800-235-5700

Design by
Frank Betz Associates, Inc.

P L A N   N O . 9 8 4 6 0

WIDTH 54'-0"
DEPTH 47'-6"

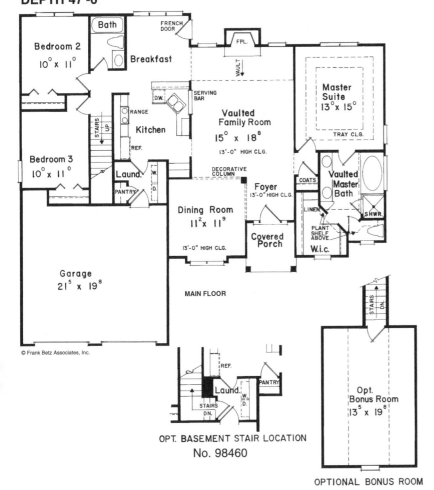

MAIN FLOOR

OPT. BASEMENT STAIR LOCATION
No. 98460

OPTIONAL BONUS ROOM

© Frank Betz Associates, Inc.

European Flair

■ This plan features:

— Three bedrooms

— Two full baths

■ Fireplace serves as an attractive focal point for the vaulted Family Room

■ Kitchen includes a serving bar for the Family Room

■ Master Suite topped by a tray ceiling over the Bedroom and a vaulted ceiling over the Master Bath

■ An optional basement or crawl space foundation — please specify when ordering

■ No materials list is available for this plan

MAIN FLOOR — 1,544 SQ. FT.
BONUS ROOM — 284 SQ. FT.
BASEMENT — 1,544 SQ. FT.
GARAGE — 440 SQ. FT.

TOTAL LIVING AREA:
1,544 SQ. FT.

Design by
Fillmore Design Group

Refer to **Pricing Schedule F** on
the order form for pricing information

Luxurious One Floor Living

■ This plan features:

— Four bedrooms

— Three full baths

■ Decorative windows enhance front entrance of elegant home

■ Formal Living Room accented by fireplace between windows overlooking rear yard

■ Breakfast bar, work island, and an abundance of storage and counter space featured in Kitchen

■ Bright alcove for informal Dining and Family Room with access to covered Patio adjoin Kitchen

■ Spacious Master Bedroom with access to covered Patio, a lavish Bath and huge walk-in closet

■ No materials list is available for this plan

MAIN FLOOR — 3,254 SQ. FT.
GARAGE — 588 SQ. FT.

TOTAL LIVING AREA:
3,254 SQ. FT.

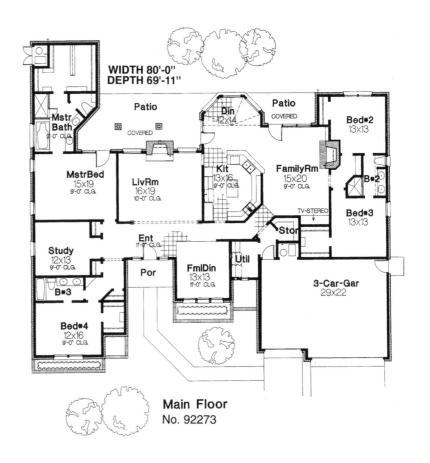

Main Floor
No. 92273

Design by
Donald A. Gardner Architects, Inc.

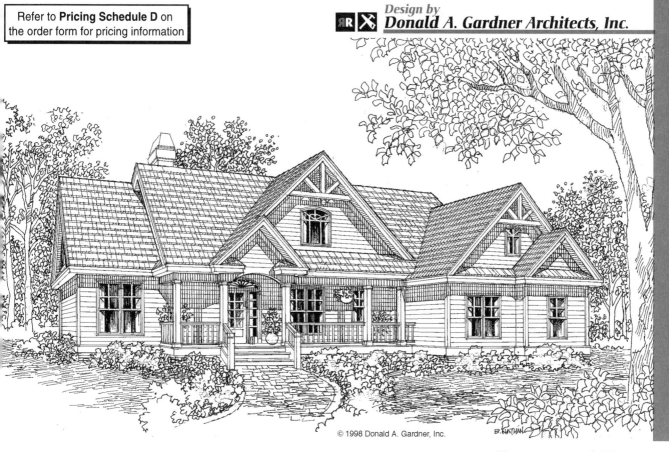

© 1998 Donald A. Gardner, Inc.

FLOOR PLAN
No. 98027

© 1998 Donald A Gardner, Inc.

BONUS RM.
10-6 x 21-0

Economical Home

■ This plan features:

— Three bedrooms

— Two full baths

■ Practical to build design offers gables, pediments and inviting front Porch

■ Tray ceiling and columns define Dining Area from Great Room

■ Great Room features a cathedral ceiling, fireplace with built-in shelves, Deck and Kitchen access

■ Open Kitchen keeps cook part of all activities

■ Corner Master Bedroom offers two walk-in closets and a double vanity Bath

■ Bonus room over Garage provides options for growing families

MAIN FLOOR — 1,544 SQ. FT.
BONUS ROOM — 320 SQ. FT.
GARAGE & STORAGE — 478 SQ. FT.

TOTAL LIVING AREA:
1,544 SQ. FT.

Design by
Donald A. Gardner Architects, Inc.

Refer to **Pricing Schedule E** on the order form for pricing information

© 1998 Donald A. Gardner, Inc.

Stately Arched Entry

- This plan features:
- — Three bedrooms
- — Two full and one half baths
- The stately arched entry Porch is supported by columns
- The Dining Room has a tray ceiling and is defined by columns
- The Great Room has a fireplace and accesses the rear Porch/Deck
- The Kitchen is full of cabinet and counter space
- The Master Bedroom has a bay window and a tray ceiling
- The Master Bath features dual vanities and walk in closets

MAIN FLOOR — 2,024 SQ. FT.
BONUS — 423 SQ. FT.
GARAGE — 623 SQ. FT.

TOTAL LIVING AREA:
2,024 SQ. FT.

SCREEN PORCH 15-6 x 14-0
DECK
BRKFST. 10-4 x 9-0
GREAT RM. 19-0 x 16-0
MASTER BED RM. 16-4 x 13-4
KIT. 10-4 x 12-0
fireplace
(cathedral ceiling)
walk-in closet
walk-in closet
BED RM./ STUDY 12-4 x 12-10
master bath
bath
DINING 12-0 x 14-0
FOYER 6-0 x 11-10
pd. rm.
74-9
up
UTIL. 6-4 x 8-10
BED RM. 12-4 x 11-0
walk-in closet
PORCH
GARAGE 22-8 x 23-0
FLOOR PLAN No. 98011
62-3
© 1998 Donald A Gardner, Inc.

attic storage
down
BONUS RM. 16-4 x 23-0

To order your Blueprints, call 1-800-235-5700

Design by
Frank Betz Associates, Inc.

© Frank Betz Associates

57'-0"

Covered Porch

Vaulted Sitting Area

Breakfast

TRAY CLG.

FRENCH DOOR

FPL

VAULT

VAULT

Bedroom 2
12⁶ x 10⁴

SERVING BAR

Master Suite
17⁰ x 13⁰

TRAY CLG.

RANGE

Kitchen

D.W.

PANTRY

REF.

Vaulted Family Room
15⁰ x 20⁷
14'-0" HIGH CEILING

Bath

NICHE

DECORATIVE COLUMNS

PLANT SHELF ABOVE

LIN.

K.S.

Vaulted M.Bath

COATS

PLANT SHELF ABOVE

W.i.c.

LINEN

Laund.

W.

D.

Foyer
14'-0" HIGH CLG.

PLANT SHELF ABOVE

Dining Room
12⁵ x 12⁷
14'-0" HIGH CEILING

Bedroom 3
10⁶ x 12⁰

SHWR.

Covered Entry

Garage
22⁵ x 20²

No. 98464
FLOOR PLAN

GARAGE LOCATION W/ BASEMENT

Vaulted M.Bath

PLANT SHELF ABOVE

SINK

W.i.c.

LINEN

Laund.

W.

D.

SHWR.

STAIRS DN.

COATS

Garage
22⁵ x 20²

OPT. BASEMENT STAIR LOCATION

European Flavor

■ This plan features:

— Three bedrooms

— Two full baths

■ A covered entry reveals a Foyer inside with a 14-foot ceiling

■ The Family Room has a vaulted ceiling and a fireplace

■ The Breakfast Area has a tray ceiling and a bay of windows

■ The Kitchen has a walk-in Pantry

■ The Dining Room is delineated by columns and has a plant shelf

■ The privately located Master Suite has a tray ceiling

■ No materials list is available for this plan

■ An optional basement or crawl space foundation — please specify when ordering

MAIN FLOOR — 1,779 SQ. FT.
BASEMENT — 1,818 SQ. FT.
GARAGE — 499 SQ. FT.

TOTAL LIVING AREA:
1,779 SQ. FT.

Design by Sun-Tel

Refer to **Pricing Schedule B** on the order form for pricing information

Carefree Comfort

■ This plan features:

— Three bedrooms

— Two full baths

■ A dramatic vaulted Foyer

■ A range top island Kitchen with a sunny eating Nook surrounded by a built-in planter

■ A vaulted ceiling in the Great Room with a built-in bar and corner fireplace

■ A bayed Dining Room that combines with the Great Room for a spacious feeling

■ A Master Bedroom with a private reading nook, vaulted ceiling, walk-in closet, and a well appointed private Bath

■ An optional basement, slab or crawl space foundation— please specify when ordering

MAIN AREA — 1,665 SQ. FT.

TOTAL LIVING AREA:
1,665 SQ. FT.

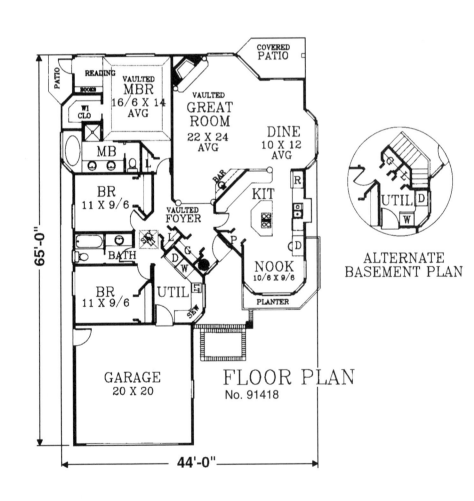

FLOOR PLAN
No. 91418

ALTERNATE
BASEMENT PLAN

Design by
Donald A. Gardner Architects, Inc.

B. NATHAN.

©1997 Donald A. Gardner Architects, Inc.

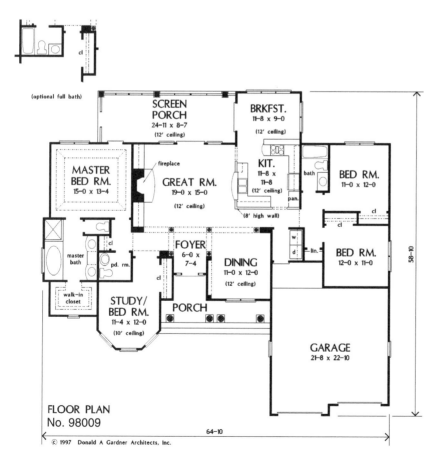

(optional full bath)

SCREEN PORCH
24-11 x 8-7
(12' ceiling)

BRKFST.
11-8 x 9-0
(12' ceiling)

KIT.
11-8 x 11-8
(12' ceiling)

MASTER BED RM.
15-0 x 13-4

fireplace

GREAT RM.
19-0 x 15-0
(12' ceiling)

bath

BED RM.
11-0 x 12-0

pan.

(8' high wall)

master bath

cl

pd. rm.

FOYER
6-0 x 7-4

w
d

lin.

cl

cl

BED RM.
12-0 x 11-0

walk-in closet

cl

DINING
11-0 x 12-0
(12' ceiling)

58-10

STUDY/BED RM.
11-4 x 12-0
(10' ceiling)

PORCH

GARAGE
21-8 x 22-10

FLOOR PLAN
No. 98009

64-10

© 1997 Donald A Gardner Architects, Inc.

Southwestern Style

■ This plan features:

— Four bedrooms

— Two full and one half baths

■ Large circle-top windows, stucco, and a tile roof add to this home

■ The common space of the home is impressive with 12' ceilings and columns

■ The Kitchen is partially enclosed by 8' high walls

■ A screen Porch in the rear is perfect for entertaining guests

■ The Master Bedroom has a tray ceiling and a private Bath

■ The Study/Bedroom has a bay in the front of it

■ An optional slab or a crawl space foundation — please specify when ordering

MAIN FLOOR — 1,954 SQ. FT.

TOTAL LIVING AREA:
1,954 SQ. FT.

Easy to Build

■ This plan features:

— Two bedrooms

— One full bath

■ Affordable Ranch with all the amenities

■ Covered entry leads into Foyer and Living and Dining rooms

■ Focal-point fireplace and bay window enhance the Living Room

■ Country style Kitchen opens to Dining Room, Nook, Utility Room and Garage

■ Master Bedroom features an oversized closet and private access to full Bath with whirlpool tub

■ Second Bedroom has an over-sized closet and access to full Bath

MAIN FLOOR — 1,313 SQ. FT.
GARAGE — 385 SQ. FT.

TOTAL LIVING AREA:
1,313 SQ. FT.

WIDTH 55'-0"
DEPTH 35'-6"

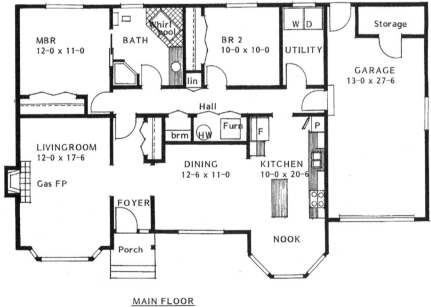

MAIN FLOOR
No. 90865

Design by
Fillmore Design Group

PLAN NO · 98511

← 65'-0" →

68'-8"

FAMILY ROOM
15 X 17

COVERED

PATIO AREA

BRKFT.
12 X 11

COVERED
LANIA

BATH

BDRM. #4
13 X 10
9" CLG.

CLOS.

COVERED

MSTR.
BATH
9" CLG.

LIVING ROOM
13 X 13
12" CLG.

KIT.
12 X 13

W-I
CLOS.

SITTING
AREA

BDRM. #3
10 X 12
9" CLG.

HALL
9" CLG.

HALL
9" CLG.

MSTR. BDRM.
14 X 18
9" CLG.

LINEN

REF

PANTRY

GALLERY
11" CLG.

UT.

PWDR.

W. D.

ENT.
11" CLG.

FORMAL
DINING
11 X 13
11" CLG.

BATH

LIN

BDRM. #2
10 X 13
10" CLG.

POR.

BOOK

THREE CAR
GARAGE

FLOOR PLAN
No. 98511

Lap of Luxury

■ This plan features:

— Four bedrooms

— Three full baths

■ Entertaining in grand style in the formal Living Room, the Dining Room, or under the covered Patio in the backyard

■ Family Room crowned in a cathedral ceiling, enhanced by a center fireplace, and built-in book shelves

■ Efficient Kitchen highlighted by a wall oven, plentiful counter space, and a Pantry

■ Master Bedroom with a Sitting Area, huge walk-in closet, private Bath, and access to a covered lanai

■ No materials list is available for this plan

MAIN FLOOR — 2,445 SQ. FT.
GARAGE — 630 SQ. FT.

TOTAL LIVING AREA:
2,445 SQ. FT.

Design by
Ahmann Designs, Inc.

Refer to **Pricing Schedule C** on
the order form for pricing information

Ranch of Distinction

■ This plan features:

— Three bedrooms

— Two full and one half baths

■ The recessed entrance has an
arched transom window over the
door and a sidelight windows
beside it

■ Once inside the Living Room
boasts a high ceiling and a warm
fireplace

■ The large Kitchen Area includes
the open Dining Area with a rear
bay that accessed the backyard

■ The Master and third Bedrooms
both have bay windows

■ No materials list is available for
this plan

MAIN FLOOR — 1,906 SQ. FT.
BASEMENT — 1,906 SQ. FT.

TOTAL LIVING AREA:
1,906 SQ. FT.

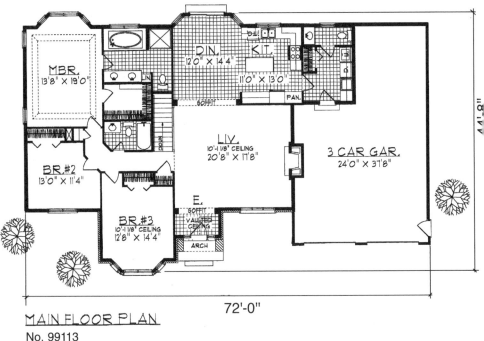

MBR.
13'8" X 19'0"

DIN.
12'0" X 14'4"

KIT.
11'0" X 13'0"

PAN.

SOFFIT

LIV.
10'-1 1/8" CEILING
20'8" X 17'8"

3 CAR GAR.
24'0" X 37'8"

BR. #2
13'0" X 11'4"

BR. #3
10'-1 1/8" CEILING
12'8" X 14'4"

E.
SOFFIT
VAULTED
CEILING

ARCH

44'-8"

72'-0"

MAIN FLOOR PLAN
No. 99113

To order your Blueprints, call 1-800-235-5700

Design by
Fillmore Design Group

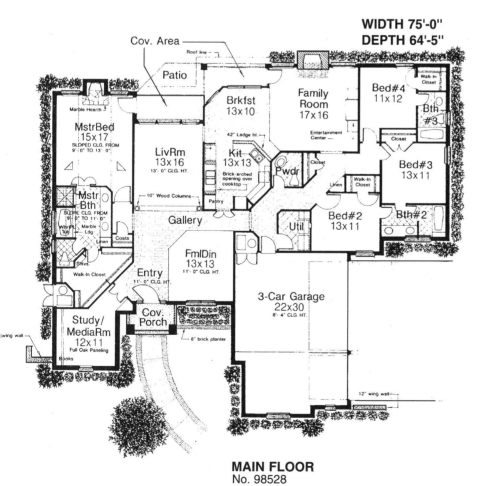

WIDTH 75'-0"
DEPTH 64'-5"

MAIN FLOOR
No. 98528

Especially Unique

■ This plan features:

— Four bedrooms

— Three full and one half baths

■ From the 11-foot entry turn left into the Study/Media Room

■ The formal Dining Room is open to the Gallery, and the Living Room beyond

■ The Family Room has a built-in entertainment center, a fireplace and access to the rear Patio

■ The private Master Bedroom has a fireplace, a private Bath and a walk-in closet

■ Three spacious Bedrooms off the Family room share two full Baths

■ No materials list is available for this plan

MAIN FLOOR — 2,748 SQ. FT.
GARAGE — 660 SQ. FT.

TOTAL LIVING AREA:
2,748 SQ. FT.

PLAN NO. 99835

Design by Donald A. Gardner Architects, Inc.

Refer to **Pricing Schedule D** on the order form for pricing information

© 1997 Donald A. Gardner Architects, Inc.

Private Master Suite

■ This plan features:

— Three bedrooms

— Two full baths

■ Working at the Kitchen island focuses your view to the Great Room with it's vaulted ceiling and a fireplace

■ Clerestory dormers emanate light into the Great Room

■ Both the Dining Room and Master Bedroom are enhanced by tray ceilings

■ Skylights floods natural light into the Bonus space

■ The private Master Suite has its own bath and an expansive walk-in closet

MAIN FLOOR — 1,515 SQ. FT.
BONUS — 288 SQ. FT.
GARAGE — 476 SQ. FT.

TOTAL LIVING AREA:
1,515 SQ. FT.

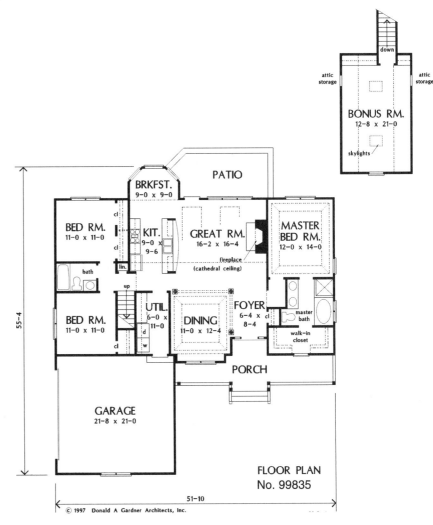

FLOOR PLAN No. 99835

© 1997 Donald A Gardner Architects, Inc.

194 To order your Blueprints, call 1-800-235-5700

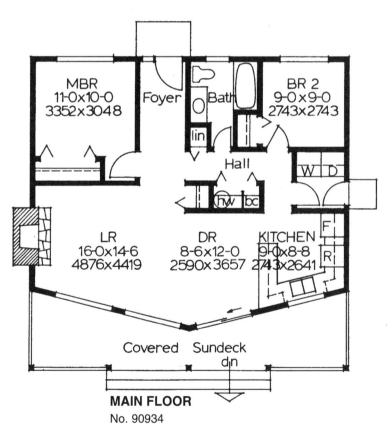

MAIN FLOOR
No. 90934

MBR
11-0x10-0
3352x3048

Foyer

Bath

lin

BR 2
9-0x9-0
2743x2743

Hall

W | D

hw bc

F
R

LR
16-0x14-6
4876x4419

DR
8-6x12-0
2590x3657

KITCHEN
9-0x8-8
2743x2641

Covered Sundeck
dn

A Nest for Empty-Nesters

■ This plan features:

— Two bedrooms

— One full bath

■ An economical design

■ A covered Sun Deck adding outdoor living space

■ A Mudroom/Laundry Area inside the side door, trapping dirt before it can enter the house

■ An open layout between the Living Room with fireplace, Dining Room and Kitchen

MAIN FLOOR — 884 SQ. FT.
WIDTH — 34'-0"
DEPTH — 28'-0"

TOTAL LIVING AREA:
884 SQ. FT.

Unique V-Shaped Home

■ This plan features:

— Two bedrooms

— Three full baths

■ Four skylights brighten the Eating Nook in the country Kitchen

■ A walk-in Pantry, range-top work island, built-in barbecue and a sink add to the amenities of the Kitchen

■ An entire wall of windows along its length illuminate the Living Room

■ Master Suite with his-n-her closets, and adjacent dressing area

■ A Guest Suite with a private Sitting Area and full Bath

■ No materials list is available for this plan

MAIN FLOOR — 3,417 SQ. FT.
GARAGE — 795 SQ. FT.

TOTAL LIVING AREA:
3,417 SQ. FT.

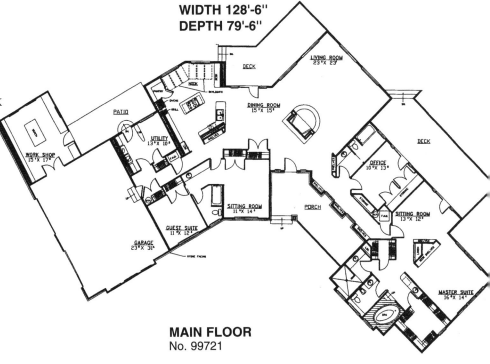

WIDTH 128'-6"
DEPTH 79'-6"

MAIN FLOOR
No. 99721

To order your Blueprints, call 1-800-235-5700

Design by
Fillmore Design Group

French Country Styling

■ This plan features:

— Four bedrooms

— Three full and one half baths

■ Brick and stone blend masterfully for an impressive French Country exterior

■ Separate Master Suite with expansive Bath and closet

■ Study containing a built-in desk and bookcase

■ Angled island Kitchen highlighted by walk-in pantry, and open to the Breakfast Bay

■ Fantastic Family Room featuring a brick fireplace and built-in entertainment center

■ No materials list is available for this plan

MAIN FLOOR — 3,352 SQ. FT.
GARAGE — 672 SQ. FT.

TOTAL LIVING AREA:
3,352 SQ. FT.

91'-0"

71'-9"

Patio Area

3-Car Gar

Brkfst
14X12'-6"

MstrBed
16X17

LivRm
16X16

Kit
14X14

FmlyRm
18X18

Util

Mstr Bath

Gallery

Entertainment
Center

Bed#4
13X16

Books

Study
12X11

Ent

FmlDin
12X13

Bed#2
13X12

Bed#3
12X11

Hallway

Linen

Cov
Por

MAIN FLOOR
No. 98513

Design by
Ahmann Design, Inc.

Perfect Plan for Busy Family

■ This plan features:

— Three bedrooms

— Two full baths

■ Covered entry opens to vaulted Foyer

■ Spacious Family Room with another vaulted ceiling, a central fireplace and expansive backyard views

■ Angular and efficient Kitchen with an eating bar, built-in desk, Dining Area with outdoor access, and nearby Laundry and Garage entry

■ Secluded Master Bedroom with a large walk-in closet and double vanity Bath

■ No materials list is available for this plan

MAIN FLOOR — 1,756 SQ. FT.
BASEMENT — 1,756 SQ. FT.

TOTAL LIVING AREA:
1,756 SQ. FT.

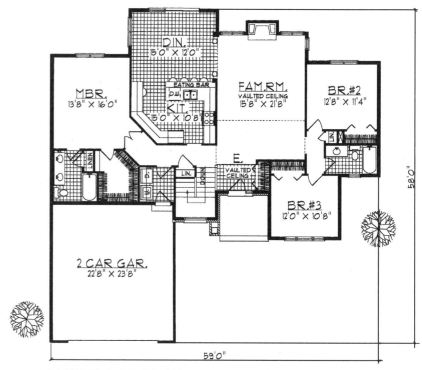

MAIN FLOOR PLAN
No. 93191

To order your Blueprints, call 1-800-235-5700

Design by
Frank Betz Associates, Inc.

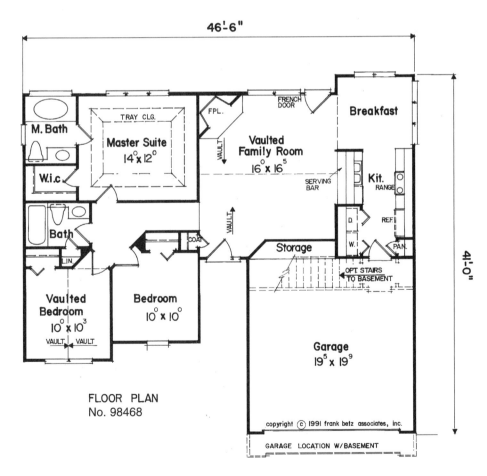

46'-6"

41'-0"

M. Bath

W.i.c.

TRAY CLG.

Master Suite
14° x 12°

FPL.

VAULT

FRENCH
DOOR

Breakfast

Vaulted
Family Room
16° x 16⁵

SERVING
BAR

Kit.

RANGE

REF.

D.

W.

PAN.

Bath

LIN.

VAULT

COAT

Storage

Vaulted
Bedroom
10° x 10³

Bedroom
10° x 10°

VAULT   VAULT

OPT. STAIRS
TO BASEMENT

Garage
19⁵ x 19⁹

FLOOR PLAN
No. 98468

copyright © 1991 frank betz associates, inc.

GARAGE LOCATION W/BASEMENT

Decorative Ceilings

■ This plan features:

— Three bedrooms

— Two full baths

■ The Family room has a vaulted ceiling, a corner fireplace, and a French door to the rear yard

■ The Breakfast Book is brightened by window on two of its walls

■ The galley Kitchen has a Pantry, and a serving bar into the Family Room

■ The Master Suite has a tray ceiling, a walk in closet, and a private Bath

■ No materials list available for this plan

■ An optional basement, slab or crawl space foundation — please specify when ordering

MAIN FLOOR — 1,104 SQ. FT.
BASEMENT — 1,104 SQ. FT.
GARAGE — 400 SQ. FT.

TOTAL LIVING AREA:
1,104 SQ. FT.

Design by
Donald A. Gardner Architects, Inc.

Refer to **Pricing Schedule D** on
the order form for pricing information

© 1997 Donald A. Gardner Architects, Inc.

B. NATHAN

Casual Country Charmer

■ This plan features:

— Three bedrooms

— Two full baths

■ Columns and arches frame the front Porch

■ The open floor plan combines the Great Room, Kitchen and Dining Room

■ The Kitchen offers a convenient breakfast bar for meals on the run

■ The Master Suite features a private Bath oasis

■ Secondary Bedrooms share a full Bath with a dual vanity

MAIN FLOOR — 1,770 SQ. FT.
BONUS — 401 SQ. FT.
GARAGE — 630 SQ. FT.

TOTAL LIVING AREA:
1,770 SQ. FT.

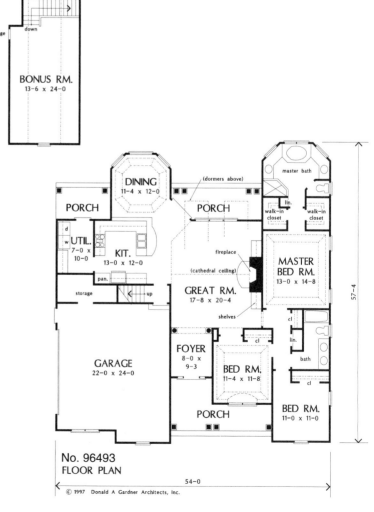

No. 96493
FLOOR PLAN
© 1997 Donald A Gardner Architects, Inc.

To order your Blueprints, call 1-800-235-5700

Floor Plan
No. 98501

Patio

FamilyRm.
16x14
Cathedral Clg.

Brkfst.
11x9
10' Clg.

Bed#4
11x10
8' Clg.

Bed#3
11x13
8' Clg.

Pantry

Kit.
10' Clg.

Linen

MstrBed
15x13
Sloped Clg. 10' Clg.

Desk

Lin

Bed#2
11x11
8' Clg.

Gallery
10' Clg.

Pwdr.

Util.

Sloped Clg.
10' Clg.

Ent.
10' Clg.

FmlDin.
11x12
10' Clg.

Liv.Rm.
14x12
10' Clg.

Gar.
20x22

Pon

57' - 0"

60' - 0"

Stunning Family Plan

■ This plan features:

— Four bedrooms

— Two full and one half baths

■ Windows, brick, and columns combine to create an eye-catching elevation

■ A pair of columns greets you as you enter the Living Room

■ The formal Dining room is located just steps away from the Kitchen

■ Set on a unique angle the Family Room has a rear wall fireplace

■ The open Kitchen has a center island

■ Set away from the active areas the Master Bedroom is a quiet retreat

■ No materials list is available for this plan

MAIN FLOOR — 2,194 SQ. FT.
GARAGE — 462 SQ. FT.

TOTAL LIVING AREA :
2,194 SQ. FT.

Design by
Vaughn A. Lauban Designs

Refer to **Pricing Schedule A** on
the order form for pricing information

One Floor Living

■ This plan features:

— Three bedrooms

— Two full baths

■ A covered front Porch is supported by columns and accented by balusters

■ The Living Room features a cozy fireplace and a ceiling fan

■ The Kitchen is distinguished by an angled serving bar

■ The Dining Room is convenient to the Kitchen and accessed the rear Porch

■ Two secondary Bedrooms share a Bath in the hall

■ The Master Bedroom has a walk in closet and a private Bath

■ A two car Garage with storage space is located in the rear of the home

MAIN FLOOR —1,247 SQ. FT.
GARAGE — 512 SQ. FT.

TOTAL LIVING AREA:
  1,247 SQ. FT.

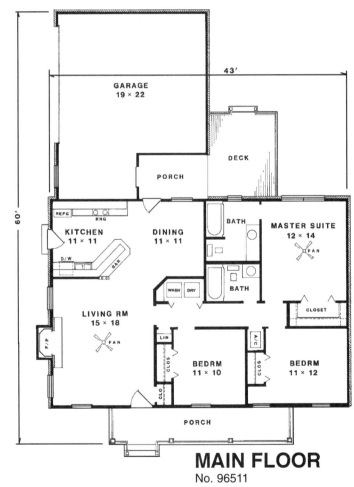

MAIN FLOOR
No. 96511

To order your Blueprints, call 1-800-235-5700

Refer to **Pricing Schedule A** on the order form for pricing information

Design by
Jannis Vann & Associates, Inc.

Drive Under Garage

- This plan features:
  — Three bedrooms
  — Two full baths
- Porch shelters Entry into living area with an inviting fireplace topped by a vaulted ceiling
- Convenient Dining Area opens to Living Room, Kitchen and Sundeck
- Efficient, U-shaped Kitchen serves Dining Area and Sun Deck beyond
- Pampering Master Bedroom with a vaulted ceiling, two closets and a double vanity Bath
- Two additional Bedrooms share a full Bath and convenient laundry center

MAIN FLOOR — 1,208 SQ. FT.
BASEMENT — 728 SQ. FT.
GARAGE — 480 SQ. FT.

TOTAL LIVING AREA:
1,208 SQ. FT.

Sundeck
10-0 x 10-0

10-0

M.Bath

Bedroom 2

Dw.

Kitchen
8-0 x 10-0

Dining
10-4 x 10-0

Opt Plant Shelf
Open To Bdrm.

W. D.

Bath 2

Ref.

Vaulted Ceil.

29-0

Master Bedroom
11-6 x 14-6

Cts.

Down

Family Room
18-4 x 13-0

Vaulted Ceil.

Bedroom 3
11-0 x 10-0

Entry

© 1989, Jannis vann & Associates, Inc.

No. 98915
MAIN FLOOR

48-0

2-4

Refer to **Pricing Schedule C** on the order form for pricing information

Plush Master Bedroom Wing

■ This plan features:

— Three bedrooms

— Two full baths

■ A raised, tiled Foyer with decorative window leading into an expansive Living Room, accented by a tiled fireplace and framed by French doors

■ An efficient Kitchen with a walk-in Pantry and serving bar adjoining the Breakfast and Utility Areas

■ A private Master Bedroom, crowned by a stepped ceiling, offering an atrium door to outside, a huge, walk-in closet and a luxurious Bath

■ No materials list is available for this plan

MAIN FLOOR — 1,849 SQ. FT.
GARAGE — 437 SQ. FT.

TOTAL LIVING AREA:
1,849 SQ. FT.

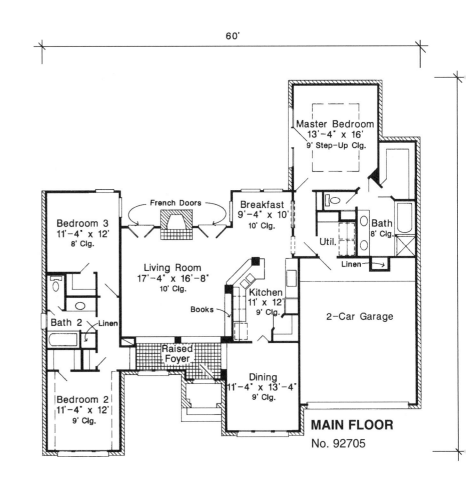

MAIN FLOOR
No. 92705

Design by
Donald A. Gardner Architects, Inc.

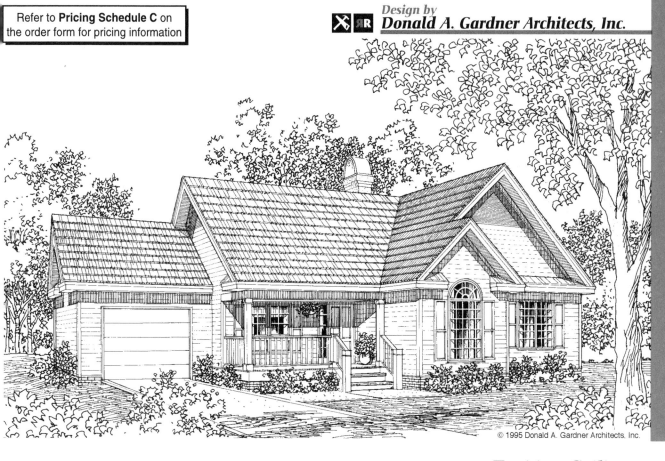

© 1995 Donald A. Gardner Architects, Inc.

Exciting Ceiling Treatments And Open Spaces

■ This plan features:

— Three Bedrooms

— Two full baths

■ Double gables and a covered Porch adding charm to the exterior

■ Common living areas in an open format topped by a cathedral ceiling

■ Front Bedroom, doubling as a Study, topped by a cathedral ceiling and accented by a picture window with circle-top

■ Master Bedroom crowned in a cathedral ceiling pampered by a lavish Bath

MAIN FLOOR — 1,298 SQ. FT.
GARAGE — 287 SQ. FT.

TOTAL LIVING AREA:
1,298 SQ. FT.

DECK

(optional two car garage)

(cathedral ceiling)

(cathedral ceiling)

walk-in closet

DINING
10–0 x 11–6

GREAT RM.
15–4 x 15–0

MASTER BED RM.
12–4 x 15–0

GARAGE
13–4 x 20–4

fireplace

master bath

KIT.
9–8 x 11–2

FOYER
6–8 x 7–8

w   d

cl

UTIL.

bath

lin.

cl

PORCH

BED RM./ STUDY
10–0 x 10–0

BED RM.
12–4 x 10–0

cl

(cathedral ceiling)

10–0

36–0

FLOOR PLAN
No. 99828

7–4   59–0

© 1995 Donald A Gardner Architects, Inc.

Design by
Donald A. Gardner Architects, Inc.

Refer to **Pricing Schedule C** on
the order form for pricing information

© Donald A. Gardner Architects, Inc.

Rustic Simplicity

■ This plan features:

— Three bedrooms

— Two full and one half baths

■ The central living area is large
and boasts a cathedral ceiling,
exposed wood beams and a
clerestory

■ A long screened Porch has a bank
of skylights

■ The open Kitchen contains a convenient serving and eating
counter

■ The generous Master Suite opens
to the screened Porch, and is
enhanced by a walk-in closet and
a whirlpool tub

■ Two more Bedrooms share a
second full Bath

MAIN FLOOR — 1,426 SQ. FT.

TOTAL LIVING AREA:
1,426 SQ. FT.

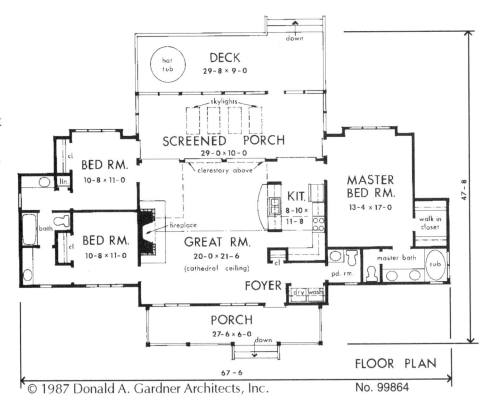

© 1987 Donald A. Gardner Architects, Inc.   No. 99864

To order your Blueprints, call 1-800-235-5700

© 1994 Donald A. Gardner Architects, Inc.

B. NATHAN

Didn't Waste An Inch of Space

■ This plan features:
— Three bedrooms
— Two full baths

■ Great Room with fireplace and built-in cabinets share a cathedral ceiling with angled Kitchen

■ Separate Dining Room allows for more formal entertaining

■ Master bedroom topped by a cathedral ceiling, walk-in closet, and well appointed Bath

■ Front and rear Covered Porches encourage relaxation

■ Skylit Bonus Room makes a great Recreation Room or Office in the future

MAIN FLOOR — 1,575 SQ. FT.
BONUS ROOM — 276 SQ. FT.
GARAGE — 536 SQ. FT.

TOTAL LIVING AREA:
1,575 SQ. FT.

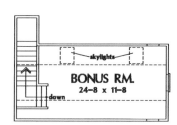

skylights
BONUS RM.
24–8 x 11–8
down

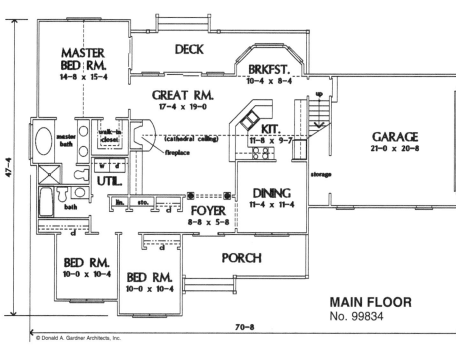

MASTER BED RM.
14–8 x 15–4

DECK

GREAT RM.
17–4 x 19–0

BRKFST.
10–4 x 8–4

up

GARAGE
21–0 x 20–8

master bath

walk-in closet

(cathedral ceiling)

KIT.
11–8 x 9–7

fireplace

w d
UTIL.

storage

bath

lin. sto.

DINING
11–4 x 11–4

FOYER
8–8 x 5–8

47–4

BED RM.
10–0 x 10–4

BED RM.
10–0 x 10–4

PORCH

MAIN FLOOR
No. 99834

70–8

© Donald A. Gardner Architects, Inc.

Design by
Design Basics, Inc.

Refer to **Pricing Schedule B** on the order form for pricing information

© design basics, inc.

Attractive Gables and Arches

■ This plan features:

— Three bedrooms

— Two full baths

■ Entry opens to formal Dining Room with arched window

■ Angles and transom windows add interest to the Great Room

■ Bright Hearth Area expands Breakfast/Kitchen Area and shares three-sided fireplace

■ Efficient Kitchen offers an angled snack bar, a large Pantry and nearby Laundry/Garage entry

■ Secluded Master Bedroom suite crowned by decorative ceiling, a large walk-in closet and a plush Bath with a whirlpool tub

MAIN FLOOR — 1,782 SQ. FT.
BASEMENT — 1,782 SQ. FT.
GARAGE — 466 SQ. FT.

TOTAL LIVING AREA:
1,782 SQ. FT.

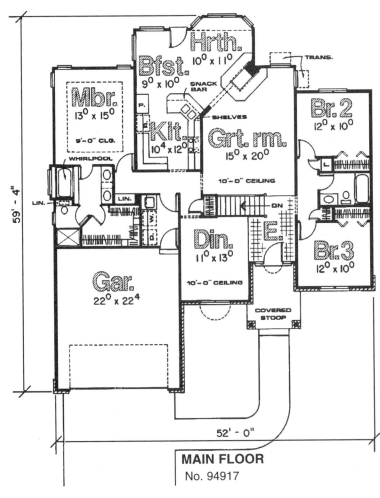

MAIN FLOOR
No. 94917

To order your Blueprints, call 1-800-235-5700

Refer to **Pricing Schedule B** on the order form for pricing information

Design by
Frank Betz Associates, Inc.

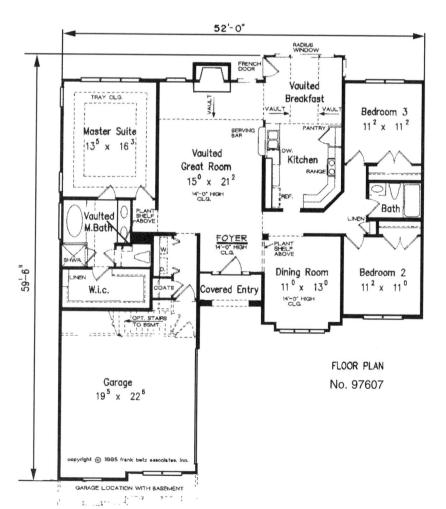

52'-0"

FLOOR PLAN
No. 97607

Charming Stucco

■ This plan features:

— Three bedrooms

— Two full baths

■ Attractive entrance with curved transom and side lights

■ A vaulted ceiling above the Great Room and Breakfast Room

■ Cozy fireplace with windows to either side in the Great Room

■ Tray ceiling crowning the Master Bedroom and a vaulted ceiling over the plush Master Bath

■ Elegant boxed bay window accenting the formal Dining Room

■ An optional basement or crawl space foundation — please specify when ordering

MAIN FLOOR — 1,696 SQ. FT.
GARAGE — 475 SQ. FT.
BASEMENT — 1,720 SQ. FT.

TOTAL LIVING AREA:
1,696 SQ. FT.

Design by
Frank Betz Associates, Inc.

Refer to **Pricing Schedule C** on the order form for pricing information

Covered Porch with Columns

■ This plan features:

— Three bedrooms

— Two full baths

■ The Foyer with 12′ ceiling leads past decorative columns into the Family Room with a center fireplace

■ The Kitchen has a serving bar and is adjacent to the Breakfast Nook which has a French door that opens to the backyard

■ The private Master Suite has a tray ceiling, a vaulted Bath with a double vanity, and a walk-in closet

■ An optional basement, slab or a crawl space foundation — please specify when ordering

MAIN FLOOR — 1,856 SQ. FT.
GARAGE — 429 SQ. FT.
BASEMENT — 1,856 SQ. FT.

TOTAL LIVING AREA:
1,856 SQ. FT.

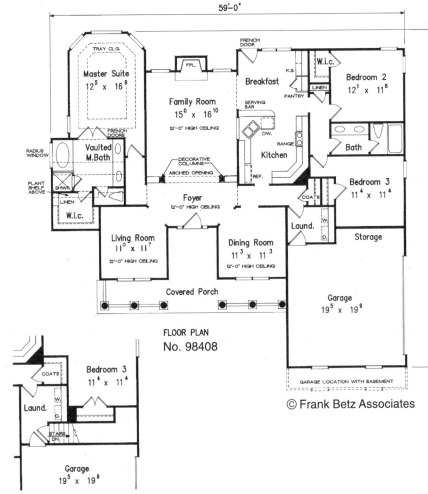

FLOOR PLAN
No. 98408

© Frank Betz Associates

OPT. BASEMENT STAIR LOCATION

Design by
Design Basics, Inc.

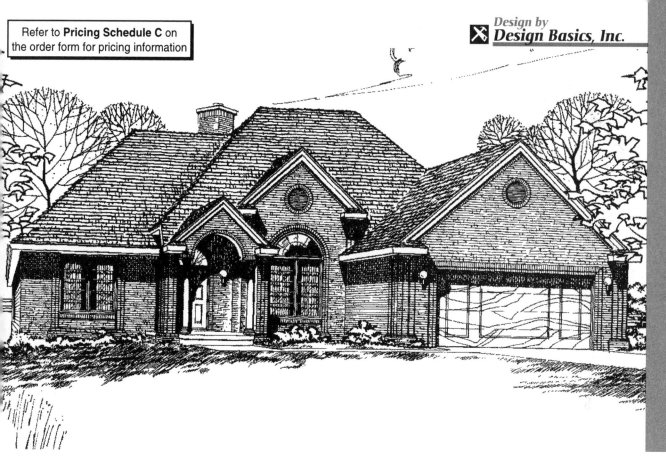

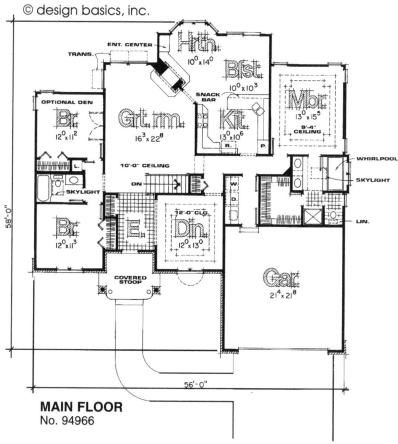

© design basics, inc.

MAIN FLOOR
No. 94966

58'-0"

56'-0"

Beautiful Arched Window

- This plan features:
- —Three bedrooms
- —Two full baths
- Ten foot ceilings top the Entry and the Great Room
- Breakfast Room and Hearth Room are in an open layout and share a see-through fireplace
- Built-in Pantry and corner sinks enhance efficiency in the Kitchen
- Split Bedroom plan assures homeowner's privacy in the Master Suite which includes a decorative ceiling, private Bath and large walk-in closet
- Two additional Bedrooms at the opposite side of the home share a full, skylit Bath in the hall

MAIN FLOOR — 1,911 SQ. FT.
GARAGE — 481 SQ. FT.

TOTAL LIVING AREA:
1,911 SQ. FT.

Design by
Frank Betz Associates, Inc.

Refer to **Pricing Schedule A** on the order form for pricing information

Open Spaces

■ This plan features:

— Three bedrooms

— Two full baths

■ Open floor plan between the Family Room and the Dining Room

■ Vaulted ceilings adding volume and a fireplace in the Family Room

■ Three Bedrooms, the Master Suite with a five-piece private Bath

■ Convenient Laundry center located outside the Bedrooms

■ No materials list is available for this plan

MAIN FLOOR — 1,135 SQ. FT.
GARAGE — 460 SQ. FT.

TOTAL LIVING AREA:
1,135 SQ. FT.

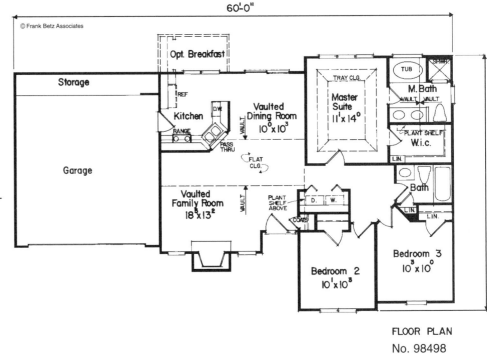

© Frank Betz Associates

60'-0"

Opt. Breakfast

Storage

REF

Kitchen

DW

RANGE

PASS THRU

Vaulted Dining Room
10⁰ x 10³

Garage

FLAT CLG.

Vaulted Family Room
18 x 13²

PLANT SHELF ABOVE

COATS

D. W.

TRAY CLG.

Master Suite
11' x 14⁰

TUB

M. Bath

VAULT VAULT

PLANT SHELF

W.i.c.

LIN.

Bath

LIN. LIN.

Bedroom 2
10' x 10³

Bedroom 3
10³ x 10⁰

FLOOR PLAN
No. 98498

To order your Blueprints, call 1-800-235-5700

WHEELCHAIR BATH
(OPT.)

Stone and Siding

- ■ This plan features:
- — Four bedrooms
- — Three full and one half baths
- ■ Attractive styling and a covered Porch create curb appeal
- ■ Formal Foyer giving access to the Bedroom wing, Library or Activity Room
- ■ Activity Room showcases a focal point fireplace
- ■ Breakfast Room is topped by a vaulted ceiling
- ■ A snack bar/peninsula counter highlights the Kitchen which also contains a built-in Pantry
- ■ Master Suite topped by a tray ceiling and pampered by five-piece Bath

MAIN FLOOR — 2,690 SQ. FT.
BASEMENT — 2,690 SQ. FT.
GARAGE — 660 SQ. FT.
DECK — 252 SQ. FT.

TOTAL LIVING AREA:
2,690 SQ. FT.

MAIN FLOOR
No. 94810

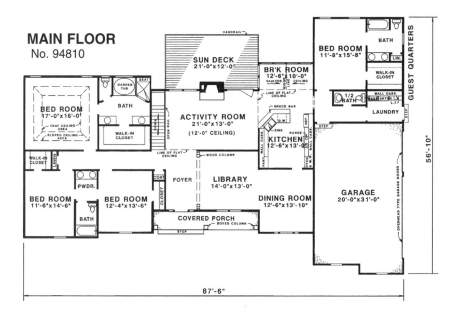

Design by
Vaughn A. Lauban Designs

Refer to **Pricing Schedule D** on the order form for pricing information

Columned Keystone Arched Entry

■ This plan features:

   Three bedrooms

   Two full baths

■ Keystone arches and arched transoms above the windows

■ Formal Dining Room and Study flank the Foyer

■ Fireplace in Great Room

■ Efficient Kitchen with a peninsula counter and bayed Nook

■ A step ceiling in the Master Suite and interesting master bath with a triangular area for the oval bath tub

■ The secondary Bedrooms share a full Bath in the hall.

MAIN FLOOR   2,256 SQ. FT.
GARAGE   514 SQ. FT.

TOTAL LIVING AREA:
   2,256 SQ. FT.

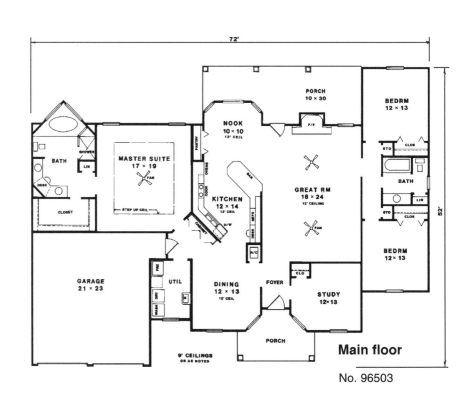

No. 96503

Design by
Frank Betz Associates, Inc.

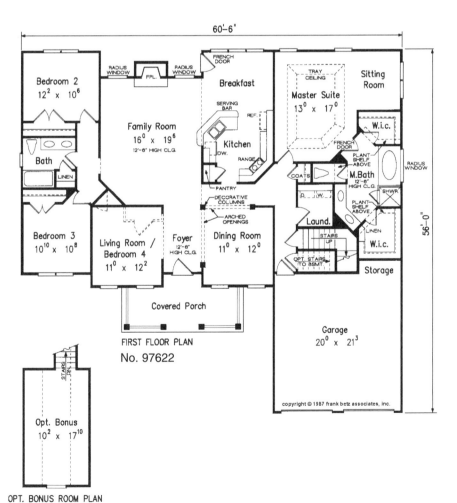

FIRST FLOOR PLAN
No. 97622

60'-6"

56'-0"

Bedroom 2
12² x 10⁶

RADIUS WINDOW

FPL.

RADIUS WINDOW

FRENCH DOOR

Breakfast

Family Room
16⁰ x 19⁶
12'-6" HIGH CLG.

SERVING BAR

REF.

Kitchen

DW.

RANGE

PANTRY

Bath

LINEN

DECORATIVE COLUMNS

ARCHED OPENINGS

Bedroom 3
10¹⁰ x 10⁸

Living Room /
Bedroom 4
11⁰ x 12²

Foyer
12'-6"
HIGH CLG.

Dining Room
11⁰ x 12⁰

COATS

Laund.

STAIRS UP

OPT. STAIRS TO BSMT.

Covered Porch

TRAY CEILING

Master Suite
13⁰ x 17⁰

Sitting Room

W.i.c.

FRENCH DOOR

PLANT SHELF ABOVE

M.Bath
12'-6" HIGH CLG.

SHWR.

PLANT SHELF ABOVE

LINEN

W.i.c.

RADIUS WINDOW

Storage

Garage
20⁰ x 21³

copyright © 1987 frank betz associates, inc.

Opt. Bonus
10² x 17¹⁰

STAIRS

OPT. BONUS ROOM PLAN

Stately Front Porch with Columns

▪ This plan features:

— Three bedrooms

— Two full baths

▪ Tray ceiling crowning Master Bedroom highlighted by a Sitting Room

▪ Arched openings accented by columns accessing the formal Dining Room

▪ Efficient Kitchen with built-in Pantry and peninsula serving bar

▪ An optional basement or crawl space foundation — please specify when ordering

▪ No materials list is available for this plan

MAIN FLOOR — 2,056 SQ. FT.
GARAGE — 454 SQ. FT.
BONUS — 208 SQ. FT.
BASEMENT — 2,056 SQ. FT.

TOTAL LIVING AREA:
2,056 SQ. FT.

Design by
Studer Residential Design, Inc.

Back Yard Views

■ This plan features:

— Three bedrooms

— Two full baths

■ Front Porch accesses open Foyer, and spacious Dining Room and Great Room with sloped ceilings

■ Corner fireplace, windows and atrium door to Patio enhance Great Room

■ Convenient Kitchen with a pantry, peninsula serving counter for bright Breakfast Area and nearby Laundry/Garage entry

■ Luxurious Bath, walk-in closet and backyard view offered in Master Bedroom

■ No materials list is available for this plan

MAIN FLOOR — 1,746 SQ. FT.
GARAGE — 480 SQ. FT.
BASEMENT — 1,697 SQ. FT.

TOTAL LIVING AREA:
1,746 SQ. FT.

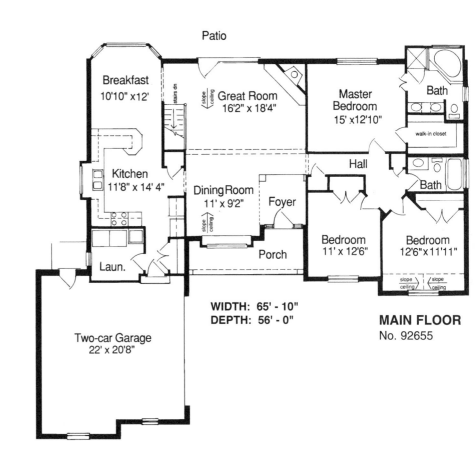

WIDTH: 65' - 10"
DEPTH: 56' - 0"

MAIN FLOOR
No. 92655

Design by
Frank Betz Associates, Inc.

PLAN NO. 98479

52'-0"

52'-6"

TRAY CLG.

Master Suite
14⁰ x 15⁰

FRENCH DOOR

Vaulted
M.Bath

SHWR.

LINEN

W.i.c.

W.   D.

PLANT SHELF
ABOVE

DESK

Vaulted
Breakfast

PANTRY

REF.

Kitchen

RANGE

D.W.

PLANT
SHELF
ABOVE

PASS
THRU

FRENCH
DOOR

FPL.

VAULT

Vaulted
Family Room
15⁰ x 21²
15'-8" HIGH CLG.

ARCHED
OPENINGS

Vaulted
Dining Room
11⁶ x 11⁴
15'-8" HIGH
CLG.

VLT.

VLT.

Foyer
15'-8" HIGH CLG.

Covered
Porch

Bedroom 2
11⁶ x 11³

LIN.

Bath

COATS

Bedroom 3
11⁶ x 11⁰

Garage
19⁵ x 20⁹

copyright © 1995 frank betz associates, inc.

GARAGE LOCATION WITH BASEMENT

No. 98479
FLOOR PLAN

SHWR.

LINEN

W.i.c.

STAIRS
DN.

W.

D.

Laun.

Garage
19⁵ x 20⁹

Opt. Basement Stair Location

Attention to Details

■ This plan features:

— Three bedrooms

— Two full baths

■ Foyer, Family Room and Dining Room have 15'8" ceilings

■ Arched openings to the Dining Room from the Family Room and Foyer

■ Split Bedroom floor plan, affording additional privacy to the Master Suite

■ Master Suite enhanced by a tray ceiling, a five-piece Master Bath and a walk-in closet

■ An optional basement or crawl space foundation — please specify when ordering

■ No materials list is available for this plan

MAIN FLOOR — 1,575 SQ. FT
BASEMENT — 1,612 SQ. FT.
GARAGE — 456 SQ. FT.

TOTAL LIVING AREA:
1,575 SQ. FT.

Design by
Ahmann Design, Inc.

Refer to **Pricing Schedule B** on
the order form for pricing information

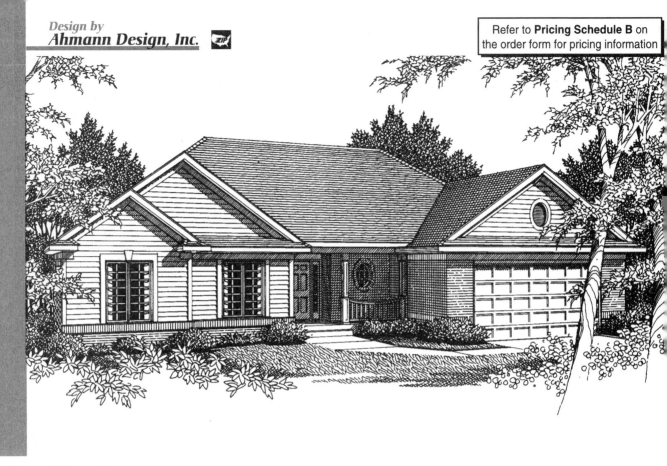

Hip Roof Ranch

■ This plan features:

— Three bedrooms

— Two full baths

■ Cozy front Porch leads into Entry with vaulted ceiling and sidelights

■ Open Living Room enhanced by a cathedral ceiling, a wall of windows and corner fireplace

■ Large and efficient Kitchen with an extended counter and a bright Dining Area with access to screen Porch

■ Convenient Utility Area with access to Garage and Storage Area

■ Spacious Master Bedroom with a walk-in closet and private Bath

■ No materials list is available for this plan

MAIN FLOOR — 1,540 SQ. FT.
BASEMENT — 1,540 SQ. FT.

TOTAL LIVING AREA:
1,540 SQ. FT.

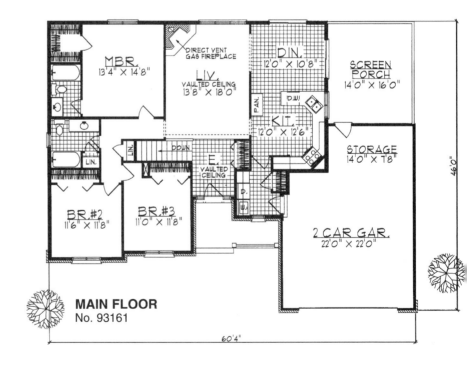

MAIN FLOOR
No. 93161

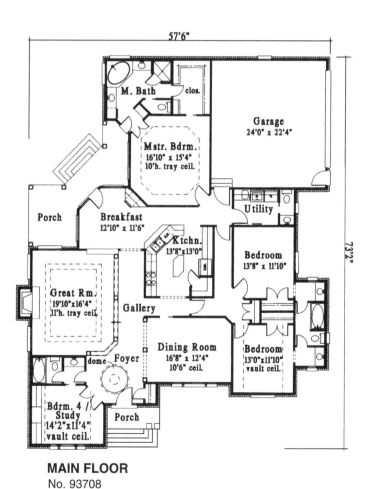

MAIN FLOOR
No. 93708

Tailored for a View to the Side

■ This plan features:

— Three/Four bedrooms

— Three full and one half baths

■ Entry Foyer highlighted by a ceiling dome and French doors leading to the private Study

■ Elegant formal Dining Room with a high ceiling, columns and arched entrance

■ Sunken Great Room with a high tray ceiling, arched openings with columns and a fireplace

■ An island and walk-in Pantry add to the Kitchen's efficiency

■ A tray ceiling and lavish Bath pamper the owner in the Master Suite

■ No materials list is available for this plan

MAIN FLOOR — 2,579 SQ. FT.
GARAGE — 536 SQ. FT.

TOTAL LIVING AREA:
2,579 SQ. FT.

Design by
Larry E. Belk

Refer to **Pricing Schedule A** on the order form for pricing information

© Larry E. Belk

For First Time Buyers

■ This plan features:

— Three bedrooms

— Two full baths

■ An efficiently designed Kitchen with a corner sink and ample counter space

■ A sunny Breakfast Room with a convenient hide-away Laundry Center

■ An expansive Family Room that includes a corner fireplace and direct access to the Patio

■ A private Master Suite with a walk-in closet and a double vanity Bath

■ No materials list is available for this plan

MAIN FLOOR — 1,310 SQ. FT.
GARAGE — 449 SQ. FT.

TOTAL LIVING AREA:
1,310 SQ. FT.

WIDTH 49–10

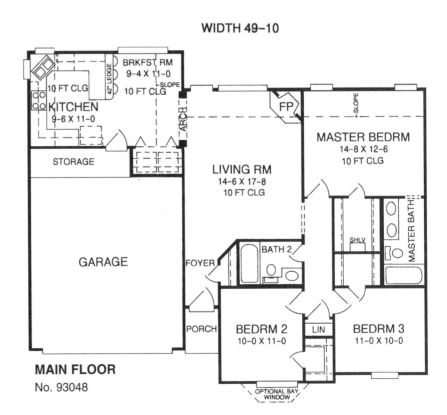

DEPTH 40–6

MAIN FLOOR
No. 93048

To order your Blueprints, call 1-800-235-5700

Design by
Frank Betz Associates, Inc.

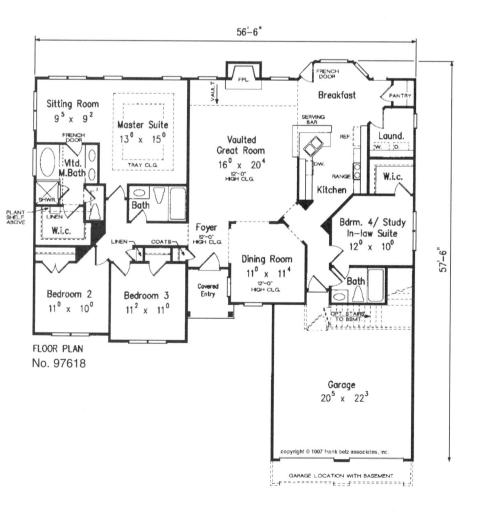

56'-6"

57'-6"

Sitting Room
9⁵ x 9²

Master Suite
13⁰ x 15⁰
TRAY CLG.

Mtd. M.Bath

Bath

W.i.c.

PLANT SHELF ABOVE

LINEN

Bedroom 2
11⁰ x 10⁰

Bedroom 3
11² x 11⁰

LINEN   COATS

Foyer
12'-0" HIGH CLG.

Covered Entry

Dining Room
11⁰ x 11⁴
12'-0" HIGH CLG.

FPL

VAULT

FRENCH DOOR

Breakfast

PANTRY

SERVING BAR

Vaulted Great Room
16⁰ x 20⁴
12'-0" HIGH CLG.

REF

Laund.
W. D.

Kitchen
RANGE

W.i.c.

Bdrm. 4/ Study In-law Suite
12⁰ x 10⁰

Bath

OPT. STAIRS TO BSMT.

FLOOR PLAN
No. 97618

Garage
20⁵ x 22³

copyright © 1997 frank betz associates, inc.

GARAGE LOCATION WITH BASEMENT

Exquisite Master Suite

■ This plan features:

— Four Bedrooms

— Three full baths

■ Formal Foyer with a convenient coat closet

■ Vaulted ceiling over the Great Room highlighted by a fireplace flanked by windows

■ Cozy Breakfast Bay with French door to rear yard

■ In-law Suite highlighted by walk-in closet and full Bath in close proximity

■ Master Suite pampered by private Sitting Room and luxurious Master Bath

■ An optional basement or crawl space foundation — please specify when ordering

MAIN FLOOR — 1,915 SQ. FT.
GARAGE — 489 SQ. FT.
BASEMENT — 1,932 SQ. FT.

TOTAL LIVING AREA:
1,915 SQ. FT.

Design by
Corley Plan Service 🗙

Refer to **Pricing Schedule A** on the order form for pricing information

No Wasted Space

■ This plan features:

— Three bedrooms

— Two full baths

■ A centrally located Great Room with a cathedral ceiling, exposed wood beams, and large areas of fixed glass

■ The Living and Dining areas separated by a massive stone fireplace

■ A secluded Master Suite with a walk-in closet and private Master Bath

■ An efficient Kitchen with a convenient Laundry Area

■ An optional basement, slab or crawl space foundation — please specify when ordering

MAIN AREA — 1,454 SQ. FT.

TOTAL LIVING AREA:
1,454 SQ. FT.

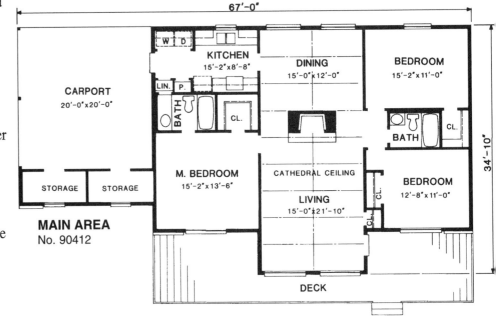

To order your Blueprints, call 1-800-235-5700

Design by
Donald A. Gardner Architects, Inc.

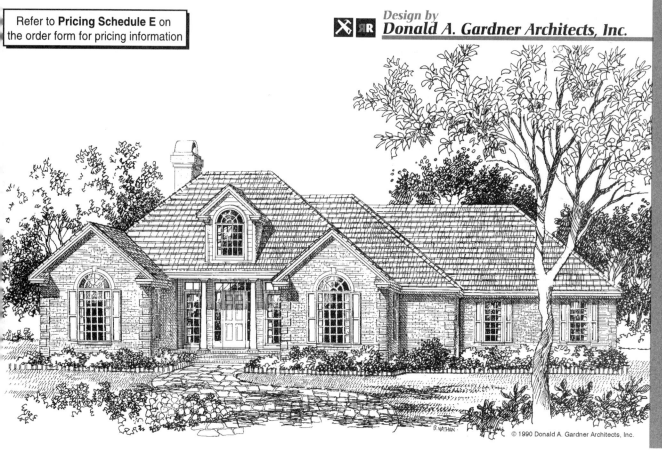

© 1990 Donald A. Gardner Architects, Inc.

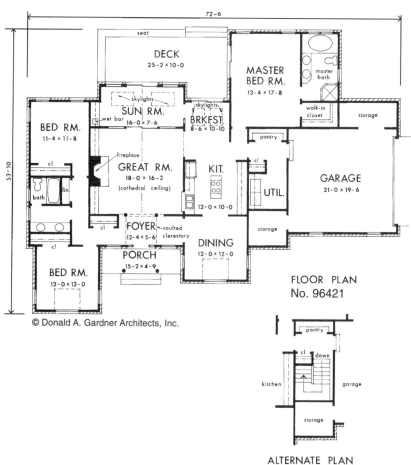

72-6

DECK
25-2 × 10-0

seat

MASTER BED RM.
13-4 × 17-8

master bath

walk-in closet

storage

BED RM.
11-4 × 11-8

skylights

SUN RM.
16-0 × 7-6

wet bar

BRKFST.
8-6 × 10-10

skylights

pantry

fireplace

GREAT RM.
18-0 × 16-2
(cathedral ceiling)

KIT.
12-0 × 10-0

cl

UTIL.

GARAGE
21-0 × 19-6

53-10

bath

lin.

cl

FOYER
12-4 × 5-6

vaulted clerestory

storage

DINING
12-0 × 12-0

cl

BED RM.
12-0 × 12-0

PORCH
15-2 × 4-9

FLOOR PLAN
No. 96421

© Donald A. Gardner Architects, Inc.

pantry

cl down

kitchen

garage

storage

ALTERNATE PLAN
FOR BASEMENT

French Influenced One-Story

■ This plan features:

— Three bedrooms

— Two full baths

■ Elegant details and arched windows, round columns and rich brick veneer

■ Arched clerestory window in the foyer introduces natural light to a large Great Room with cathedral ceiling and built-in cabinets

■ Great Room adjoins a skylit Sun Room with a wetbar which opens onto a spacious Deck

■ Kitchen with cooking island

■ Large Master Bedroom with Deck access

■ An optional basement or crawl space foundation — please specify when ordering

MAIN FLOOR — 2,045 SQ. FT.
GARAGE & STORAGE — 563 SQ. FT.

TOTAL LIVING AREA:
2,045 SQ. FT.

Design by
James Fahy, P.E., P.C.

Refer to **Pricing Schedule C** on the order form for pricing information

Small, But Not Lacking

■ This plan features:

— Three bedrooms

— One full and one three quarter baths

■ Great Room adjoins the Dining Room for ease in entertaining

■ Kitchen highlighted by a peninsula counter/snackbar extending work space and offering convenience in serving informal meals or snacks

■ Split-bedroom plan allows for privacy in the Master Bedroom with a Bath and a walk-in closet

■ Two additional Bedrooms share the full family Bath in the hall

■ Garage entry convenient to the Kitchen

MAIN AREA — 1,546 SQ. FT.
BASEMENT — 1,530 SQ. FT.
GARAGE — 440 SQ. FT.

TOTAL LIVING AREA:
1,546 SQ. FT.

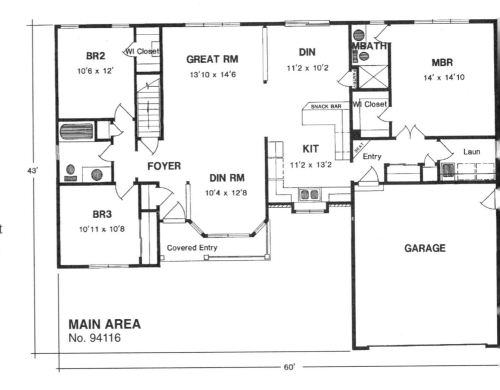

BR2
10'6 x 12'

WI Closet

GREAT RM
13'10 x 14'6

DIN
11'2 x 10'2

MBATH

MBR
14' x 14'10

SNACK BAR

WI Closet

KIT
11'2 x 13'2

FOYER

DIN RM
10'4 x 12'8

Entry

Laun

43'

BR3
10'11 x 10'8

GARAGE

Covered Entry

MAIN AREA
No. 94116

60'

To order your Blueprints, call 1-800-235-5700

Design by
Jannis Vann & Associates, Inc.

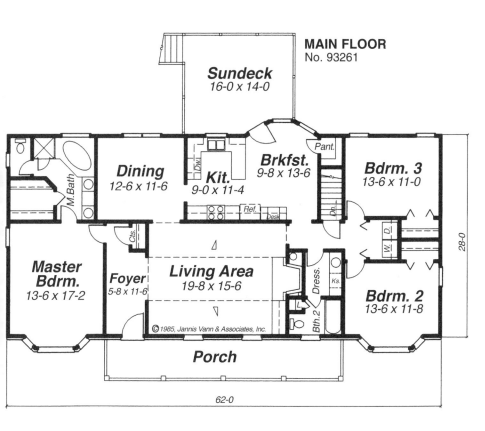

MAIN FLOOR
No. 93261

Sundeck
16-0 x 14-0

Pant.

Dining
12-6 x 11-6

Kit.
9-0 x 11-4

Brkfst.
9-8 x 13-6

Bdrm. 3
13-6 x 11-0

Ref.

Desk

M. Bath

Cts.

Master Bdrm.
13-6 x 17-2

Foyer
5-8 x 11-6

Living Area
19-8 x 15-6

Dress.

Bth. 2

Ks.

W. D.

Bdrm. 2
13-6 x 11-8

© 1985, Jannis Vann & Associates, Inc.

Porch

62-0

28-0

Bay Windows and a Terrific Front Porch

■ This plan features:

— Three bedrooms

— Two full baths

■ A Country style front Porch

■ An expansive Living Area that includes a fireplace

■ A Master Suite with a private Master Bath and a walk-in closet, as well as a bay window view of the front yard

■ An efficient Kitchen that serves the sunny Breakfast Area and the Dining Room with equal ease

■ A built-in Pantry and a desk add to the conveniences in the Breakfast Area

■ A convenient main floor Laundry Room

MAIN FLOOR — 1,778 SQ. FT.
BASEMENT — 1,008 SQ. FT.
GARAGE — 728 SQ. FT.

TOTAL LIVING AREA:
1,778 SQ. FT.

Design by
Fillmore Design Group

Refer to **Pricing Schedule B** on
the order form for pricing information

Brilliance in Brick and Fieldstone

■ This plan features:

— Three bedrooms

— Two full baths

■ Stately appearance of entrance and arched windows gives style to modest plan

■ Hub of home is Great Room opening to Study/Formal Dining Area, covered Patio and Dining/Kitchen

■ An efficient Kitchen features a pantry, serving ledge and bright Dining Area

■ Master Bedroom wing offers access to covered Patio, a huge walk-in closet and a whirlpool Bath

■ No materials list is available for this plan

MAIN FLOOR — 1,640 SQ. FT.
GARAGE — 408 SQ. FT.

TOTAL LIVING AREA:
1,640 SQ. FT.

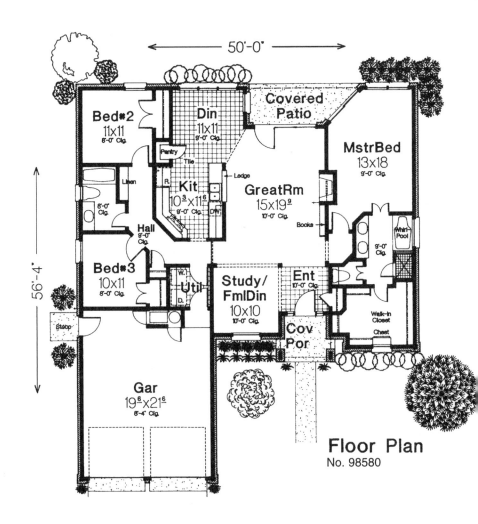

Floor Plan
No. 98580

To order your Blueprints, call 1-800-235-5700

Design by
Wesplan Building Design

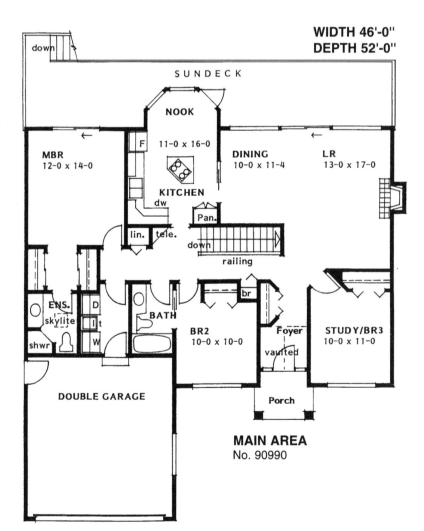

WIDTH 46'-0"
DEPTH 52'-0"

SUNDECK

NOOK

MBR
12-0 x 14-0

F

11-0 x 16-0

DINING
10-0 x 11-4

LR
13-0 x 17-0

KITCHEN
dw

Pan.

lin. tele.

down

railing

ENS.
skylite

D
lt

shwr

W

BATH

br

BR2
10-0 x 10-0

Foyer
vaulted

STUDY/BR3
10-0 x 11-0

DOUBLE GARAGE

Porch

MAIN AREA
No. 90990

Comfort and Style

■ This plan features:

— Two bedrooms with possible third bedroom/den

— One full and one three quarter baths

■ An unfinished daylight basement, providing possible space for family recreation

■ A Master Suite complete with private Bath and skylight

■ A large Kitchen including an eating Nook

■ A Sun Deck that is easily accessible from the Master Suite, Nook and the Living/Dining Area

MAIN AREA — 1,423 SQ. FT.
BASEMENT — 1,423 SQ. FT.
GARAGE — 399 SQ. FT.

TOTAL LIVING AREA:
1,423 SQ. FT.

Design by
Jannis Vann & Associates, Inc.

Refer to **Pricing Schedule A** on the order form for pricing information

For an Established Neighborhood

■ This plan features:

— Three bedrooms

— Two full baths

■ A Living Room enhanced by natural light streaming in from the large front window

■ A bayed formal Dining Room with direct access to the Sun Deck and the Living Room

■ An efficient, galley Kitchen

■ An informal Breakfast Room with direct access to the Sun Deck

■ A large Master Suite equipped with a walk-in closet and a full private Bath

MAIN AREA — 1,276 SQ. FT.
FINISHED STAIRCASE — 16 SQ. FT.
BASEMENT — 392 SQ. FT.
GARAGE — 728 SQ. FT.

TOTAL LIVING AREA:
1,292 SQ. FT.

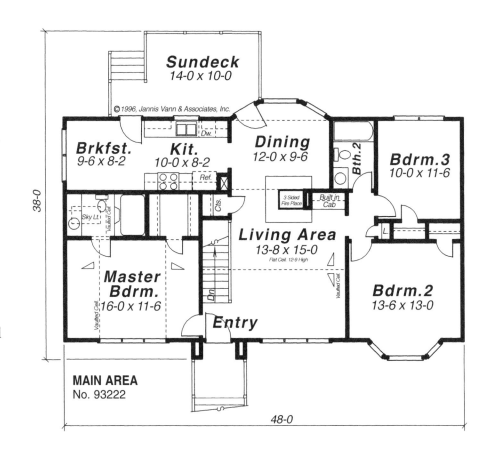

Design by
Ahmann Design, Inc.

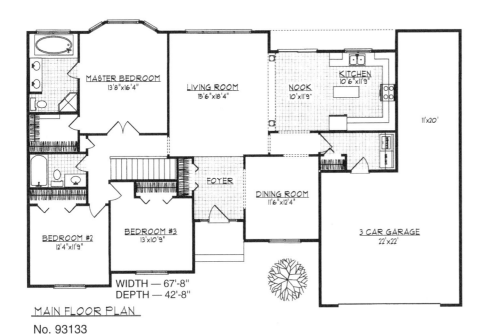

WIDTH — 67'-8"
DEPTH — 42'-8"

MASTER BEDROOM
13'8"x16'4"

LIVING ROOM
15'6"x18'4"

NOOK
10'x11'9"

KITCHEN
10'6"x11'9"

11'x20'

FOYER

DINING ROOM
11'6"x12'4"

3 CAR GARAGE
22'x22'

BEDROOM #2
12'4"x11'9"

BEDROOM #3
13'x10'9"

MAIN FLOOR PLAN
No. 93133

Triple Tandem Garage

■ This plan features:

— Three bedrooms

— Two full baths

■ A large Foyer leads to the bright and spacious Living Room

■ The open Kitchen has a central work island

■ The handy Laundry Room has a Pantry and Garage access

■ The Master Suite has a bay windowed Sitting Area and French doors, as well as a private Master Bath

■ A triple tandem garage with space for a third car, boat or just extra space

■ No materials list is available for this plan

MAIN FLOOR — 1,761 SQ. FT.
BASEMENT — 1,761 SQ. FT.
GARAGE — 658 SQ. FT.

TOTAL LIVING AREA:
1,761 SQ. FT.

Design by
Larry E. Belk

Refer to **Pricing Schedule A** on
the order form for pricing information

A Stylish, Open Concept Home

■ This plan features:

— Three bedrooms

— Two full baths

■ An angled Entry creates the illusion of space

■ Two square columns flank the bar and separate the Kitchen from the Living Room

■ The Dining Room may service both formal and informal occasions

■ The Master Bedroom has a large walk-in closet

■ The Master Bath has a dual vanity, linen closet and whirlpool tub/shower combination

■ No materials list is available for this plan

MAIN FLOOR — 1,282 SQ. FT.
GARAGE — 501 SQ. FT.

TOTAL LIVING AREA:
1,282 SQ. FT.

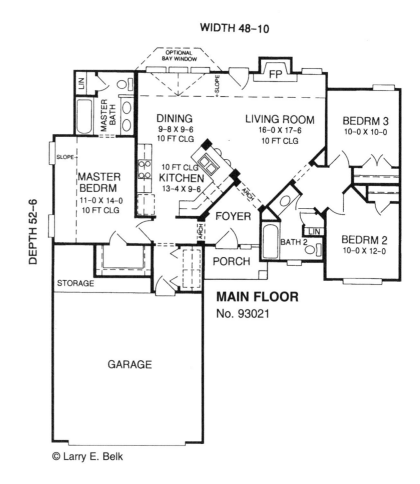

WIDTH 48-10

DEPTH 52-6

OPTIONAL BAY WINDOW

LIN

MASTER BATH

SLOPE

MASTER BEDRM
11-0 X 14-0
10 FT CLG

DINING
9-8 X 9-6
10 FT CLG

LIVING ROOM
16-0 X 17-6
10 FT CLG

FP

BEDRM 3
10-0 X 10-0

10 FT CLG
KITCHEN
13-4 X 9-6

ARCH

FOYER

ARCH

BATH 2

LIN

BEDRM 2
10-0 X 12-0

PORCH

STORAGE

MAIN FLOOR
No. 93021

GARAGE

© Larry E. Belk

To order your Blueprints, call 1-800-235-5700

Design by
Landmark Designs, Inc.

L-Shaped Front Porch

- This plan features:
— Three bedrooms
— Two full baths
- Attractive wood siding and a large L-shaped covered Porch
- Generous Living Room with a vaulted ceiling
- Large two car garage with access through Utility Room
- Kitchen highlighted by a built-in Pantry and a garden window
- Vaulted ceiling adds volume to the Dining Room
- Master Suite in isolated location enhanced by abundant closet space, separate vanity, and linen storage

MAIN FLOOR — 1,280 SQ. FT.

TOTAL LIVING AREA:
1,280 SQ. FT.

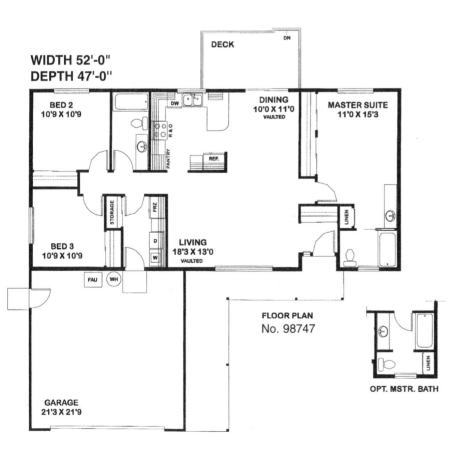

WIDTH 52'-0"
DEPTH 47'-0"

FLOOR PLAN
No. 98747

OPT. MSTR. BATH

Design by
Vaughn A. Lauban Designs

Refer to **Pricing Schedule A** on the order form for pricing information

Country Trimmings

■ This plan features:

— Three bedrooms

— Two full baths

■ A Country style Porch giving curb appeal to the exterior and extending living space

■ An L-shaped open floor plan between the Dining Room and the Great Room for a feeling of spaciousness

■ Fireplace in Great Room creating a warm atmosphere

■ Split-bedroom layout assuring the Master Suite of privacy

■ Bayed area in front Bedroom adding architectural interest

■ No material list is available for this plan

MAIN FLOOR — 1,455 SQ. FT.
GARAGE — 453 SQ. FT.

TOTAL LIVING AREA:
1,455 SQ. FT.

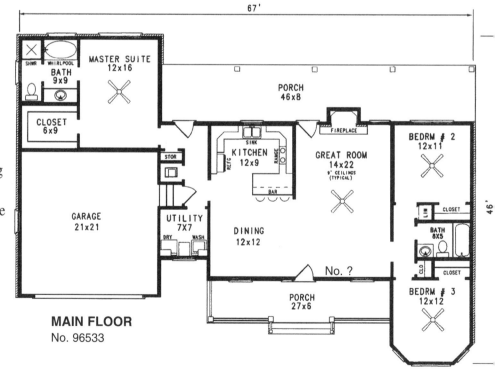

MAIN FLOOR
No. 96533

To order your Blueprints, call 1-800-235-5700

Design by
Frank Betz Associates, Inc.

PLAN NO · 98411

WIDTH 50'-4"
DEPTH 45'-0"

© Frank Betz Associates

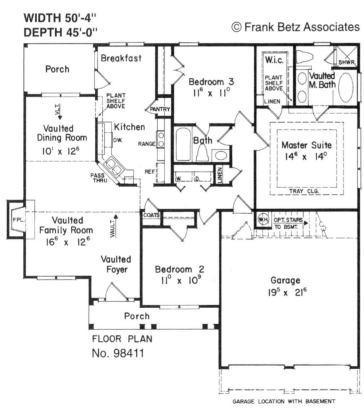

FLOOR PLAN
No. 98411

GARAGE LOCATION WITH BASEMENT

Style and Convenience

■ This plan features:

— Three bedrooms

— Two full baths

■ Large front windows, dormers
and an old-fashioned Porch add a
pleasing style

■ A Formal Dining Room flows
from the Family Room crowned
in an elegant vaulted ceiling

■ The efficient Kitchen is enhanced
by a Pantry and direct access to
the Dining Room and Breakfast
Room

■ A decorative tray ceiling, a
five-piece private Bath and a
walk-in closet in the Master Suite

■ An optional basement or crawl
space foundation — please
specify when ordering

MAIN FLOOR — 1,373 SQ. FT.
BASEMENT — 1,386 SQ. FT.

TOTAL LIVING AREA:
1,373 SQ. FT.

Design by
Fillmore Design Group

Packed with Options

▪ This plan features:

— Three bedrooms

— Three full baths

▪ This home has a tiled Entry and Gallery that connects the living space

▪ The Great Room has a rear wall fireplace that is set between windows

▪ Both Dining Areas are located steps away from the Kitchen

▪ The Study has a sloped ceiling and a front bay of windows

▪ The Master Bedroom has a private Bath and a galley-like walk- in closet

▪ No materials list is available for this plan

MAIN FLOOR — 2,081 SQ. FT.
GARAGE — 422 SQ. FT.

TOTAL LIVING AREA:
2,081 SQ. FT.

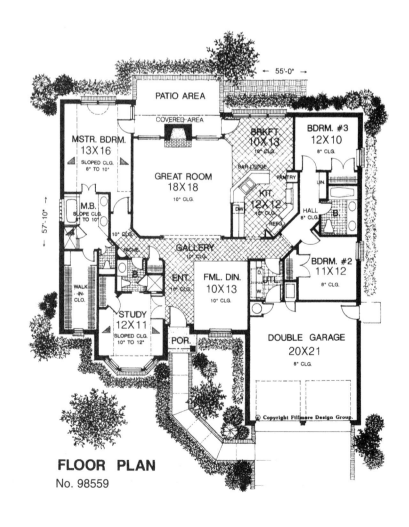

FLOOR PLAN
No. 98559

© Copyright Fillmore Design Group

Design by
Design Basics, Inc.

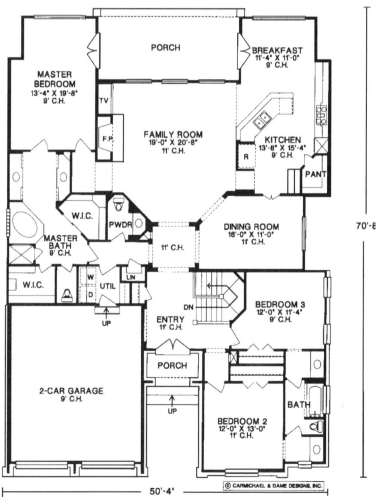

PORCH

BREAKFAST
11'-4" X 11'-0"
9' C.H.

MASTER
BEDROOM
13'-4" X 19'-8"
9' C.H.

TV

F.P.

FAMILY ROOM
19'-0" X 20'-8"
11' C.H.

KITCHEN
13'-8" X 15'-4"
9' C.H.

R

PANT

W.I.C.

PWDR

DINING ROOM
16'-0" X 11'-0"
11' C.H.

MASTER
BATH
9' C.H.

11' C.H.

70'-8

W.I.C.

W
D

UTIL

LIN

DN

BEDROOM 3
12'-0" X 11'-4"
9' C.H.

UP

ENTRY
11' C.H.

2-CAR GARAGE
9' C.H.

PORCH

UP

BEDROOM 2
12'-0" X 13'-0"
11' C.H.

BATH

50'-4"

© CARMICHAEL & DAME DESIGNS, INC.

MAIN FLOOR
No. 97446

Classic Brick Exterior

■ This plan features:

— Three bedrooms

— Two full and one half baths

■ An eleven-foot ceiling adorning the Foyer

■ Private access to the full Bath from the secondary Bedrooms

■ Central Family Room accented by a fireplace and a built in entertainment center

■ Secluded Master Suite highlighted by a lavish Master Bath

■ An angled peninsula counter/snack bar in the Kitchen extending work space

■ Rear porch with access from the Master Suite and the Breakfast Room

MAIN FLOOR — 2,404 SQ. FT.
GARAGE — 493 SQ. FT.

TOTAL LIVING AREA:
2,404 SQ. FT.

Design by
Ahmann Design, Inc.

Refer to **Pricing Schedule C** on the order form for pricing information

Beautiful and Functional

■ This plan features:

— Three bedrooms

— Two full baths

■ Gracious, keystone arch entry opens to formal Dining Room and Great Room beyond

■ Spacious Great Room features fireplace surrounded by windows topped by a cathedral ceiling

■ Kitchen/Nook layout ideal for busy household with easy access to Deck, Dining Room, Laundry and Garage

■ Corner Master Bedroom offers privacy, double vanity Bath and a huge walk-in closet

■ No materials list is available for this plan

MAIN FLOOR — 2,007 SQ. FT.
GARAGE — 748 SQ. FT.

TOTAL LIVING AREA:
2,007 SQ. FT.

WD. DECK
12'0" X 12'0"

BR. #2
12'0" X 11'8"

GRT. RM.
CATHEDRAL CLG.
16'0" X 20'0"

NK.
10'6" X 12'0"

KIT.
10'6" X 12'0"

MBR.
16'0" X 13'0"

PAN.

ARCH NICHE

DN.

BUTLER PAN.

BR. #3
12'0" X 11'0"

E.
11' 1-1/8"
CEILING HGT.

DIN.
TRAY CEILING
12'0" X 13'0"

3 CAR GAR.
34'0" X 22'0"

53'0"

67'0"

MAIN FLOOR PLAN

No. 97151

To order your Blueprints, call 1-800-235-5700

Design by
Vaughn A. Lauban Designs

Open Spaces

■ This plan features:

— Three bedrooms

— Two full baths

■ An open layout between the Living Room, Dining Room and Kitchen creating and illusion of spaciousness

■ A peninsula counter/eating bar for a quick meal separating the Kitchen from the Living Room

■ A vaulted ceiling in the Living Room adding volume to the room

■ A Laundry center located near the bedrooms for efficiency

■ No material list available for this plan

MAIN FLOOR — 1,120 SQ. FT.
GARAGE — 288 SQ. FT.

TOTAL LIVING AREA:
1,120 SQ. FT.

PATIO
10x8

D/W SINK REFG
KITCHEN
9x9

DINING
9x10

RANGE

BAR

BATH
9x5

MASTER SUITE
12x14

BATH
9x5

(OPTIONAL)
GARAGE
12x24

DRY WASH
UTILITY

LIN

A/C

CLOSET

VAULT

VAULT

LIVING ROOM
13x18

BEDRM #2
11x10

CLOSET

CLOSET

BEDRM #3
13x10

34'

PORCH
25x6

52'

MAIN FLOOR
No. 96538

Design by
Donald A. Gardner Architects, Inc.

Refer to **Pricing Schedule C** on the order form for pricing information

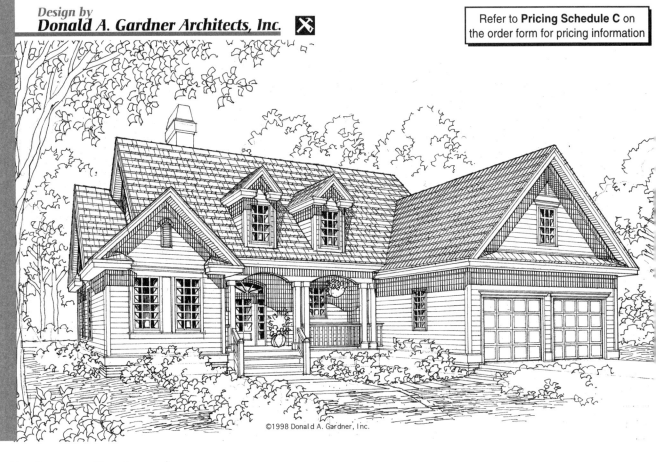

©1998 Donald A. Gardner, Inc.

Split-Bedroom Design

■ This plan features:

— Three bedrooms

— Two full baths

■ Engaging Country home starts with front Porch and leads into Great Room with cathedral ceiling above an inviting fireplace, Deck access and Dining area

■ Compact Kitchen ideal for busy cooks with loads of counter space and serving bar

■ Private Master Suite enhanced decorative ceiling, huge walk-in closet and twin vanity Bath

■ Two secondary Bedrooms with ample closets, share a full Bath in the hall

MAIN FLOOR — 1,460 SQ. FT.
GARAGE — 490 SQ. FT.

TOTAL LIVING AREA:
1,460 SQ. FT.

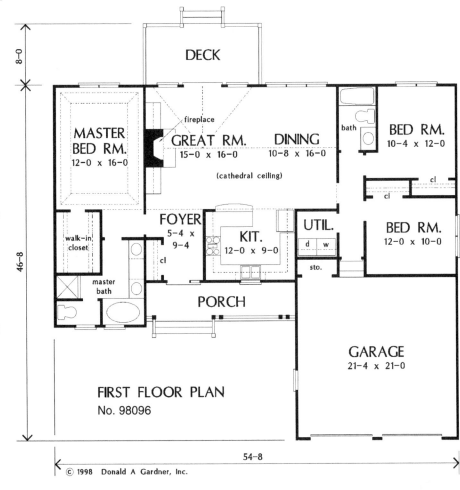

DECK

MASTER BED RM.
12-0 x 16-0

GREAT RM.
15-0 x 16-0

fireplace

DINING
10-8 x 16-0

(cathedral ceiling)

bath

BED RM.
10-4 x 12-0

cl
cl

walk-in closet

FOYER
5-4 x 9-4

KIT.
12-0 x 9-0

UTIL.

d   w

sto.

BED RM.
12-0 x 10-0

cl

master bath

PORCH

GARAGE
21-4 x 21-0

FIRST FLOOR PLAN
No. 98096

54-8

8-0

46-8

© 1998   Donald A. Gardner, Inc.

To order your Blueprints, call 1-800-235-5700

Cozy Front Porch

Design by
Design Basics, Inc.

Price Code: A

■ This plan features:
— Three bedrooms
— Two full baths

■ Terrific Great Room with twelve-foot ceiling and fireplace flanked by windows

■ Kitchen/Breakfast Room with ample counter space and storage

■ Laundry Room doubles as a Mudroom

■ The Master bedroom includes a private, double vanity Bath and a walk-in closet

■ The two additional Bedrooms are in close proximity to the full Bath in the hall.

MAIN FLOOR — 1,433 SQ. FT.
GARAGE — 504 SQ. FT.

TOTAL LIVING AREA:
1,433 SQ. FT.

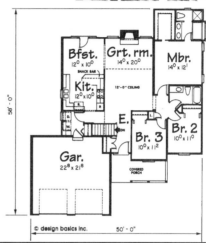

Four Bedroom

Design by
Garrell Associates, Inc.

Price Code: B

■ This plan features:
— Four bedrooms
— Two full baths

■ A vaulted ceiling of the Foyer with convenient coat closet

■ A vaulted ceiling crowning the Family Room with a French door to the rear yard and a cozy fireplace

■ Efficient Kitchen located between the formal and informal dining areas for ease in serving

■ Tray ceiling topping the Master Bedroom and a vaulted ceiling crowning the Master Bath

■ Secondary Bedrooms located near the full Bath in the hall with a window seat accenting one Bedroom and a vaulted ceiling highlighting another

■ An optional basement, slab or crawl space foundation — please specify when ordering

■ No materials list is available for this plan

MAIN FLOOR — 1,688 SQ. FT.
BASEMENT — 1,702 SQ. FT.
GARAGE — 402 SQ. FT.

TOTAL LIVING AREA:
1,688 SQ. FT.

Design by
Donald A. Gardner Architects, Inc.

Refer to **Pricing Schedule D** on
the order form for pricing information

Stunning Stone and Stucco

■ This plan features:

— Three bedrooms

— Two full baths

■ Unusual gable detailing compliments this design and the grand fieldstone entrance

■ Expansive Great Room offers a cathedral ceiling, fireplace nestled between book shelves and access to Deck, Dining Area and screen Porch

■ Efficient Kitchen with curved serving counter and Pantry easily accesses Breakfast and Dining Areas, and Utility and Garage

■ Comfortable Master Bedroom suite with Deck access, walk-in closet and plush Bath

MAIN FLOOR — 1,933 SQ. FT.
GARAGE — 526 SQ. FT.

TOTAL LIVING AREA:
1,933 SQ. FT.

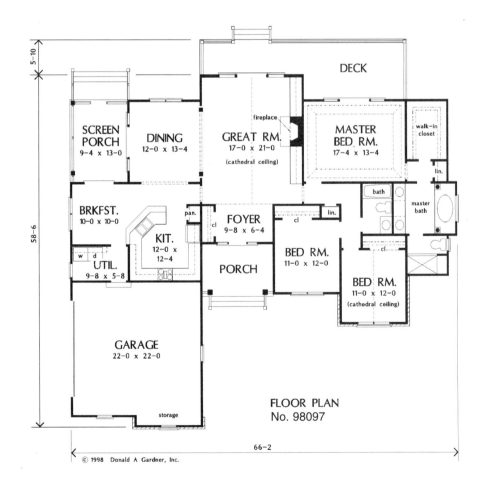

DECK

SCREEN PORCH
9-4 x 13-0

DINING
12-0 x 13-4

GREAT RM.
17-0 x 21-0
(cathedral ceiling)

fireplace

MASTER BED. RM.
17-4 x 13-4

walk-in closet

BRKFST.
10-0 x 10-0

KIT.
12-0 x 12-4

pan.

FOYER
9-8 x 6-4

cl

lin.

bath

master bath

lin.

w d

UTIL.
9-8 x 5-8

PORCH

BED RM.
11-0 x 12-0

cl

BED RM.
11-0 x 12-0
(cathedral ceiling)

GARAGE
22-0 x 22-0

storage

FLOOR PLAN
No. 98097

5-10

58-6

66-2

© 1998 Donald A Gardner, Inc.

Design by
Frank Betz Associates, Inc.

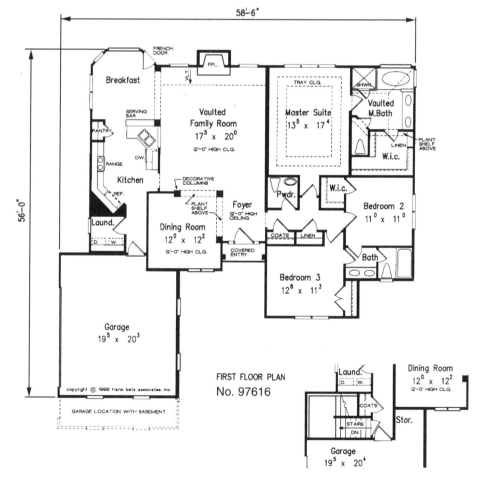

FIRST FLOOR PLAN
No. 97616

copyright © 1996 frank betz associates, inc.

GARAGE LOCATION WITH BASEMENT

OPT. BASEMENT STAIR LOCATION

Attention to Detail

■ This plan features:

— Three bedrooms

— Two full and one half baths

■ A twelve-foot ceiling, large window and decorative columns highlight the elegant Dining Room

■ Vaulted ceiling tops the Family Room, which is further accented by a fireplace

■ A tray ceiling tops the Master Bedroom and a vaulted ceiling crowns the Master Bath

■ An optional basement or crawl space foundation — please specify when ordering

■ No material list is available for this plan

MAIN FLOOR — 1,861 SQ. FT.
GARAGE — 450 SQ. FT.
BASEMENT — 1,898 SQ. FT.

TOTAL LIVING AREA:
1,861 SQ. FT.

Design by
Frank Betz Associates, Inc.

Eye-Catching Dining Room

Price Code: A

- This plan features:
  — Three bedrooms
  — Two full baths
- Two-story window allows for streaming sunlight to enter the Dining Room
- Crowning vaulted ceiling over the Great Room
- Tray ceiling highlighting the Master Bedroom and a vaulted ceiling over the Master Bath
- French door from the Breakfast Room leading to the rear yard
- Laundry Center located at the end of the Breakfast Room
- An optional basement or crawl space foundation — please specify when ordering
- No materials list is available for this plan

MAIN FLOOR — 1,271 SQ. FT.
BASEMENT — 1,292 SQ. FT.
GARAGE — 400 SQ. FT.

TOTAL LIVING AREA:
1,271 SQ. FT.

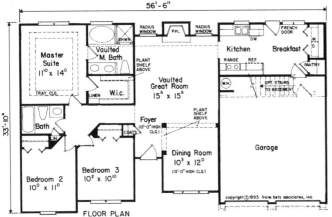

56'-6"

33'-10"

Master Suite 11¹⁰ x 14⁰
TRAY CLG.
Bath
Vaulted M. Bath
LINEN
W.i.c.
RADIUS WINDOW
FPL.
RADIUS WINDOW
SHWR.
PLANT SHELF ABOVE
Vaulted Great Room 15⁶ x 15⁸
PLANT SHELF ABOVE
Foyer (13'-0" HIGH CLG.)
COATS
Bedroom 2 10⁰ x 11⁰
Bedroom 3 10² x 10¹⁰
Dining Room 10³ x 12⁰ (13'-0" HIGH CLG.)
Kitchen
RANGE
REF
W.H.
DW
FRENCH DOOR
W. D.
Breakfast
PANTRY
OPT. STAIRS TO BASEMENT
Garage
copyright ©1993 frank betz associates, inc.

FLOOR PLAN

Design by
Vaughn A. Lauban Designs

Gingerbread Trim

Price Code: B

- This plan features:
  — Three bedrooms
  — Two full baths
- The vaulted Foyer presents a terrific first impression
- A fireplace and access to the rear Porch highlight the Family Room
- A center cooktop island and a peninsula counter/snack bar add efficiency to the Kitchen
- A whirlpool Bath and a walk-in closet pamper the secluded Master Bedroom
- Front Study with closet space to easily become an additional Bedroom
- No materials list is available for this plan

MAIN FLOOR — 1,917 SQ. FT.
GARAGE — 474 SQ. FT.

TOTAL LIVING AREA:
1,917 SQ. FT.

68'

57'

MASTER SUITE 20x13
MASTER BATH 10x11
CLOSET 8x8
SHELF
WORK BENCH
GARAGE 20x22
DINING 14x14
KITCHEN 15x12 COOKTOP
BAR
FOYER 7x10
HOBBY NICHE 7x7
UTILITY 8x7
STUDY/BEDRM 4 12x10
PORCH 33x8
FAMILY ROOM 21x16 11' FLAT CEILING
BEDRM #2 12x11
CLOSET
BATH #2 8x5
CLOSET
BEDRM #3 12x13
PORCH 24x5

MAIN AREA

To order your Blueprints, call 1-800-235-5700

Decorative Ceiling Treatments

Price Code: B

- This plan features:
  — Three bedrooms
  — Two full baths
- Covered front Porch creating curb appeal and extending living space
- A tray ceiling crowning the Great Room which includes a corner fireplace and access to the rear Deck
- Dining Area open to the Kitchen with angled snack bar for meals on the go
- Split Bedroom floor plan assuring the Master Suite of privacy.
- A tray ceiling topping the Master Bedroom which has direct access to a whirlpool Master Bath

MAIN FLOOR — 1765 SQ. FT.
GARAGE — 440 SQ. FT.

TOTAL LIVING AREA:
1,765 SQ. FT.

Design by
Vaughn A. Lauban Designs

MAIN FLOOR

PLAN NO. 96534

Eye-Catching Elevation

Price Code: C

- This plan features:
  — Four bedrooms
  — Two full baths
- Expansive Great Room with a vaulted ceiling and a fireplace with windows to either side
- Arched openings accented by columns accessing the formal Dining Room
- Efficient Kitchen with built-in Pantry, serving bar and double sinks
- Tray ceiling topping the Master Bedroom and a vaulted ceiling over the luxurious Master Bath
- Super walk-in closet in Master Suite with a plant shelf
- No materials list is available for this plan

MAIN FLOOR — 2,032 SQ. FT.
BASEMENT — 1,471 SQ. FT.
GARAGE — 561 SQ. FT.

TOTAL LIVING AREA:
2,032 SQ. FT.

Design by
Frank Betz Associates, Inc.

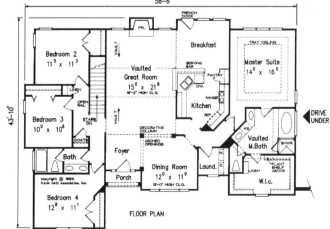

FLOOR PLAN

PLAN NO. 97619

Design by
Frank Betz Associates, Inc.

Stone and Siding

Price Code: B

■ This plan features:
— Three bedrooms
— Two full baths
■ An arched opening with decorative columns accenting the Dining Room
■ Ample cabinet and counter space with a built-in pantry and serving bar in the Kitchen
■ French door to the outdoors or an optional bay window in the Breakfast Room
■ A vaulted ceiling crowning the Great Room highlighted by a fireplace
■ Lavish Master Suite topped by a tray ceiling and pampered by a plush Master Bath

MAIN FLOOR — 1,571 SQ. FT.
BONUS — 334 SQ. FT.
BASEMENT — 1,642 SQ. FT.
GARAGE — 483 SQ. FT.

TOTAL LIVING AREA:
1,517 SQ. FT.

FIRST FLOOR PLAN

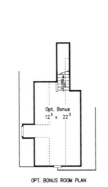

OPT. BONUS ROOM PLAN

Design by
Frank Betz Associates, Inc.

Outstanding Arched Window

Price Code: D

■ This plan features:
— Three bedrooms
— Two full and one half baths
■ An outstanding front window accents the formal Dining Room enhanced by a fourteen-foot high ceiling
■ Expansive Family Room accented a fireplace and active dormer with radius window
■ Luxurious Master Suite highlighted by a tray ceiling, private Sitting Room, and plush Master Bath
■ Formal Living Room entered through French doors and sporting a bay window
■ Efficient Kitchen including double oven, work island and built-in Pantry
■ An optional basement, crawl space, or slab foundation — please specify when ordering
■ No materials list is available for this plan

MAIN FLOOR — 2,322 SQ. FT.
BASEMENT — 2,322 SQ. FT.
GARAGE — 453 SQ. FT.

TOTAL LIVING AREA:
2,322 SQ. FT.

FLOOR PLAN

To order your Blueprints, call 1-800-235-5700

Country Styled Home

Price Code: B

- This plan features:
  — Three bedrooms
  — Two full baths
- Covered Porch shelters front entrance of home and adds to the old-fashioned appeal
- Half wall with columns separating the formal Dining Room from the Family Room
- Efficient Kitchen direct accesses the formal and informal dining areas and includes a snack bar
- A fireplace and French doors to the rear Porch accent the Family Room
- Secluded Master Suite includes a private whirlpool Bath with separate shower
- An optional crawl space or slab foundation — please specify when ordering
- No materials list is available for this plan

MAIN FLOOR — 1,926 SQ. FT.
GARAGE — 441 SQ. FT.

TOTAL LIVING AREA:
1,926 SQ. FT.

Design by
Vaughn A. Lauban Designs

MAIN FLOOR

Cute Starter Home

Price Code: B

- This plan features:
  — Three bedrooms
  — Two full bathsW
- Simple design with quality details provides charm inside and out
- Spacious Living/Dining room allows comfortable gatherings with multiple windows and outdoor access
- Open Kitchen/Nook easily accesses Dining Area, Laundry closet and Garage
- Corner Master Bedroom boasts full view of rear yard, walk-in closet and private Bath
- Two additional Bedrooms with ample closets, share a full Bath
- No materials list is available for this plan

MAIN FLOOR — 1,557 SQ. FT.
BASEMENT — 1,557 SQ. FT.
GARAGE — 400 SQ. FT.

TOTAL LIVING AREA:
1,557 SQ. FT.

Design by
Ahmann Design, Inc.

MAIN FLOOR PLAN

Everything You Need...
...to Make Your Dream Come True!

You pay only a fraction of the original cost for home designs by respected professionals.

You've Picked Your Dream Home!

You can already see it standing on your lot... you can see yourselves in your new home... enjoying family, entertaining guests, celebrating holidays. All that remains ahead are the details. That's where we can help. Whether you plan to build-it-yourself, be your own contractor, or hand your plans over to an outside contractor, your Garlinghouse blueprints provide the perfect beginning for putting yourself in your dream home right away.

We even make it simple for you to make professional design modifications. We can also provide a materials list for greater economy.

For over 90 years, homeowners and builders have relied on us for accurate, complete, professional blueprints. Our plans help you get results fast... and save money, too! These pages will give you all the information you need to order. So get started now... I know you'll love your new Garlinghouse home!

EXTERIOR ELEVATIONS

Elevations are scaled drawings of the front, rear, left and right sides of a home. All of the necessary information pertaining to the exterior finish materials, roof pitches and exterior height dimensions of your home are defined.

CABINET PLANS

These plans, or in some cases elevations, will detail the layout of the kitchen and bathroom cabinets at a larger scale. This gives you an accurate layout for your cabinets or an ideal starting point for a modified custom cabinet design. Available for most plans in our collection. You may also show the floor plan without a cabinet layout. This will allow you to start from scratch and design your own dream kitchen.

TYPICAL WALL SECTION

This section is provided to help your builder understand the structural components and materials used to construct the exterior walls of your home. This section will address insulation, roof components, and interior and exterior wall finishes. Your plans will be designed with either 2x4 or 2x6 exterior walls, but most professional contractors can easily adapt the plans to the wall thickness you require. Available for most plans in our collection.

FIREPLACE DETAILS

If the home you have chosen includes a fireplace, the fireplace detail will show typical methods to construct the firebox, hearth and flue chase for masonry units, or a wood frame chase for a zero-clearance unit. Available for most plans in our collection.

FOUNDATION PLAN

These plans will accurately dimension the footprint of your home including load bearing points and beam placement if applicable. The foundation style will vary from plan to plan. Your local climatic conditions will dictate whether a basement, slab or crawlspace is best suited for your area. In most cases, if your plan comes with one foundation style, a professional contractor can easily adapt the foundation plan to an alternate style.

ROOF PLAN

The information necessary to construct the roof will be included with your home plans. Some plans will reference roof trusses, while many others contain schematic framing plans. These framing plans will indicate the lumber sizes necessary for the rafters and ridgeboards based on the designated roof loads.

TYPICAL CROSS SECTION

A cut-away cross-section through the entire home shows your building contractor the exact correlation of construction components at all levels of the house. It will help to clarify the load bearing points from the roof all the way down to the basement.

DETAILED FLOOR PLANS

The floor plans of your home accurately dimension the positioning of all walls, doors, windows, stairs and permanent fixtures. They will show you the relationship and dimensions of rooms, closets and traffic patterns. The schematic of the electrical layout may be included in the plan. This layout is clearly represented and does not hinder the clarity of other pertinent information shown. All these details will help your builder properly construct your new home.

STAIR DETAILS

If stairs are an element of the design you have chosen, the plans will show the necessary information to build these, either through a stair cross section, or on the floor plans. Either way, the information provides your builders the essential reference points that they need to build the stairs.

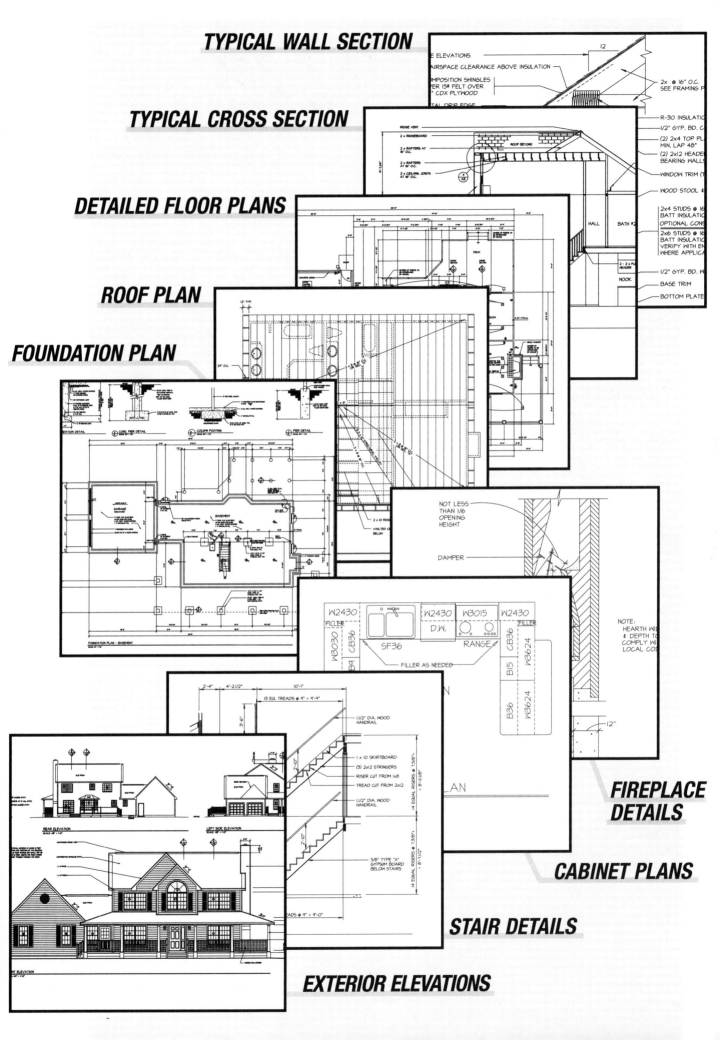

TYPICAL WALL SECTION

TYPICAL CROSS SECTION

DETAILED FLOOR PLANS

ROOF PLAN

FOUNDATION PLAN

FIREPLACE DETAILS

CABINET PLANS

STAIR DETAILS

EXTERIOR ELEVATIONS

Garlinghouse Options & Extras ...Make Your Dream A Home

Reversed Plans Can Make Your Dream Home Just Right!

"That's our dream home...if only the garage were on the other side!"

You could have exactly the home you want by flipping it end-for-end. Check it out by holding your dream home page of this book up to a mirror. Then simply order your plans "reversed." We'll send you one full set of mirror-image plans (with the writing backwards) as a master guide for you and your builder.

The remaining sets of your order will come as shown in this book so the dimensions and specifications are easily read on the job site...but most plans in our collection come stamped "REVERSED" so there is no construction confusion.

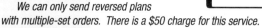
As Shown   Reversed

We can only send reversed plans with multiple-set orders. There is a $50 charge for this service.

Some plans in our collection are available in Right Reading Reverse. Right Reading Reverse plans will show your home in reverse, with the writing on the plan being readable. This easy-to-read format will save you valuable time and money. Please contact our Customer Service Department at (860) 343-5977 to check for Right Reading Reverse availability. (For this service there is a $150 charge for plan series 998', 964', 980' and $125 for all other plans.)

Specifications & Contract Form

We send this form to you free of charge with your home plan order. The form is designed to be filled in by you or your contractor with the exact materials to use in the construction of your new home. Once signed by you and your contractor it will provide you with peace of mind throughout the construction process.

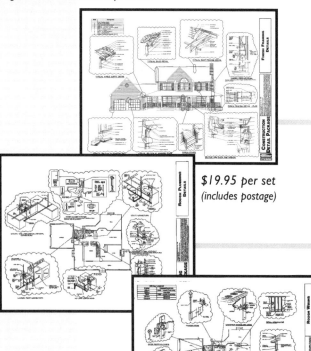

$19.95 per set
(includes postage)

Remember To Order Your Materials List

It'll help you save money. Available at a modest additional charge, the Materials List gives the quantity, dimensions, and specifications for the major materials needed to build your home. You will get faster, more accurate bids from your contractors and building suppliers — and avoid paying for unused materials and waste. Materials Lists are available for all home plans except as otherwise indicated, but can only be ordered with a set of home plans. Due to differences in regional requirements and homeowner or builder preferences... electrical, plumbing and heating/air conditioning equipment specifications are not designed specifically for each plan. However, non-plan specific detailed typical prints of residential electrical, plumbing and construction guidelines can be provided. Please see below for additional information. If you need a detailed materials cost you might need to purchase a Zip Quote. (Details follow)

Detail Plans Provide Valuable Information About Construction Techniques

Because local codes and requirements vary greatly, we recommend that you obtain drawings and bids from licensed contractors to do your mechanical plans. However, if you want to know more about techniques — and deal more confidently with subcontractors — we offer these remarkably useful detail sheets. These detail sheets will aid in your understanding of these technical subjects. **The detail sheets are not specific to any one home plan and should be used only as a general reference guide.**

RESIDENTIAL CONSTRUCTION DETAILS

Ten sheets that cover the essentials of stick-built residential home construction. Details foundation options — poured concrete basement, concrete block, or monolithic concrete slab. Shows all aspects of floor, wall and roof framing. Provides details for roof dormers, overhangs, chimneys and skylights. Conforms to requirements of Uniform Building code or BOCA code. Includes a quick index and a glossary of terms.

RESIDENTIAL PLUMBING DETAILS

Eight sheets packed with information detailing pipe installation methods, fittings, and sized. Details plumbing hook-ups for toilets, sinks, washers, sump pumps, and septic system construction. Conforms to requirements of National Plumbing code. Color coded with a glossary of terms and quick index.

RESIDENTIAL ELECTRICAL DETAILS

Eight sheets that cover all aspects of residential wiring, from simple switch wiring to service entrance connections. Details distribution panel layout with outlet and switch schematics, circuit breaker and wiring installation methods, and ground fault interrupter specifications. Conforms to requirements of National Electrical Code. Color coded with a glossary of terms.

Modifying Your Favorite Design, Made *EASY*!

OPTION #1

Modifying Your Garlinghouse Home Plan

Simple modifications to your dream home, including minor non-structural changes and material substitutions, can be made between you and your builder by marking the changes directly on your blueprints. However, if you are considering making significant changes to your chosen design, we recommend that you use the services of The Garlinghouse Co. Design Staff. We will help take your ideas and turn them into a reality, just the way you want. Here's our procedure!

When you place your Vellum order, you may also request a free Garlinghouse Modification Kit. In this kit, you will receive a red marking pencil, furniture cut-out sheet, ruler, a self addressed mailing label and a form for specifying any additional notes or drawings that will help us understand your design ideas. Mark your desired changes directly on the Vellum drawings. NOTE: Please use only a **red pencil** to mark your desired changes on the Vellum. Then, return the redlined Vellum set in the original box to The Garlinghouse Company at, 282 Main Street Extension, Middletown, CT 06457. **IMPORTANT**: Please **roll** the Vellums for shipping, **do not fold** the Vellums for shipping.

We also offer modification estimates. We will provide you with an estimate to draft your changes based on your specific modifications before you purchase the vellums, for a $50 fee. After you receive your estimate, if you decide to have The Garlinghouse Company Design Staff do the changes, the $50 estimate fee will be deducted from the cost of your modifications. If, however, you choose to use a different service, the $50 estimate fee is non-refundable. (Note: Personal checks cannot be accepted for the estimate.)

Within 5 days of receipt of your plans, you will be contacted by a member of The Garlinghouse Co. Design Staff with an estimate for the design services to draw those changes. A 50% deposit is required before we begin making the actual modifications to your plans.

Once the design changes have been completed to your vellum plan, a representative from The Garlinghouse Co. Design Staff will call to inform you that your modified Vellum plan is complete and will be shipped as soon as the final payment has been made. For additional information call us at 1-860-343-5977. Please refer to the Modification Pricing Guide for estimated modification costs. Please call for Vellum modification availability for plan numbers 85,000 and above.

OPTION #2

Reproducible Vellums for Local Modification Ease

If you decide not to use the Garlinghouse Co. Design Staff for your modifications, we recommend that you follow our same procedure of purchasing our Vellums. You then have the option of using the services of the original designer of the plan, a local professional designer, or architect to make the modifications to your plan.

With a Vellum copy of our plans, a design professional can alter the drawings just the way you want, then you can print as many copies of the modified plans as you need to build your house. And, since you have already started with our complete detailed plans, the cost of those expensive professional services will be significantly less than starting from scratch. Refer to the price schedule for Vellum costs. Again, please call for Vellum availability for plan numbers 85,000 and above.

IMPORTANT RETURN POLICY: Upon receipt of your Vellums, if for some reason you decide you do not want a modified plan, then simply return the Kit and the unopened Vellums. Reproducible Vellum copies of our home plans are copyright protected and only sold under the terms of a license agreement that you will receive with your order. Should you not agree to the terms, then the Vellums may be returned, **unopened,** for a full refund less the shipping and handling charges, plus a 15% restocking fee. For any additional information, please call us at 1-860-343-5977.

MODIFICATION PRICING GUIDE

CATEGORIES	ESTIMATED COST
KITCHEN LAYOUT — PLAN AND ELEVATION	$175.00
BATHROOM LAYOUT — PLAN AND ELEVATION	$175.00
FIREPLACE PLAN AND DETAILS	$200.00
INTERIOR ELEVATION	$125.00
EXTERIOR ELEVATION — MATERIAL CHANGE	$140.00
EXTERIOR ELEVATION — ADD BRICK OR STONE	$400.00
EXTERIOR ELEVATION — STYLE CHANGE	$450.00
NON BEARING WALLS (INTERIOR)	$200.00
BEARING AND/OR EXTERIOR WALLS	$325.00
WALL FRAMING CHANGE — 2X4 TO 2X6 OR 2X6 TO 2X4	$240.00
ADD/REDUCE LIVING SPACE — SQUARE FOOTAGE	QUOTE REQUIRED
NEW MATERIALS LIST	QUOTE REQUIRED
CHANGE TRUSSES TO RAFTERS OR CHANGE ROOF PITCH	$300.00
FRAMING PLAN CHANGES	$325.00
GARAGE CHANGES	$325.00
ADD A FOUNDATION OPTION	$300.00
FOUNDATION CHANGES	$250.00
RIGHT READING PLAN REVERSE	$575.00
ARCHITECTS SEAL (Available for most states)	$300.00
ENERGY CERTIFICATE	$150.00
LIGHT AND VENTILATION SCHEDULE	$150.00

Questions?

Call our customer service department at **1-860-343-5977**

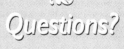

"How to obtain a construction cost calculation based on labor rates and building material costs in <u>your</u> Zip Code area!"

ZIP-QUOTE!
HOME COST CALCULATOR

ZIP QUOTE
HOME COST CALCULATOR

WHY?

Do you wish you could quickly find out the building cost for your new home without waiting for a contractor to compile hundreds of bids? Would you like to have a benchmark to compare your contractor(s) bids against? *Well, Now You Can!!,* with **Zip-Quote** Home Cost Calculator. Zip-Quote is only available for zip code areas within the United States.

HOW?

Our new **Zip-Quote** Home Cost Calculator will enable you to obtain the calculated building cost to construct your new home, based on labor rates and building material costs within your zip code area, without the normal delays or hassles usually associated with the bidding process. Zip-Quote can be purchased in two separate formats, an itemized or a bottom line format.

"How does **Zip-Quote** actually work?" When you call to order, you must choose from the options available, for your specific home, in order for us to process your order. Once we receive your **Zip-Quote** order, we process your specific home plan building materials list through our Home Cost Calculator which contains up-to-date rates for all residential labor trades and building material costs in your zip code area. "The result?" A calculated cost to build your dream home in your zip code area. This calculation will help you (as a consumer or a builder) evaluate your building budget. This is a valuable tool for anyone considering building a new home.

All database information for our calculations is furnished by Marshall & Swift, L.P. For over 60 years, Marshall & Swift L.P. has been a leading provider of cost data to professionals in all aspects of the construction and remodeling industries.

OPTION 1

The **Itemized Zip-Quote** is a detailed building material list. Each building material list line item will separately state the labor cost, material cost and equipment cost (if applicable) for the use of that building material in the construction process. Each category within the building material list will be subtotaled and the entire Itemized cost calculation totaled at the end. This building materials list will be summarized by the individual building categories and will have additional columns where you can enter data from your contractor's estimates for a cost comparison between the different suppliers and contractors who will actually quote you their products and services.

OPTION 2

The **Bottom Line Zip-Quote** is a one line summarized total cost for the home plan of your choice. This cost calculation is also based on the labor cost, material cost and equipment cost (if applicable) within your local zip code area.

COST

The price of your **Itemized Zip-Quote** is based upon the pricing schedule of the plan you have selected, in addition to the price of the materials list. Please refer to the pricing schedule on our order form. The price of your initial **Bottom Line Zip-Quote** is $29.95. Each additional **Bottom Line Zip-Quote** ordered in conjunction with the initial order is only $14.95. **Bottom Line Zip-Quote** may be purchased separately and does NOT have to be purchased in conjunction with a home plan order.

FYI

An **Itemized Zip-Quote** Home Cost Calculation can ONLY be purchased in conjunction with a Home Plan order. The **Itemized Zip-Quote** can not be purchased separately. The **Bottom Line Zip-Quote** can be purchased separately and doesn't have to be purchased in conjunction with a home plan order. Please consult with a sales representative for current availability. If you find within 60 days of your order date that you will be unable to build this home, then you may exchange the plans and the materials list towards the price of a new set of plans (see order info pages for plan exchange policy). The **Itemized Zip-Quote** and the **Bottom Line Zip-Quote** are NOT returnable. The price of the initial **Bottom Line Zip-Quote** order can be credited towards the purchase of an **Itemized Zip-Quote** order only. Additional **Bottom Line Zip-Quote** orders, within the same order can not be credited. Please call our Customer Service Department for more information.

Zip-Quote is available for plans where you see this symbol. Please call for current availability.

SOME MORE INFORMATION

The Itemized and Bottom Line Zip-Quotes give you approximated costs for constructing the particular house in your area. These costs are not exact and are only intended to be used as a preliminary estimate to help determine the affordability of a new home and/or as a guide to evaluate the general competitiveness of actual price quotes obtained through local suppliers and contractors. However, Zip-Quote cost figures should never be relied upon as the only source of information in either case. Land, sewer systems, site work, landscaping and other expenses are not included in our building cost figures. The Garlinghouse Company and Marshall & Swift L.P. can not guarantee any level of data accuracy or correctness in a Zip-Quote and disclaim all liability for loss with respect to the same, in excess of the original purchase price of the Zip-Quote product. All Zip-Quote calculations are based upon the actual blueprint materials list with options as selected by customer and do not reflect any differences that may be shown on the published house renderings, floor plans, or photographs.

Ignoring Copyright Laws Can Be
A $1,000,000 Mistake

Recent changes in the US copyright laws allow for statutory penalties of up to **$100,000** per incident for copyright infringement involving any of the copyrighted plans found in this publication. The law can be confusing. So, for your own protection, take the time to understand what you can and cannot do when it comes to home plans.

••• WHAT YOU CANNOT DO •••

You Cannot Duplicate Home Plans

Purchasing a set of blueprints and making additional sets by reproducing the original is **illegal**. If you need multiple sets of a particular home plan, then you must purchase them.

You Cannot Copy Any Part of a Home Plan to Create Another

Creating your own plan by copying even part of a home design found in this publication is called "creating a derivative work" and is **illegal** unless you have permission to do so.

You Cannot Build a Home Without a License

You must have specific permission or license to build a home from a copyrighted design, even if the finished home has been changed from the original plan. It is **illegal** to build one of the homes found in this publication without a license.

What Garlinghouse Offers

Home Plan Blueprint Package

By purchasing a multiple set package of blueprints or a vellum from Garlinghouse, you not only receive the physical blueprint documents necessary for construction, but you are also granted a license to build one, and only one, home. You can also make simple modifications, including minor non-structural changes and material substitutions, to our design, as long as these changes are made directly on the blueprints purchased from Garlinghouse and no additional copies are made.

Home Plan Vellums

By purchasing vellums for one of our home plans, you receive the same construction drawings found in the blueprints, but printed on vellum paper. Vellums can be erased and are perfect for making design changes. They are also semi-transparent making them easy to duplicate. But most importantly, the purchase of home plan vellums comes with a broader license that allows you to make changes to the design (ie, create a hand drawn or CAD derivative work), to make copies of the plan, and to build one home from the plan.

License To Build Additional Homes

With the purchase of a blueprint package or vellums you automatically receive a license to build one home and only one home, respectively. If you want to build more homes than you are licensed to build through your purchase of a plan, then additional licenses may be purchased at reasonable costs from Garlinghouse. Inquire for more information.

Order Code No. H9SL7

Order Form

Plan prices guaranteed until 08/01/00 — After this date call for updated pricing

_____ set(s) of blueprints for plan #_____ $_____

_____ Vellum & Modification kit for plan #_____ $_____

_____ Additional set(s) @ $35 each for plan #_____ $_____

_____ Mirror Image Reverse @ $50 each $_____

_____ Right Reading Reverse @ $150 each for plan series
998', 964', 980', and $125 for all other plans $_____

_____ Materials list for plan #_____ $_____

_____ Detail Plans @ $19.95 each

    ❏ Construction ❏ Plumbing ❏ Electrical $_____

_____ Bottom line ZIP Quote@$29.95 for plan #_____ $_____

_____ Additional Bottom Line Zip Quote

    @ $14.95 for plan(s) #_____

_____ $_____

_____ Itemized ZIP Quote for plan(s) #_____ $_____

Shipping (see charts on opposite page) $_____

Subtotal $_____

Sales Tax (CT residents add 6% sales tax, KS residents add
6.15% sales tax) (Not required for other states) $_____

TOTAL AMOUNT ENCLOSED $_____

Send your check, money order or credit card information to:
(No C.O.D.'s Please)

Please submit all <u>United States</u> & <u>Other Nations</u> orders to:

Garlinghouse Company
P.O. Box 1717
Middletown, CT. 06457

Please Submit all <u>Canadian</u> plan orders to:

Garlinghouse Company
60 Baffin Place, Unit #5
Waterloo, Ontario N2V 1Z7

ADDRESS INFORMATION:

NAME:_____

STREET:_____

CITY:_____

STATE:_____ **ZIP:**_____

DAYTIME PHONE:_____

Credit Card Information		
Charge To:	❏ Visa	❏ Mastercard
Card #		
Signature		Exp. ____ / ____

Payment must be made in U.S. funds. Foreign Mail Orders: Certified bank checks in U.S. funds only

IMPORTANT INFORMATION TO READ BEFORE YOU PLACE YOUR ORDER

How Many Sets Of Plans Will You Need?

The Standard 8-Set Construction Package

Our experience shows that you'll speed every step of construction and avoid costly building errors by ordering enough sets to go around. Each tradesperson wants a set — the general contractor and all subcontractors; foundation, electrical, plumbing, heating/air conditioning and framers. Don't forget your lending institution, building department and, of course, a set for yourself. * Recommended For Construction *

The Minimum 4-Set Construction Package

If you're comfortable with arduous follow-up, this package can save you a few dollars by giving you the option of passing down plan sets as work progresses. You might have enough copies to go around if work goes exactly as scheduled and no plans are lost or damaged by subcontractors. But for only $50 more, the 8-set package eliminates these worries.
* Recommended For Bidding *

The Single Study Set

We offer this set so you can study the blueprints to plan your dream home in detail. They are stamped "study set only-not for construction", and you can-not build a home from them. In pursuant to copyright laws, it is <u>illegal</u> to repro-duce any blueprint.

Our Reorder and Exchange Policies:

If you find after your initial purchase that you require additional sets of plans you may purchase them from us at special reorder prices (please call for pricing details) provided that you reorder within 6 months of your original order date. There is a $28 reorder processing fee that is charged on all reorders. For more information on reordering plans please contact our Customer Service Department at (860) 343-5977.

We want you to find your dream home from our wide selection of home plans. However, if for some reason you find that the plan you have purchased from us does not meet your needs, then you may exchange that plan for any other plan in our col-lection. We allow you sixty days from your original invoice date to make an exchange. At the time of the exchange you will be charged a processing fee of 15% of the total amount of your original order plus the difference in price between the plans (if appli-cable) plus the cost to ship the new plans to you. Call our Customer Service Department at (860) 343-5977 for more information. Please Note: Reproducible vel-lums can only be exchanged if they are unopened.

Important Shipping Information

Please refer to the shipping charts on the order form for service availability for your specific plan number. Our delivery service must have a street address or Rural Route Box number — never a post office box. (PLEASE NOTE: Supplying a P.O. Box number <u>only</u> will delay the shipping of your order.) Use a work address if no one is home during the day.

Orders being shipped to APO or FPO must go via First Class Mail. Please include the proper postage.

For our International Customers, only Certified bank checks and money orders are accepted and must be payable in U.S. currency. For speed, we ship internation-al orders Air Parcel Post. Please refer to the chart for the correct shipping cost.

Important Canadian Shipping Information

To our friends in Canada, we have a plan design affiliate in Kitchener, Ontario. This relationship will help you avoid the delays and charges associated with ship-ments from the United States. Moreover, our affiliate is familiar with the building requirements in your community and country. We prefer payments in U.S. Currency. If you, however, are sending Canadian funds please add 40% to the prices of the plans and shipping fees.

An Important Note About Building Code Requirements:

All plans are drawn to conform to one or more of the industry's major national building standards. However, due to the variety of local building regulations, your plan may need to be modified to comply with local requirements — snow loads, energy loads, seismic zones, etc. Do check them fully and consult your local building officials.

A few states require that all building plans used be drawn by an architect registered in that state. While having your plans reviewed and stamped by such an architect may be prudent, laws requiring non-conforming plans like ours to be completely redrawn forces you to unnecessarily pay very large fees. If your state has such a law, we strongly recommend you contact your state representative to protest.

The rendering, floor plans, and technical information contained within this publication are not guaranteed to be totally accurate. Consequently, no information from this publication should be used either as a guide to constructing a home or for estimating the cost of building a home. Complete blueprints must be purchased for such purposes.

Garlinghouse 1999 Blueprint Price Code Schedule

Additional sets with original order $35

PRICE CODE	A	B	C	D	E	F	G	H
SETS OF SAME PLAN	$405	$445	$490	$530	$570	$615	$655	$695
4 SETS OF SAME PLAN	$355	$395	$440	$480	$520	$565	$605	$645
1 SINGLE SET OF PLANS	$305	$345	$390	$430	$470	$515	$555	$595
VELLUMS	$515	$560	$610	$655	$700	$750	$795	$840
MATERIALS LIST	$60	$60	$65	$65	$70	$70	$75	$75
ITEMIZED ZIP QUOTE	$75	$80	$85	$85	$90	$90	$95	$95

Shipping — (Plans 1-84999)

	1-3 Sets	4-6 Sets	7+ & Vellums
Standard Delivery (UPS 2-Day)	$25.00	$30.00	$35.00
Overnight Delivery	$35.00	$40.00	$45.00

Shipping — (Plans 85000-99999)

	1-3 Sets	4-6 Sets	7+ & Vellums
Ground Delivery (7-10 Days)	$15.00	$20.00	$25.00
Express Delivery (3-5 Days)	$20.00	$25.00	$30.00

International Shipping & Handling

	1-3 Sets	4-6 Sets	7+ & Vellums
Regular Delivery Canada (7-10 Days)	$25.00	$30.00	$35.00
Express Delivery Canada (5-6 Days)	$40.00	$45.00	$50.00
Overseas Delivery Airmail (2-3 Weeks)	$50.00	$60.00	$65.00

Option Key

Zip Quote Available | Right Reading Reverse
Duplex Plan | Materials List Available

Index

T O P   S E L L I N G
GARAGE PLANS

Save money by Doing-It-Yourself using our Easy-To-Follow plans. Whether you intend to build your own garage or contract it out to a building professional, the Garlinghouse garage plans provide you with everything you need to price out your project and get started. Put our 90+ years of experience to work for you. Order now!!

No. 06016C $86.00

Apartment Garage With One Bedroom

- 24' x 28' Overall Dimensions
- 544 Square Foot Apartment
- 12/12 Gable Roof with Dormers
- Slab or Stem Wall Foundation Options

No. 06015C $86.00

Apartment Garage With Two Bedrooms

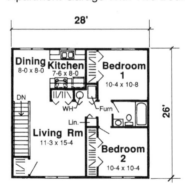

- 26' x 28' Overall Dimensions
- 728 Square Foot Apartment
- 4/12 Pitch Gable Roof
- Slab or Stem Wall Foundation Options

No. 06012C $54.00

30' Deep Gable &/or Eave Jumbo Garages

- 4/12 Pitch Gable Roof
- Available Options for Extra Tall Walls, Garage & Personnel Doors, Foundation, Window, & Sidings
- Package contains 4 Different Sizes
- 30' x 28'   • 30' x 32'   • 30' x 36'   • 30' x 40'

No. 06013C $68.00

Two-Car Garage With Mudroom/Breezeway

- Attaches to Any House
- 24' x 24' Eave Entry
- Available Options for Utility Room with Bath, Mudroom, Screened-In Breezeway, Roof, Foundation, Garage & Personnel Doors, Window, & Sidings

No. 06001C $48.00

12', 14' & 16' Wide-Gable 1-Car Garages

- Available Options for Roof, Foundation, Window, Door, & Sidings
- Package contains 8 Different Sizes
- 12' x 20' Mini-Garage • 14' x 22' • 16' x 20' • 16' x 24'
- 14' x 20'   • 14' x 24' • 16' x 22' • 16' x 26'

No. 06003C $48.00

24' Wide-Gable 2-Car Garages

- Available Options for Side Shed, Roof, Foundation, Garage & Personnel Doors, Window, & Sidings
- Package contains 5 Different Sizes
- 24' x 22'   • 24' x 24'   • 24' x 26'
- 24' x 28'   • 24' x 32'

No. 06007C $60.00

Gable 2-Car Gambrel Roof Garages

- Interior Rear Stairs to Loft Workshop
- Front Loft Cargo Door With Pulley Lift
- Available Options for Foundation, Garage & Personnel Doors, Window, & Sidings
- Package contains 5 Different Sizes
- 22' x 26' • 22' x 28' • 24' x 28' • 24' x 30' • 24' x 32'

No. 06006C $48.00

22' & 24' Deep Eave 2 & 3-Car Garages

- Can Be Built Stand-Alone or Attached to House
- Available Options for Roof, Foundation, Garage & Personnel Doors, Window, & Sidings
- Package contains 6 Different Sizes
- 22' x 28'   • 22' x 32'   • 24' x 32'
- 22' x 30'   • 24' x 30'   • 24' x 36'

No. 06002C $48.00

20' & 22' Wide-Gable 2-Car Garages

- Available Options for Roof, Foundation, Garage & Personnel Doors, Window, & Sidings
- Package contains 7 Different Sizes
- 20' x 20'   • 20' x 24'   • 22' x 22'   • 22' x 28'
- 20' x 22'   • 20' x 28'   • 22' x 24'

No. 06008C $60.00

Eave 2 & 3-Car Clerestory Roof Garages

- Interior Side Stairs to Loft Workshop
- Available Options for Engine Lift, Foundation, Garage & Personnel Doors, Window, & Sidings
- Package contains 4 Different Sizes
- 24' x 26'   • 24' x 28'   • 24' x 32'   • 24' x 36'

Order Code No: **G9SL7**

Garage Order Form

Please send me 3 complete sets of the following GARAGE PLANS:

Item no. & description	Price
Additional Sets	$ _____
(@ $10.00 EACH)	$ _____
Shipping Charges: UPS-$3.75, First Class-$4.50	$ _____
Subtotal:	$ _____
Resident sales tax: KS-6.15%, CT-6% (NOT REQUIRED FOR OTHER STATES)	$ _____

Total Enclosed: $ _____

My Billing Address is:
Name: _____

Address: _____

City: _____

State: _____ Zip: _____

Daytime Phone No. (_____) _____

My Shipping Address is:
Name: _____

Address: _____
(UPS will not ship to P.O. Boxes)

City: _____

State: _____ Zip: _____

For Faster Service...Charge It!
U.S. & Canada Call
1(800)235-5700

All foreign residents call 1(860)343-5977

MASTERCARD, VISA

Card # |_|_|_|_|_|_|_|_|_|_|_|_|_|_|_|_|_|_|

Signature _____ Exp.____/____

If paying by credit card, to avoid delays:
billing address must be as it appears on credit card statement
or FAX us at (860) 343-5984

Here's What You Get

• Three complete sets of drawings for each plan ordered
• Detailed step-by-step instructions with easy-to-follow diagrams on how to build your garage (not available with apartment garages)
• For each garage style, a variety of size and garage door configuration options
• Variety of roof styles and/or pitch options for most garages
• Complete materials list
• Choice between three foundation options: Monolithic Slab, Concrete Stem Wall or Concrete Block Stem Wall
• Full framing plans, elevations and cross-sectionals for each garage size and configuration

Build-It-Yourself PROJECT PLAN

Order Information For Garage Plans:

All garage plan orders contain three complete sets of drawings with instructions and are priced as listed next to the illustration. Additional sets of plans may be obtained for $10.00 each with your original order. UPS shipping is used unless otherwise requested. Please include the proper amount for shipping.

Send your order to:
(With check or money order payable in U.S. funds only)
The Garlinghouse Company
P.O. Box 1717
Middletown, CT 06457

No C.O.D. orders accepted; U.S. funds only. UPS will not ship to Post Office boxes, FPO boxes, APO boxes, Alaska or Hawaii. Canadian orders must be shipped First Class.
Prices subject to change without notice.